Ernest Ingersole

Rand, McNally & Co.'s Handy Guide to the Country around New York

For the Wheelman, Driver, and Excursionist

Ernest Ingersole

Rand, McNally & Co.'s Handy Guide to the Country around New York
For the Wheelman, Driver, and Excursionist

ISBN/EAN: 9783337190200

Printed in Europe, USA, Canada, Australia, Japan

Cover: Foto ©Lupo / pixelio.de

More available books at **www.hansebooks.com**

Tribune Bicycles

The Easiest Running Wheel in The World

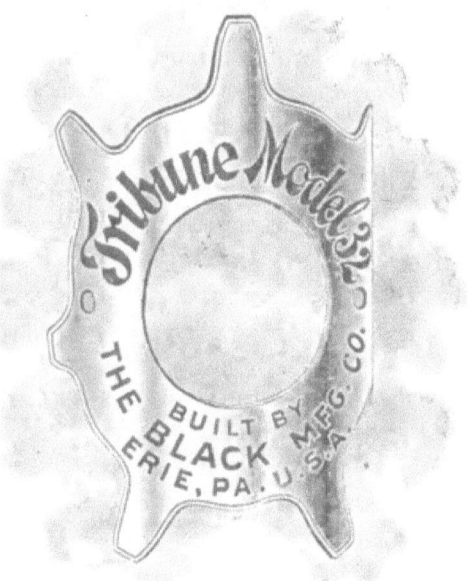

DISTRIBUTING AGENTS

UNITED STATES NET & TWINE CO.

316 Broadway, NEW YORK

Brooklyn Agency, 1261 BEDFORD AVENUE

SEND FOR CATALOGUE

Rand, McNally & Co.'s
SERIES OF
HANDY GUIDES

This new series of American Guide Books gives, in volumes of "handy" size, the information generally desired by travelers seeking pleasure, health, or business. The books are uniform in size and general arrangement. Places or objects of particular importance or interest are noted in black-faced type, and those of less importance in italics. Care has been taken to present everything in the most candid and helpful light, saying little or nothing about that which is deemed worth little attention. Numerous illustrations from photographs, and colored maps supplement the text.

PRICE OF EACH GUIDE.

In Paper Binding, - - - - 25 Cents.
In Flexible Cloth Binding, Rounded Corners, 50 Cents.

The following are now ready and will be revised annually:

NEW YORK CITY, including Brooklyn, Staten Island, and other suburbs. 210 pages; 44 illustrations. Maps of New York City, 28 x 17; Central Park, 10 x 28, and New York and New Jersey Suburbs, 28 x 26.

BOSTON AND ENVIRONS. 154 pages; 24 illustrations. Maps of Boston, 28 x 21; *Environs of Boston*, 11 x 13½, and *Business Portion of Boston*, 9¼ x 9.

PHILADELPHIA AND ENVIRONS, including Atlantic City and Cape May. 187 pages; 22 illustrations. Maps of Philadelphia, 28 x 22, and *One Hundred Miles Around Philadelphia*, 28 x 21.

WASHINGTON AND THE DISTRICT OF COLUMBIA. 161 pages; 40 illustrations. Map of Washington, 21 x 28.

CHICAGO. 215 pages; 46 illustrations. Map of Chicago, 31 x 33.

HUDSON RIVER AND CATSKILL MOUNTAINS. 240 pages; 18 illustrations. Five large scale sectional maps showing both sides of the river from New York to Troy.

SOUTHEASTERN STATES. Includes Florida, Georgia, the Carolinas, and the Gulf Coast; 246 pages; illustrations. Map of Southeastern States, 24 x 28.

NEW ENGLAND STATES. 260 pages; numerous illustrations. Maps of Maine, New Hampshire, Vermont, Massachusetts, Rhode Island, and Connecticut, printed in colors, each 11 x 14 in size.

COUNTRY AROUND NEW YORK. 180 pages. Describing resorts and routes in Westchester County on Staten Island and Long Island, and in Northeastern and Seaside New Jersey. Forty half-tone illustrations. Twelve route maps in black and white and map of region around New York, north to Hastings-on-the-Hudson; east to Garden City, Long Island; south to South Amboy, N. J.; west to Lake Hopatcong.

Our publications are for sale by booksellers and newsdealers generally, or will be sent postpaid to any address on receipt of price.

RAND, McNALLY & CO., Publishers,

61 East Ninth Street, near Broadway, NEW YORK.
166-168 Adams Street, CHICAGO, ILL.

Is your club fitted up with these Holders?
If not, why not?

Snow Adjustable Bicycle Holders

FOR USE IN
PUBLIC BUILDINGS, CLUBS, STORES, AND
PRIVATE DWELLINGS.

Attractive ⋯ Artistic ⋯ Simple ⋯ Strong

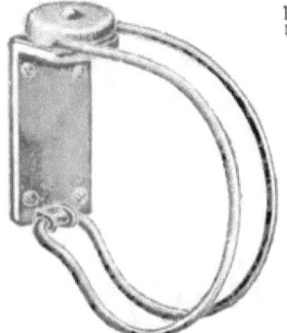

Patents applied for in the
United States and foreign countries.

They adjust to any angle

Although our Holders have been on the market less than one year, there are to-day more of them in use than all others combined.

PRICE 50c.   WEIGHT 16 oz.

FOR INSIDE USE.
The spring wire is nickel-plated and the cap and bracket are finished in gold bronze or enameled. Finished in antique copper, electro bronze, or full nickeled.

FOR OUTSIDE USE.
The Holders are fully enameled.

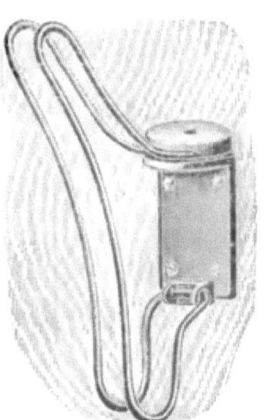

MANUFACTURED BY
THE SNOW WIRE WORKS,
76-84 Exchange street,

Established 1834.   ROCHESTER, N. Y.   PRICE 75c.   WEIGHT 20 oz.

If you can not obtain them from your dealer we will send them prepaid.

"Search-Light" Always Bright

All Riders Say it is the Best

The only lantern that you can feel sure will not go back on you. A lantern that does not jar or blow out. Reflecting surfaces are always bright.

THE BRIDGEPORT BRASS CO.,
BRIDGEPORT, CONN.

Something New in Bicycle Lamps

RETAIL PRICE, $3.00.

Have You Seen it?

If so, you know what it is; can heartily recommend it; and vouch for the truthfulness of the statement that

There is Nothing Like it.

Constructed on the principle of all first-class outdoor lamps—the Tubular—and is the only Tubular Bicycle Lamp on the market. Will not jar out or blow out. A lamp that can positively be depended upon at all times. For sale by all first-class dealers. Write for circular.

C. T. HAM MFG. CO.,
Sole Manufacturers,
ROCHESTER, N.Y.

HAM'S "DIAMOND" TUBULAR.

The 20th Century.

BICYCLE HEAD-LIGHT AND DRIVING LAMP.

Acknowledged leader of all Bicycle Lamps.
Endorsed by riders everywhere.

Standard Size.		Tandem Size.	
Nickel,	$3.00	Nickel,	$4.00
Japanned,	3.00	Japanned,	4.00
Aluminum,	3.75	Aluminum,	5.00

ON SALE EVERYWHERE.

TO THE

NTRY AROUND NEW YORK

FOR THE WHEELMAN, DRIVER, AND EXCURSIONIST

With Original Maps and Illustrations.

CONTENTS.

CHAPTER.	PAGE.
I. IN WESTCHESTER COUNTY	7
BICYCLING ROUTES	9

      1. Along the Hudson River, 9; 2. Along the Harlem Valley, 19; 3. New York to Portchester, 24; Cross Routes, 32.

   STEAMBOATS AND RAILROADS 38

      Up the Hudson by Steamboat, 38; Railroads, 40; New York & Putnam Railroad, 46; The Harlem Railroad, 49; The New Haven Railroad, 53; Suburban Railroads, 55; A Rural Walk — Bronx Park, etc., 55; East River Steamboats, 58.

II. ON LONG ISLAND 62
   BICYCLING ROUTES 63

      1. To Coney Island, 63; 2. To the South Side, 64; 3. To the North Shore, 72.

   DRIVES ON LONG ISLAND 75
   RAILROAD AND STEAMBOAT ROUTES 79

      Long Island Railroad, 79; Local Suburban Lines, 86; Steamboats to Long Island Ports, 87.

III. ON STATEN ISLAND 89
   BICYCLE TOURS 91

      Tour of the South Shore, 91; North Shore and Fort Wadsworth, 94.

   RAILROADS AND STEAMBOATS 98

      Rapid Transit Lines, 98; Electric Railways, 99; Steamboats to Staten Island, 100.

IV. SUBURBAN NEW JERSEY 101
   BICYCLING ROUTES 101

      1. To Englewood and Nyack, 101; 2. To Hackensack and Paramus, 107; 3. Up the Ramapo Valley, 109; 4. To Morristown, via Paterson and Boonton, 113; 5. New York to Lake Hopatcong, 116; 6. Through the Oranges to Morristown, 119.

   RAILROAD ROUTES 125

      1. Electric Lines along the Palisades, 125; 2. The Fort Lee Road Line to Englewood, 127; 3. Northern Railroad of New Jersey, 129; 4. West Shore Railroad, 129; 5. New Jersey & New York Railroad, 134; 6. The Susquehanna Railroad, 138; 7. The Erie Railway, 139; 8. New York & Greenwood Lake Railway, 142; 9. Electric Lines to Passaic and Paterson, 143; 10. Electric Lines in Paterson and to Little Falls, 144; 11. Boonton Branch, Delaware, Lackawanna & Western Railroad, 144; 12. Morris & Essex (D., L. & W.) Railroad, 145; 13. Electric Cars to Newark and Beyond, 147; 14. Electric Line to Arlington, 149; 15. Electric Line, Newark and Passaic, 149; 16. Electric Cars to Bloomfield and Montclair, 149; 17. Electric Cars to the Oranges, 150.

V. CENTRAL AND SEASIDE NEW JERSEY 155
   BICYCLING ROUTES 155

      1. New York to Somerville, 155; 2. Newark to Plainfield, through Orange, 159; 3. New Brunswick to Newark, via Springfield, 159; 4. To Long Branch, Asbury Park, etc., 163.

   RAILROAD AND STEAMBOAT ROUTES 170

      1. Pennsylvania Railroad, 170; 2. Central Railroad of New Jersey, 171; 3. Lehigh Valley Railroad, 174; 4. Electric Lines, 173; Steamboats to New Jersey Ports, 174.

(3)

Dayton Wheels

Win Races!

Note Waller's two six-day triumphs at Washington and Pittsburg, and Becker's at San Francisco, the latter breaking all world's records.

THE MOST ELEGANT, RIGID, EASY-RUNNING WHEELS IN THE WORLD.

DAYTON BICYCLE CO.,
76 READE STREET,
NEW YORK.

LIST OF ILLUSTRATIONS.

Riverside Drive and Tomb of Gen. U S. Grant,	Frontispiece
The Bronx River, below Bronxdale,	Opposite page 18
Country Clubhouse of the New York Athletic Club,	" 28
Christ's Church, Pelham Manor, N. Y.,	" 30
The Old Van Cortlandt Saw Mill in Van Cortlandt Park,	" 40
Lake and Country Clubhouse, Park Hill, Yonkers,	" 46
The Bronx River,	" 56
The Lake, Prospect Park, Brooklyn,	" 76
Richmond Turnpike, at Silver Lake, Castleton,	" 94
Tompkinsville and the Narrows of New York Bay,	" 96
East Side Park, Paterson, N. J.,	" 108
Pompton Plains, N. J.,	" 110
Lake Hopatcong, New Jersey,	" 116
Eagle Rock, on Orange Mountain, elevation 620 feet,	" 120
The Village of Pompton Plains, N. J.,	" 138
The Passaic River, above Paterson, N. J.,	" 144
Road in Llewellyn Park, Orange, N. J.,	" 146
Harrison Street, East Orange,	" 148
Munn Avenue, East Orange,	" 150
Main Street, Orange,	" 152
Entrance to Llewellyn Park, Orange, N. J.,	" 154
Lake on Orange Mountain, near Eagle Rock,	" 156
A Street in Shrewsbury, N. J.,	" 162
On the Rumson Road, looking west,	" 166

DIXON'S CYCLE CHAIN GRAPHITES

Graphite cycle chain lubricants are infinitely superior to any other lubricant. The stick is in a convenient form, yet the paste is always in good demand, as it lubricates and cleans the chain and sprockets, and does not get too soft in summer. Dixon's Graphites are made of only the finest materials.

If it is Quality You Want Use Dixon's.

No. 678 IS IN POWDER FORM.
No. 679 IS LARGE STICK.
No. 691 IS SMALL STICK.

Full Size.

No. 692 IS IN COLLAPSIBLE TUBE.

Reduced Cut.

Ask your dealer for Dixon's and take no other.

JOS. DIXON CRUCIBLE CO
Jersey City, N. J.

PREFATORY NOTE.

A preface for a book of this kind must take the form, if any, of an explanation. The purpose—for which originality may be claimed—has been to suggest to citizens of the more crowded parts of New York and the adjacent cities, the means for taking recreation trips, at a small expense of time and money, into the suburban districts. The situation of New York provides for an almost inexhaustible variety of scenes and outdoor pleasures, attractive to the rambler along the seashore, upon the rivers or inland ; and it is believed that a book that attempts to indicate the character of the country in all directions from the city, the nature of the roads and stopping places, and the means of reaching each to best advantage, will be welcomed by a large class of citizens.

Little or nothing is said of those popular resorts like Coney Island and the New Jersey watering places, which scarcely come into the scope of this book, and are already well known; nor is time spent on the suburban towns and residence "parks," however admirable as dwelling places, the whole of the necessarily limited space being needed for an account of what the *country* can offer to "wheelmen, drivers, and excursionists" out for a day's pleasure.

The editor bespeaks charity for any shortcomings of this experimental first edition, and promises to endeavor to make amends in future editions, where addition or correction seems desirable.

E. I.

DEAN TIRES

(Single Tube)

A Pointer on Tires

$15.00 Per Pair

A good wheel is made perfect by a good tire.

DEAN TIRES ARE ... PERFECTION

DO NOT SLIP...

Resilient and Fast

Guaranteed Against PUNCTURE

No Repairs To Make

WRITE FOR BOOKLET

DEAN TIRE CO. 25 Warren St. NEW YORK CITY

I.

IN WESTCHESTER COUNTY.

Nowhere can the person, who seeks an outing-trip of a day or a week, or a month, turn his steps with more confidence than to the region north of the city of New York. The city now extends its boundary in that direction to Yonkers, Mount Vernon, and Pelham, several miles from the Harlem River; but for the purposes of this book of suggestions to the rambler, municipal lines may be disregarded, and anything beyond the built-up streets may be considered to be of interest to the reader. This would include, as, in fact, such a consideration must, many beautiful and retired spaces south of the Harlem and Spuyten Duyvil, especially along the highlands bordering upon the Hudson. One may find in the region beyond Fort George a rural space and greenness very refreshing; Kingsbridge is always attractive; while there are large areas on the heights of Fort Washington and Inwood — especially in this rocky corner of Manhattan Island — where the pedestrian can get entirely away from the noise, glare, and feeling of the city, and stroll for hours amid green lanes and beneath ancient trees, or climb about rocks and among thickets that seem rarely to have felt the foot of man. Much the same is true of the country just north (or east) of the Harlem, especially along the line of the old aqueduct, in Bronx, Crotona, and Van Cortlandt parks, and all along the heights from Spuyten Duyvil to Yonkers, where, in ten minutes, at the end of your strength or time, you may descend to a railway or street-car line, and be whisked speedily and comfortably back to town. It is surprising that one encounters so few walkers or riders in these romantic and primitive solitudes. The reason can only be that so few persons realize the rural privileges they afford. It is for this reason that most of the plans for excursions inland, outlined in the succeeding pages, have been made to begin at the Harlem River rather than at the conventional city line.

This region between the Hudson and East rivers is remarkable for its accessibility. Steamboats run to almost every port upon its shore; four steam railways traverse it from the heart of the metropolis, running frequent accommodations at low rates of fares; electric roads are day by day penetrating farther and farther into its quiet valleys, and it is covered by a network of improved roads, along which are scattered an uncounted number of houses of rest and refreshment. These means of public conveyance so interlock that it is rare that one needs to return the way he came; while the opportunities for ending your journey at a point convenient for a delightful walk or 'cycle ride to some other point whence you can quickly return, make this form of round trip one especially to be recommended. Plans for several such round trips, including a section afoot, are given in the following pages.

Westchester County abounds in flourishing cities and villages, more or less attractive; these are increasing and broadening, and new ones are constantly arising at the behest of skillful manipulators of "parks" and various real-estate projects. Description of these does not enter into the purpose, except so far as the facts may be supposed to be of interest or value to the rambler as stations on his route or means to further progress. This is one of the most pleasing districts for bicycle riding in the whole country; and when the tours outlined below are studied in connection with the maps, and with the succeeding remarks upon the railroad routes and other similar data, the reader will find himself able to start fearlessly upon any ramble, in a carriage, by wheel, or afoot, with a definite knowledge of what he may expect and where he will come out. The information is fresh and accurate, having been obtained especially for these pages.

BICYCLING ROUTES.

1. Along the Hudson River.

New York to Tarrytown and Northward.— Leaving the city at Central Park we go up Seventh Avenue to *Central Bridge*, on the site of the old McComb's Dam Bridge, cross it, and enter upon our route north of the Harlem, by immediately turning into *Sedgwick Avenue*, the diverging road to the left, along the water's edge. This gives us a fine view of the rugged heights on the western shore of the Harlem, already reserved as a park, and of the Speedway along its base. We hasten beneath the arches of High Bridge and

Washington Bridge.* Beyond the latter structure we rise to higher ground and overlook toward the west the Fort George and Washington Heights, and a little latter Marble Hill and Kingsbridge, all identified with the stirring story of '76, and the American struggle or liberty, while the Hudson and its Palisades form the background of a picture now so rapidly becoming citified. There is an especially fine view near the Webb Institute for Shipbuilding; and near here roads strike eastward into the interesting region about Fordham and beyond. Just beyond the Institute we take the left fork of the road (Bailey Avenue) and descend into *Kingsbridge*, cross the railroad tracks, and turn to the right at the footbridge into *Broadway* (7 m.). This is the old Albany post-road, now known as "Broadway" pretty much all the way from the Battery, in New York, to Albany. It is level and permits us to put on as high speed as we like along the margin of the Tibbett's Brook marshes, and then, slowly rising, along the western border of Van Cortlandt Park, with the old Manor House and Vault Hill in plain sight. The high ground at the left is Spuyten Duyvil (p. 40), to which several pleasant roads lead up; and ahead on the left, opposite the Park, was Mosholu, now lost in a maze of streets, and included by the postoffice in the Riverdale district. A mile farther brings us opposite Mount St. Vincent and to the gateway of an old country road winding across Van Cortlandt Park, and then continuing westward as Mosholu Avenue and Cuthbert's Lane over to the convent and bank of the Hudson. A run down a slight grade, passing on the right Lawrence Street leading to Lowerre, carries us over the line from New York City into

Yonkers. The road is now asphalt; and at the fountain we take the left fork up over the hill passing on the right the new high school and public library building, then on the left the new Dutch Reformed Church, and dismount at *Getty Square* (4 m. = 11 m.). This is the center of the city, and here are clustered the most interesting objects in the city, for which see page 41. Yonkers will well repay a long ramble through its streets, most of which are excellently surfaced. Several restaurants furnish good fare. Ordinances requiring lamps and prohibiting speeding and sidewalk riding are enforced.

---

* For a full account of these bridges, the Harlem Valley, and other places within the more densely populated borders of the city, consult Rand, McNally & Co.'s *Handy Guide to New York City* (illustrated), for sale by booksellers and at all news-stands, price 50 and 25 cents.

Leaving Yonkers from Getty Square, we follow Broadway (macadamized) up a long, steep climb to the heights of Glenwood, where a *magnificent picture* of the valley of the American Rhine bursts upon our view. We are still on the old post-road, and from now on shall follow the river in all its windings—a rare vista at every turn. Handsome estates succeed one another along the way, each in the midst of a park facing the river. Prominent among them, in succession, are those of J. B. Trevor, somewhat below Broadway; C. H. Lilienthal, with its brownstone, battlemented tower, and, adjoining it, the elegant grounds of "Greystone," the country seat of the late Samuel J. Tilden. Here and there we catch glimpses of the river stretching northward, and of the basaltic crags of the Palisades beyond it. The road is finely macadamed and so well graded that one hardly notices the hills and vales it traverses. Suddenly the little village of *Hastings* (5 m. = 16 m.), nestling on the river-front, breaks upon us. It is prettier at a distance than near at hand, however, and calls for little if any pause. It has a railway station and steamboat landing, and is the terminus of the Warburton Avenue extension—a boulevard designed to skirt the river-front from Yonkers to this point.

In revolutionary days this locality was the domain of Peter Post, whose patriotism cost him dear. He once assisted the patriots, under Colonel Sheldon, to surprise a party of marauding Hessians, beguiling them into the belief that the Americans, whom they were pursuing, had moved on in a certain direction, while they were ambushed conveniently in the rear.

"The Hessians, deceived by his answer," says the story, according to Bolton, in his *History of the County of Westchester*—a rare and valuable book to which every student of this region must be indebted—"were proceeding at full gallop through the lane, when a shrill whistle rang through the air, instantly followed by the impetuous charge of Sheldon's horse. Panic-stricken, the enemy fled in every direction, but the fresh horses of the Americans carried their gallant riders wherever a wandering ray disclosed the steel cap of the brilliant accouterments of a Hessian. A bridle-path leading from the place of ambush to the river was strewed with the dead and dying, while those who sought safety in the water were captured, cut to pieces, and drowned. The conflict, so short and bloody, was decisive. One solitary horseman was seen galloping off in the direction of Yonkers, and he alone, wounded and unarmed, reached the camp of Colonel Emmerick in safety. Here he related the particulars of the march, the sudden onset and retreat. Astonished and maddened with rage, Emmerick started his whole command in pursuit. Poor Post was stripped for his fidelity, and after having a sufficient number of blows inflicted upon his person, left for dead."

Earlier than this, however, Hastings had acquired notoriety from the fact that there Cornwallis embarked his army for the subjugation of Fort Lee, following the capture of Fort Washington.

We turn to the left up a steep incline and are rewarded by a grand view of the river, expanding into the Tappan Sea. The dark wall of the Palisades is here highest and most precipitous. Its loftiest point (550 feet), called Indian Head, is a mile or two below, and the northernmost high point of the Palisades, nearly opposite us, marks where the northern New Jersey boundary comes to the river and Rockland County, N. Y., begins. Beyond that the wall breaks down, and we see the rolling Nyack Hills and the long wharf at Piermont. The lofty clock tower and windmill of Dr. Huyler's residence is just below us, and next to it "Sabine Farm," the home of Mr. Foster. Rolling on down the little hill we enter *Edgar's Lane*, opened in 1644, level and straightaway for nearly three-fourths of a mile, and in early times used as a trotting course. We bowl merrily along the tree-bordered old speedway, passing on the right the handsome Shepard estate, and enter **Dobbs Ferry** (1½ m. = 17½ m.), a pretty little village deriving its name from the family of Jan Dobbs, who lived here as early as 1698, and operated a small ferry to Sneeden's Landing on the opposite shore, where a road came down from the Dutch settlements in Northern New Jersey. Its special object of interest is the Livingston mansion and monument.

Dobbs Ferry was an important post in the Revolution, and the rendezvous of each army alternately It was here that the British troops mustered after the battle of White Plains, and before marching to the assault upon Fort Washington. In January, 1777, Lincoln and his detachment of the patriot army encamped here a while. Later (1781), Washington established the American army headquarters at the large farmhouse on the post-road, now known as the Livingston Mansion. Here he and Rochambeau planned and started to execute the Yorktown campaign; and there, on May 6, 1783, George Clinton and Sir Guy Carleton, the British commander, met to confer on the subject of the evacuation of the city of New York by the British forces. This house did not come into the possession of the Livingston family until after the Revolution. It was originally built by a Dutch farmer, who leased it from the lord of the Philipse Manor; the Philipse estate being sequestrated by the Government at the close of the war, this farm was purchased by Peter Van Brugh Livingston, with 500 acres, and it became henceforth known as the "Livingston Manor." (See also page 44.) In front of the house now stands a granite shaft, erected by the New York Society of the Sons of the Revolution, commemorating this glorious history.

From Dobbs Ferry the road is fairly level to Irvington, and is bordered on each side with elegant estates, here and there permitting, through their grand old trees, pleasing views of the river and hills beyond. *Irvington* (2 m.=20 m.) itself contains little of casual interest, save the new and handsome building of The Cosmopolitan (magazine), lying just south of the little main street which runs from the post-road down to the railroad station. Near by is the Main Street Hotel ($2), where good refreshment can be obtained. The quaint, petite Episcopal chapel on the post-road, and the stately Presbyterian Church adjoining it, will claim passing notice, when, after a short, level run of half a mile, we reach Sunnyside Avenue, which leads (to the left) to "Sunnyside," the home of Washington Irving. This is down on the river-front (see p. 44). The road onward is solid and smooth, bordered by handsome properties, and gives a very enjoyable ride. A delightful walk is along the old aqueduct, half way down the hill. Shortly, on our left, we pass "*Lyndhurst*," the country seat of the late Jay Gould, but before him of the gifted Paulding family (p. 45); and a short, fairly level run farther, over fine macadam, brings us into

Tarrytown (2½ m.=22½ m.)—This is a very ancient village settled by the Dutch, upon the site of Indian stockaded villages which are said to have persisted as late as 1644. It is now a flourishing town of considerable mercantile and manufacturing importance. There is a steam ferry to Nyack, near the railway station and steamboat wharf; and from Nyack a fine driving and cycling road goes west through Orange County to Suffern, etc. (p. 113), and southward along the valley of the Hackensack (p. 101), which makes a fine round trip from New York. Tarrytown's hillside avenues are beautifully shaded and run between lines of luxurious cottage homes. Nowhere does Broadway present a more pleasing appearance. One of the finest of the up-and-down streets is the Nepara road, which winds up to the top of Castle Heights (a name that goes back to Patroon Philipse's time), giving admirable views far across and up the Hudson.

Tarrytown's principal hotels are the long established and excellent Franklin House, on Broadway ($2.50, L. A. W. $2), and the Mott House. The latter is in a more retired position on the high Nepara road and is shaded by immense oaks and elms.—See p. 45.

The Mott homestead on the east side of Broadway, a few steps north of Main Street, is a relic worth special attention from the thoughtful. It was built long previous to 1712, when a Martlings was the owner; it was his descendant who is called the Martyr of Sleepy Hollow. Until the Revolutionary War the house saw nothing eventful so far as the records relate; but during that war it was converted into a public house kept by Elizabeth Van Tassel and known as the Van Tassel Tavern, and it saw not only the riotous "skinners" and "cowboys" of the Neutral Ground, but the leading officers of both armies, for it was sometimes within British lines and sometimes under the Continental flag. Its most stirring incident, probably, was the capture, in its taproom, of a party of British raiders, who were surprised by the American Major Hunt and a band of militiamen and captured to a man. But the legendary interest surpasses the actual. Here lived Katrina Van Tassel to whom Ichabod Crane lost his heart, and for whom he ran the ghastly risks of being chased by the Headless Horseman and having other dreadful things happen to him. Irving knew the old tavern well, and drew thence no small part of the imaginary scenes and portraits which have made Tarrytown immortal in literature. This house will perhaps become a local museum.

☞ *The Nepara road* leads along the highlands behind Tarrytown, past stations on the New York & Putnam Railroad and over to Kensico—a very pretty ride. Another interesting old road (Benedict Avenue) leads inland from the southern edge of the city and straight east through Elmsford to White Plains, it is this way that the proposed connection by electric cars will be made between Tarrytown, White Plains, and Portchester. Both of these roads are attractive to wheelmen and pedestrians, though rather hilly.

Continuing out Broadway from the center of Tarrytown northward, we pass on the left the church which Irving attended, to commemorate which, the vestrymen have erected a marble tablet in its wall; and just beyond Wildey Street we pause to view the *André*

Monument on the left of the road — a plain shaft of native marble, surmounted by a bronze statue of a minute-man, and containing a fine bronze panel by Theodore Bauer, depicting incidents of the capture. On its face is a circumstantial inscription recording that

> " ON THIS SPOT,
> The 23d day of September, 1780, the Spy,
> MAJOR JOHN ANDRE,
> Adjutant-General of the British Army, was captured by
> John Paulding, David Williams, and Isaac Van Wait,
> All natives of this County.
> History has told the Rest."

The monument was dedicated October 7, 1853, but has only recently acquired its prominent position, due to the building near by of the handsome series of " colonial " residences which add so much to the beauty of that part of town.

At the brick church (St. Paul's), a short distance north of the André Monument, Broadway turns down the hill to the left, while Jones Avenue goes straight along the high ground at the right of the church. Passing the pretty grounds of the Tennis Club the rider, in two or three minutes, will find himself at the *bridge over the Pocantico* — the stream which drains Sleepy Hollow, the scene of one of Washington Irving's most perfect romances. This present bridge is of recent construction, the direction of the road having been slightly changed, and the old bridge, over which frantically galloped poor Ichabod Crane, in his mad endeavor to escape the ghostly companionship of the Headless Horseman, disappeared long ago. But the tranquil, weedy little millpond is still the same as when Irving strolled upon its grassy shores, and the old mill is still standing by its moss-grown dam; and near it is the manor-house occupied by the Philipse family before the completion of their grand new one at Yonkers. Here Washington was a guest, and its history is closely interwoven with that of his time. Upon the hill on our right, overlooking the Pocantico Valley and the quiet little pond, is the small *Dutch Church*, probably the oldest church edifice now standing in the State. It is a small, rectangular structure of bricks brought from Holland for the purpose, strictly Dutch in architecture, and surmounted by an antique roof and square belfry. The windows are small, square, and old fashioned, and in the wall, north of the little doorway, is a tablet of marble, testifying that it was " Erected and built by Frederick Philipse and Catherine Van Cortlandt, his wife, in 1699." On the western peak is a curious weather-vane in the shape of a pennant bearing the monogram of the Philipse family. Many old and interesting tombstones, several bearing rude letters and carvings, surround the little edifice, while the newer monuments of the Sleepy Hollow Cemetery dot the hills to the north and east. *Irving's grave* is in this portion, on the slope of Battle Hill, which was fortified and garrisoned by revolutionary soldiers, and from which a very interesting view may be obtained (1 m. = 23½ m.).

☞ *Sleepy Hollow* was the name long ago given to the Pocantico Vale, lying between the heights bordering the Hudson and the Pocantico Hills to the east; and one who does not dread a poor bit of road will enjoy the interesting and pretty ride through it, as follows: Keeping due north at St. Paul's Church, go out Jones Avenue. The road skirts a deep ravine, through which tumbles a small branch of the river, called Gory Brook, and, threading prettily wooded glens, ascends to the summit of *Prospect Hill*, which overlooks the valley. Turn to the right at the second cross-road, called the Long Hill road, and bear to the right into the old Sleepy Hollow road. It is very poor riding, but is wild and picturesque. Still bear to the right as far as the lake which supplies Tarrytown with water, then, skirting the lake, mount a slight hill and follow the old road down the river valley until that strikes into the Bedford road near the base of Kaakeout Hill, the second highest in the county. On its easterly base is Raven Rock, which, tradition says, is haunted by the wraith of a woman in white, who perished there in the snow a hundred years ago.

☞ A direct road to the Tarrytown Railroad station leads to the right (as you face south) from the Pocantico Bridge, which is far shorter than to return by way of Broadway; but it passes through the poorer part of town, and the streets are not in very good condition for bicycles.

Continuing northward from the Pocantico Bridge and old Dutch Church, we rise to the top of an easy hill between the cemetery and the richly-wooded Kingsland estate on the left, which includes all of Kingsland Point. From the brow of the hill the road reaches into a long embowered avenue, and through the waving foliage our eyes are greeted with a vista across the majestic Hudson to the varicolored hills back of Nyack. A fine bit of road follows—a long, gradual descent between parks, whose great trees overhang the roadway. These are, on the left, the country seats of Messrs. R. E. Hopkins, J. G. Phillips, and "Rockwood Hall," the baronial estate of William Rockefeller, by whose gate stands an ancient milestone, still bearing plainly on its face the legend, "30 m. from New York." We now pass under the massive granite arch of the Croton Aqueduct and begin the climb of a steep, sandy hill. Heretofore the road has been of good, smooth macadam, and though hilly the grades have been easy and ridable, but from here on the traveling will be poor, relieved here and there by a side-path or occasional bits of good road. As we toil up the rise we pass, near the top, a little roadhouse, where a rest may be taken and light refreshment obtained. To the west we get a glimpse of the river through the trees and of the Verdrietig range of hills beyond. On our right is a little brick schoolhouse of some antiquity, over which proudly waves "Old Glory," while yonder the stately residence of the late Elliot F. Shepard looms above the tree-tops. The road now makes a dip and is here macadamized, thanks to the generosity of the adjacent property holders. Opposite the Shepard estate, which we now skirt, lies that of H. Walter Webb of the New York Central Railroad, and at the crossroad, on the right, stands the handsome Elliot F. Shepard Memorial Church, a fine structure of native marble (3¼ m.=26¾ m.).

☞ *The road branching to the left* here leads to the little village of Sparta, on the river front; that to the right, to the *Briar-cliff Church* and the heights behind Sing Sing. The latter offers a very pretty ride, the climb of the hill being offset by the rare prospects and the pleasure of a visit to the little ivy-covered chapel, with its handsome windows. The road directly east is called the Long Hill road, and leads to Prospect Hill and the Sleepy Hollow road.

Taking the straight road to the right of the farmhouse on the corner, we encounter a slight hill. On its westerly slope lies the old *Sparta burying-ground*, in the center of which, half hidden by a boxwood hedge, is the Ladieu plot, inclosed by a low wall of brick. Imbedded in the face of the wall are the headstones at which the British sloop of war, "Vulture," fired, supposing the structure a fortification, when, in 1780, that vessel lay anchored off this point, awaiting the return of André from his treason-hatching interview with Arnold. The shot struck the center headstone and the mark is discernible. Although Mr. Ingersoll does not mention this in his book on the Hudson River, already referred to, he gives a carefully studied and very full account of the whole sad incident of the André-Arnold conspiracy, to which the reader is referred. The road here is poor and sandy, but ridable on the side-path. As we reach the brow of the hill we see the houses of **Sing Sing** clustered upon the rocky hills opposite (1¼ m.=28½ m.), and soon cross the valley and enter the main avenue of that charming village, which, owing to the proximity of the State Prison, the general public is prone to regard as a penal colony. On the contrary, it is a prosperous, attractive town, of considerable mercantile importance. It possesses several churches of architectural beauty, notably the white marble Methodist Episcopal edifice—on our right as we enter the town.

At few places along the Hudson can more inspiring **views of the river** and its mountains be had than from the highlands of Sing Sing, and they will repay travelers who take pains to search out the best points of view. One of the most pleasing landscapes is that from the old Cedar Lane road, which branches to the east from Broadway, just opposite Snowden Avenue on the northern outskirts of the town. To the north, through the vale, the Croton River winds its way to its estuary, with here and there a clump of stately trees, or a quiet farmhouse breaking the expanse of velvety green. The river is crossed near its mouth by the sinuous old post-road, and beyond, jutting out into the Hudson, is the irregular, rocky, tree-covered peninsula of Croton Point, forming a boundary to the sail-dotted extent of Haverstraw Bay. Far to the northward rise the blue-topped mountains of Orange County, whence the eye sweeps southward with increasing pleasure along the highlands of New Jersey to the purple ramparts of the Palisades.

Several very good restaurants and hotels are clustered near the junction of Broadway and Main Street, both charging $2 a day to L. A. W. members.

From Sing Sing we take the left road out of the square by the stone bank-building down the hill, cross the bridge over Sing Sing Creek, then up over a rise and down again on a bit of good macadam road, shaded by a double row of trees, to a fork of the road (1½ m.), when we turn sharply to the left, a signboard pointing the way.

☞ The road to the *right* leads to the new Quaker Bridge Dam, on the Croton, some two miles above this point.

The road now becomes a poor bit of sand, quite the worst yet encountered and hardly ridable. The Croton winds through the hills, bordered by marsh land, from which rise abruptly the wooded heights, and is presently crossed upon a bridge, at the farther extremity of which stands the original Van Cortlandt manor-house, built by Stephen Van Cortlandt in 1683, one of the most valuable colonial relics in the country, long ante-dating the mansions on the banks of the Mosholu erected by the scions of this fine old patroon. Poor and hilly riding through a wooded space follows, until the road makes a sudden turn to the right and traverses the brickyards below Croton Landing (4 m.—32½ m.) to the banks of the Hudson (here forming Haverstraw Bay), with Haverstraw and the Verdrietig Mountains rising green and graceful beyond the blue plain.

☞ *The road branching to the east* from the post-road, opposite the railroad station, leads into the Somerstown Pike, which follows the Croton Valley northeasterly past Croton Lake to Somers and Croton Falls — about twelve miles.

Our route takes us straight on through Croton, and up a long, unridable hill, then bears to the left, skirting the ridge on the river-front over a better surface, with now and then a glimpse of the stream. On the east the wooded slope rises to the eminence of Hessian Hill, noted during the Revolution as the camp of a large force of those hirelings of the British army from the Duchy of Hesse. At a turn in the road here we are treated to a charming view of the river, bending lakelike around Verplank's Point. Opposite us lies the low promontory of Grassy Point, and just beyond it Wayne's battlefield at Stony Point. For the story of this battle see pages 68 to 72 of the "Guide to the Hudson River" — one of the most original chapters in the book. The road begins to improve and bears inland through oak groves, meadows, and farms, to the small settlement of *Oscawana*. The post-road crosses the little Furnace Brook, and trends away from the river, through *Cruger's*, where, beyond the bridge over the railroad, a bit of good macadam permits a rapid spin along under the base of the Spitzenberg Mountains into the town of Montrose.

☞ *The cross-road* here leads on the right to the railroad station at Montrose, and on the left over the old King's Ferry road to Verplank's Point, a straggling settlement of old houses — now principally occupied by employes of the ice company and brickyards — which stand on the site of the camps and fortifications of this strategic peninsula, so important in the defense of the Highlands made by the patriots of 1776. Here was the principal ferry over the river; and here, when the pressure of actual conflict was lifted, Steuben carried forward the drilling of the recruits which did so much to increase the effectiveness of the army. Finally, it was here, amid joyous festivities, that the French allies took leave of their American acquaintances and then marched to Boston to embark for home.

The road northward, now very good and shady, clings closely to the railroad as we near Lent's Cove, where suddenly the white cliffs of Dunderberg break into view at the southern gateway of the Highlands that tower up behind it. In the foreground, sloping down to the river-front, is the town of **Peekskill** (8 m.=40½ m.), outlined against the background of Red Hook. A long climb is required, however, before we enter the town by South Street. The Allen House ($2.50) recommends itself to wheelmen, and the older Eagle Hotel is still open to travelers.

The exploration of the country about Peekskill is rather more difficult for wheelmen than for others, since the region is very hilly and most of the roads poor. There are, however, many places of great interest near by, which are more or less accessible. A good road (with the exception of some three miles over the mountain), from which a rough track leads to the tip of Anthony's Nose, may be followed northward to Garrison's (steam ferry to West Point), Fishkill, Poughkeepsie, etc. At Fishkill you may cross to Newburgh, and there find good roads to return on the west side of the Hudson, described in Chapter IV.

The northern interior of Westchester County is reached from Peekskill by two roads — one, the *Five-mile Pike*, northeast, via Lake Mohegan, Shrub Oak, Jefferson Valley, and Baldwin's, to Lake Mahopac or Croton Falls and North Salem (about twelve miles); and the other, the *Crom Pond road*, leading due east through Yorktown, Somers, and Purdy's, to Salem, or from Somers down to Katonah. Both these roads connect with good routes leading back to New York by way of White Plains or Portchester.

2. Along the Harlem Valley.

New York to Croton Falls.—Leaving Manhattan Island at Central Bridge, we wheel out Jerome Avenue through *Fordham* to the entrance to Woodlawn Cemetery (9 m.). At Grand Avenue, beyond, we turn to the right, inasmuch as the straight road, although more direct, is very poor riding and uninteresting to the mind.

☞ The branch *to the left* leads down a winding hill to Van Cortlandt Lake, and is intersected by Mosholu Avenue, a beautiful woodland avenue of hard dirt, traversing the northerly section of Van Cortlandt Park, and connecting with Broadway just south of the city line; it forms a charming cross-route for Riverdale, Mount St. Vincent, or Yonkers.

Taking the road to the right (at present very poor and hilly, but presently to be graded and macadamized), we skirt the northern boundary of the cemetery to Woodlawn station, on the Harlem Railroad; turning left here we enter the Bronx River road, commonly known as the *Pipe Line*, from the fact that it is built upon the conduit leading from the Kensico reservoir to the city. This road follows closely the course of the Bronx, and is replete with charming scenery. The river winds through the meadow-lands to the east, here overhung with drooping willows, there shrouded in a dense

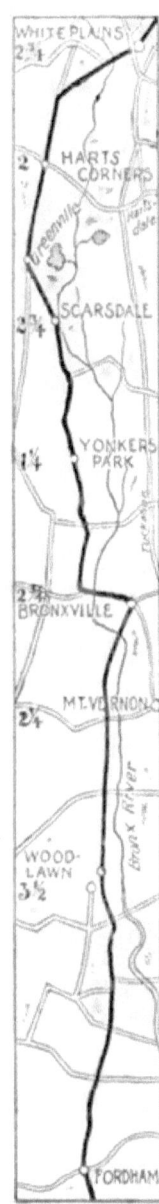

growth of bushes, occasionally widening out into a placid, shimmering pool, quickening its currents through the narrow confines of mossy banks, or dividing its course to avoid a jagged rock or wooded islet. We pass a small reservoir, and then meet a cross-road winding down through the trees from the ridge on the left to the old Hunt's Bridge down in the valley (a narrow, tree-shaded lane). From this rural bit we suddenly emerge into all the life and bustle of a suburban town, and the jarring buzz of the electric cars between Yonkers and Mount Vernon on *Yonkers Avenue* (1½ m. = 11¼ m.).

Our road (straight on north) is now of smooth macadam, skirting the villa-site of Sherwood Park, but the macadam is soon succeeded by a level surface of dirt, running along the base of a low, wooded ridge, with the river winding in and out among the trees, in a glen to the right; now skirting the road so closely that we can see the fish disporting in its lucid depths, then making a bend afar around some knoll or bit of rock, until we meet a cross-road winding down the hill on our left and disappearing through the trees into the river vale. We keep straight on, and, as the road bears around to the right at half a mile distance, cross a bridge spanning the Harlem Railroad tracks and the river, and turn sharply to the left at the next cross-road into the Pondfield road to Bronxville station (2¾ m. = 14 m.), past the half hidden marble gateway of Lawrence Park. Crossing the tracks again, we run down the hill onto the little bridge, crossing the Bronx by the old *Underhill Mill*. This is one of the prettiest bits of scenery along the river's course. The stream widens above the dam into the little mill-pond, and Beaver Pond is only just beyond, densely shaded by drooping willows and elms, and bordered with long, waving grasses. The stone mill, the tumbling stream feeding the placid pool beneath the bridge, and the rich, green meadows lower down, form a picture that never fails to charm the eye. Several old stone houses face the road on the right as we mount the hill, among them an old tavern—the Bronxville Hotel ($2)—where refreshment may be had.

Just beyond the inn, where a signboard reads "To Tuckahoe," we turn to the right and enter another section of the Pipe Line. Upon the hillside are the pretty villas composing Armour Park, and the wooded ravine on our right contains the river on its way into Beaver Pond. We cross the *Tuckahoe road*, a well macadamized avenue leading from the Sawmill Valley north of Yonkers over the ridge on our west down to the hamlet of Tuckahoe on the railroad, and, following the Pipe Line, reach another intersecting road close by a neat church of native marble. Here we bear to the right on the center road over the bridge spanning the turbulent mill stream, called Troublesome Brook, and pass the highly civilized villa property of the Yonkers Park Association (1¼ m. = 15¼ m.), in the southerly corner of which the river, partly by natural and partly by artificial means, forms a shady miniature lake dotted with tiny islets of rocks and bush. Electric roads will soon open this region to excursionists.

Our way is shaded by fine trees, and the river flows through a deep, wooded ravine to the right, its banks a tangle of shrubbery and flowering weeds that often hides the water and forms a safe retreat for numberless birds. A narrow road leads off to the right across the valley, while just beyond, on the left, perched on a rocky ledge up among the old trees, is the *Scarsdale Hotel* ($2.50) (2¾ m. = 18 m.).

☞ Ardsley Avenue, crossed soon after leaving the hotel, is a hilly, wooded road leading eastward over the ridge to Ardsley (p. 48), where it connects with Ashford Avenue direct to Dobbs Ferry on the Hudson. To the right it terminates at Scarsdale station, on the Harlem Railroad.

We bowl along under the edge of a rocky ledge, surmounted by a fine grove of spruce, with the river in a densely wooded glen on the right, where, at this moment, a family from New York, who have come out by train, are merrily picnicking by a camp-fire built upon the rocks beside the dashing currents. Presently we emerge through the avenue of trees, on the railroad side. From here on to Hartsdale the road traverses a ledge of the ridge, with the railroad tracks below, and the river, always changing and beautiful, in the lowlands beyond. At *Hartsdale* (1¼ m. = 19¼ m.), a scattering settlement, with a railroad station and a solitary store, we turn to the left onto a roadway of marble macadam, its white surface glistening in the sunlight, and mount a gradual ascent to *Hart's Corners* (½ m.), where we turn to the right onto Central **Park** Avenue, a continuation of Central Avenue in New York. It is a broad, sandy road, poor for riding, but has a hard side-path on the left. To the **northward** rise the tree-covered summits of the hills above White Plains. Several fine places border the road, one of which, that of J. Dickman Brown, rightly suggests, by its cluster of clean, roomy stables, that it is a blooded stock farm. The numberless dwellings which now meet the eye in every direction denote the proximity of **a town,** and turning to the right at the fountain we **wheel into White Plains, the** county seat of Westchester, prettily situated among the hills, with a local history dating back beyond two centuries ($2\frac{3}{4}$ m. = $22\frac{1}{2}$ m.).

This was originally the site of the chief village of the **Necquaskeck** Indians, and was called by them "**Quarroppas,**" or "**White Plains,**" supposedly from the large quantities of balsam which once covered the fields with white blossoms. The town figured prominently during the Revolution, for on the heights of Chatterton Hill, opposite the Brown farm, was fought, in October, 1776, the battle of White Plains. On Spring Street is the house occupied by Lafayette, and about a mile out Broadway, near the cemetery, is that one selected by Washington as his headquarters. The city is one of the principal stations on the Harlem division of the New York Central Railroad, and has **an electric railway running from** Broadway along Railroad Avenue, and past the fair grounds to Elmsford, on the New York & Putnam Railroad. This tramway is to be extended to Tarrytown. White Plains has several good *hotels*, prominent among which are the **Orawampum** ($2.50, **L. A. W. $2),** Leland's Standard ($2.50), and Carpenter's ($2), and the **little hotel and** restaurant ($1.50, L. A. W. $1) on Depot Place, presided over by the world-famous "Admiral Dot." Several good restaurants, luncheon, and ice **cream** places may be found on Main Street.

White Plains forms an excellent center for cycling expeditions in all directions.

Northward to Croton Falls the **road leads out** Broadway and up the valley of the Bronx past Kensico **Cemetery** and through Unionville. Here a **road at the left leads northward, at the** right of Buttermilk Hill, **to Sing Sing, or south of the hill to the** Sawmill Valley and Tarrytown. Keeping on **to Pleasantville—a** quaint, old-fashioned village—we meet, just beyond the cemetery, **the Bedford road, which** furnishes a good **route back to** Tarrytown. Our **route then proceeds through a** beautiful country, offering **some interesting landscapes, on through Chappaqua to** Mount Kisco. **The Harlem** Railroad has been **at the left since** leaving Pleasantville, **but** is crossed at Bedford station. **A short** distance beyond **this is the** large summer town, *Katonah*, and then follow Golden's Bridge, Purdy's, and Croton Falls (28¾ m. from White Plains). From Katonah a good road may be followed down the Croton Valley to Sing Sing, or straight west over the Crom Pond road to Peekskill, or southeast to South Salem, and back to the shore of the Sound. From Purdy's good roads go west to the Hudson, and east and south to North Salem and Portchester. From Croton Falls you may make easy runs west to Peekskill, including a detour to Lake Mahopac; or northeast to Peach Lake and into Putnam County.

☞ For details of all this region, condition of roads, etc., consult Rand, McNally & Co.'s "Road Map and Cycling Guide to Westchester County" (50 cents).

Another route to the North from White Plains is that which takes you to the borders of Connecticut. Going out Broadway and over the hill take the right fork and make your way to the old village of Kensico, then up the valley of Bear Gutter Creek to Armonk. This is a wild hilly region, full of lakes and forests and old-fashioned farms and cross-roads hamlets on the edge of Connecticut. You can here turn back, if you wish, and follow King Street to Portchester. Going on, you proceed northward through Northcastle, past Cobamong Pond, with Byram Lake in the distance, and down the Mianus Valley to Bedford —a very interesting old town, several miles from the railroad, with which it is connected by a stage line. Its revolutionary and legendary history is interesting and has been somewhat embodied in Cooper's "Spy." If you consider this far enough a good road may be followed northwestward through an interesting country to Katonah. Many very pretty side trips may be made in this romantic neighborhood. The roads northward are not very good, and lead across the hills to Cross River, Lake Waccabuc, Salem Center (whence a good road leads west to Purdy's and beyond), and to North Salem. From Cross River

good roads lead eastward to Titicus and Ridgefield, and from North Salem to Peach Lake and eastward into the borders of Connecticut; and these all connect with the main routes southward to Stamford and Portchester.

From White Plains to Tarrytown the road is nearly straight, following the electric car tracks as far as Elmsford, and then over the hills into the southern part of Tarrytown. It is all macadam, and the distance is about 6½ miles.

From White Plains to Rye, Portchester, or Greenwich, Conn., take Harrison Street straight east from Broadway. It is hilly but has a good surface, and passes through "The Purchase," where, 2½ miles from White Plains, a good road turning to the right will lead straight south to Rye. Two miles farther brings you to King Street, the great north-and-south thoroughfare (p. 32), upon which you turn to the right three-quarters of a mile to the intersection of Ridge Street. A turn to the right would lead to Rye; to the left this street leads through Glenville, and across the Byram River in Connecticut, and by a somewhat circuitous route to Greenwich, where the macadamized shore road may be followed back to New York.

From White Plains to Rye a very direct route is down North Street, which forks to the right near where Harrison Avenue leaves Broadway, and takes a straight course southeastward across the Mamaroneck Valley into Locust Avenue.

From White Plains to Rye Pond is a pleasant day's excursion. Go north on Broadway to the first turn to the right beyond the Soldiers' Monument. Keep to the left around the bend in the road and then to the right to St. Mary's Lake, a small, oval sheet of water, bordered with high, rocky, wooded hills. Beyond the lake the route forks to the right over a new road and continues through a rock-strewn bit of woodland, sloping down in rolling hills and hollows to the valley of the Mamaroneck on the right. Henceforth keep to the center road by the little smithy and out Lake Street, through a negro settlement, bearing to the right at the first fork, then to the left at the next, passing the little African chapel, and then wheel direct to Rye Pond. The roadbed is here sandy and stony, and the way a succession of hills and hollows, through deep forests, with here and there a clearing, until you reach the top of the ridge and have before you, on the left, the broad expanse of Rye Pond. Precipitous hills rise from the water's edge on every side, and tangled forests half hide and half reveal the jutting crags.

One half expects to see the antlers of a deer as it stoops to lap the waters on that bit of strand, or a canoe, laden with savages, shoot out from the shelter of yon shady cove. It is but a short distance on to King Street, where you can turn north or south indefinitely.

3. New York to Portchester.

From Central Park we whirl up Seventh Avenue to 116th Street, turn to the left upon St. Nicholas Avenue, and make a long, gradual ascent over smooth macadam, to 161st Street. Taking the west fork, we cross the cable-road into the Kingsbridge road (See Route 1), traverse Washington Heights, turn in at Christ's Hotel (3⅝ m.), and cross *Washington Bridge*. Leaving the bridge, we turn to the left, pass the Ogden estate, swing to the right through Featherbed Lane (once narrow, cool, and shady), then turn to the left on the Macomb's Dam road, where, at the top of the hill, we pass on the left the old stone mansion of the Morrises; then down the hill and by "Fairlawn" and the Berkeley Oval. Now the way leads up a slight hill, through a bower of trees, and presently brings us to the Fordham Landing road, where we turn to the right, over the aqueduct, cross Jerome Avenue, and run down hill to *Fordham* (3⅝ m. = 7¼ m.). Crossing the sunken tracks of the Harlem Railroad we go out Pelham Avenue, passing, on the left, the extensive grounds of St. John's College. Now comes a gradual ascent, and then a race down the hill, across the Southern Boulevard and the bridge over the Bronx. To the left lies Bronx Park, with the Lorillard mansion and the old snuff mill close by. Proceeding over a slight rise, we find that the road forks. The branch to the left leads to the park; the right fork, which we follow, leads over the hill and through the small settlement of *Bronxdale*, where we cross the old Boston road and keep straight out, following the trolley-line to Mount Vernon as far as Morris Park, where the tracks bend sharply to the right, toward West Farms. Leaving the rails, we keep straight on by the handsome race track, down the hill under the New Haven Railroad, and turn to the left into **Westchester** (3¼ m. = 10½ m.), following the street-car line on Westchester Avenue straight into the village, which has little to detain us except the beautiful shaded old graveyard around the handsome church. The great juvenile corrective institution, known as the Catholic Protectory, is conspicuous in the distance.

☞ From **Brooklyn, etc.**—It will not be amiss to mention here the best routes of approach to this route and the interior of Westchester County from Brooklyn and the eastern side of New York City. From *East Twenty-third Street* (*Williamsburg*) *Ferry*, go up to First Avenue (block pavement), turn to the right three blocks to Twenty-sixth Street (asphalt), then to the left to Madison Avenue, at the northeast corner of Madison Square.

From here you must go up Madison Avenue (asphalt) to Sixtieth Street, thence to the left one block to Central Park, where you follow the East Drive to the Lenox Avenue exit (macadam) and up to 115th Street, where you turn to the right one block to Fifth Avenue, and go up that avenue (asphalt) to 131st Street. Turn to the right, here, one block, to the Madison Avenue Bridge, over it and on through 138th Street (block pavement) to Willis Avenue, which is of asphalt, and leads to Westchester Avenue, where you have block pavement, succeeded by macadam as far as Westchester, which is entered as before. *From Brooklyn Bridge to Madison Square* the best route is up Park Row to Chatham Square, then to the right along Division Street (asphalt), then to the left up Forsyth Street (asphalt) to Houston, then one block to the left to Second Avenue (asphalt) and up to Twenty-second Street. Here turn to the left to Lexington Avenue, and then to the left through Twenty-sixth Street to Madison Avenue. *From Desbrosses Street* (Jersey City) or *Christopher Street* (Hoboken) ferry, the best route is to go directly to Hudson Street (belgian), up to and along Eighth Avenue (asphalt) to West Twenty-sixth Street (asphalt), and then east to Madison Avenue.

Leaving Westchester Village we follow the main street on to the bridge crossing Westchester Creek, then turn to the left where the road branches.

☞ The fork to the right leads to **Throg's Neck and Fort Schuyler.** Throg's Neck is the peninsula reaching eastward at the place where Long Island Sound contracts into East River. It is the easternmost point of the city of New York, and in the longitude of Rockaway Beach. The first three miles of this smooth, park-like road to Fort Schuyler is bordered by elaborate country homes of wealthy families, such as the Havemeyers, the Morrises of race-track fame, and others; and along each side stand aged and lofty elms, oaks, and other noble shade-trees, their roots buried beneath green grass. "The trees here and there," notes a recent traveler, "thicken into small groves, and every turn of the road reveals great trunks and high overhanging branches. It is an ideal path for walking, driving, or bicycling. There are fascinating byways, but the high road is never crowded. The Sound is revealed from time to time across the greenery of the fields, an ideal summer sea, dotted with sails and bounded by the purplish, wooded shores of Long Island."

Three-quarters of a mile from Westchester Center, and a somewhat less distance beyond the bridge over Westchester Creek, the Eastern Boulevard is crossed, and here is a settlement with two or three busy road-houses. A few rods eastward this boulevard turns sharply north to Baychester. To the west it runs across the creek and its marshes into Unionport, a settlement on **Cornell Neck,** south of Westchester Avenue; this part of it, however, is unimproved, and a country road extends southward to the mouth of Westchester Creek at Old Ferry Point. For a mile or more after this, the blue water is almost constantly in sight. Locust Point and Old Ferry Point come into view, and are edged with tropical-looking ailantus trees. A succession of embowered country seats is in view, each held in the embrace of the Sound. Two miles below the cross-roads, where a road leads off to the left to Locust Point on the Sound side, Throg's Neck suddenly becomes a very narrow peninsula, the trees cease, and the Government Military Reservation begins. The road narrows and becomes white with the dust of oyster shells. New York has its shell roads as well as New Orleans. A narrow causeway finally leads across a stretch of marsh, and *Fort Schuyler* is at hand. The fortifications are only grassy mounds, with old smooth-bore guns forming picturesque foreground adjuncts to the sweet sea-pictures north and south. The officers' houses, and residences for two artillery companies, are in the interior, facing landward and sheltered from the winter gales by the ramparts.

On this promontory of Throg's Neck, called by the Indians "Quimshung," a settlement was established as early as 1642, by John Throgmorton, a Baptist, and thirty-five families, who had been driven from Massachusetts with Roger Williams, the patriarch of Rhode Island and the Providence plantations. These settlers were attracted hither by the Dutch guarantee of civil and religious liberty to all comers who meant to be law-abiding citizens, and soon brought together, during the next quarter-century, many families of Quakers, Church of England people, and others unable to live contentedly under the severe regimen of the Puritan rulers of New England, who scattered all along the shore, and have left their names upon the various creeks, bays, headlands, and "necks" that are found upon our present maps. This peninsula takes its name from the shortened and misspelled Throgmorton family. It is a delightful experience to lie at ease of a summer day upon these ramparts, or, even better, upon the little bluff a few hundred yards distant, and watch the procession of the commerce of New York as it defiles through this gateway to the metropolis. "Sails are disappearing under the round and others are rising into view every few minutes. For an instant a single schooner, so set upon her way that her sails look like mere ribbons, with strips of sky between, has the whole horizon to herself. Ten minutes later she has half a dozen consorts, filmy-winged yachts, merchant schooners, their sails bleached and etherealized by the distance, a steam yacht, and excursion steamers. They wax and wane until the horizon is again completely transformed. New risen steamers come on with swift paddles, pass the fort, and disappear southward. Tiny sloops are outlined against the Long Island shore, now backed with the purplish blue of woodlands, now by warm yellow where a bare little cliff rises from the water. There is a sound of paddles in all directions, rhythmic, dreamy, peaceful. All the sights and sounds breathe a summer peace. The blue is almost a snowstorm of canvas where pleasure-craft tilt and tack. The noises from the sparkling plain of water are all smothered and softened."

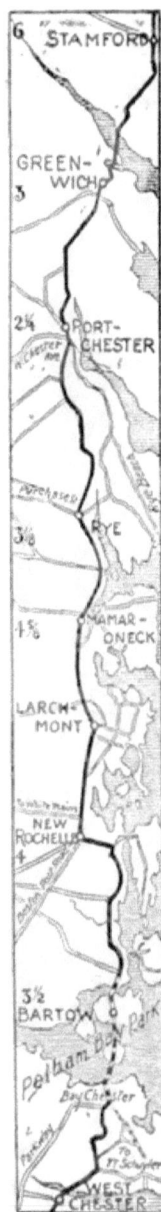

Beyond Westchester Creek our route (the Pelham road) makes a gradual ascent of a bluff, skirting the broad salt-meadows along the creek verge, which are wet at high tide yet grow good hay.

☞ A third of a mile beyond the fork a macadamized road striking off to the right leads (⅔ m.) to the gates of the Westchester Country Club, whose grounds and handsome house are on the shore of Pelham Bay, at the head of a cove east of Throg's Neck Village. This is the oldest and most fashionable country club in the neighborhood of New York.

A short distance farther, where the road turns, there stands a wayside inn, built in 1753. We bear to the right beyond this relic of colonial good cheer, and up over the hill through a little settlement, and then enter *Pelham Bay Park*, at the point where a (poor) road leads to the right down to the country club and Throg's Neck. From here on through the Park the road has been broadened and is to be improved as "Pelham Parkway;" beyond the Park the Pelham road resumes its name. The Parkway is now in fair condition, and the side-path offers good wheeling and leads us rapidly across a stretch of shoreland, then up a slight hill, and down on to Pelham Bay bridge.

This bay and river were formerly of great commercial importance to the farmers and merchants of this shore; and Eastchester grew into a village because it was at the head of navigation for boats big enough to sail to New York. Even now the bridges must be built with draws, for the river is used for heavy freights, such as coal and building materials; and a small steamboat plys regularly between Eastchester (Mount Vernon) and New York.

Baychester is half a mile north of the bridge, by a good road, and here the Bronx Parkway of the future comes in. We wheel along a shady avenue through *Bartow*, past the railroad station, where a road leads to the right to City Island and to pretty spots along the shore of Pelham Bay Park (3½ m. = 10½ m.).

City Island is two miles south off the extremity of Rodman "Neck," itself an island. This string of islands forms the eastern shore of Pelham Bay, separating it from the Sound. A horse-car line

New Aladdin Lamp
For the Bicycle.
PRICE, $2.50.

LENS, Oilwell, or Springs can not be lost. Springs extra strong, can be **instantly removed and replaced without use of solder or rivets.** Can be lit in highest wind, without opening lamp. Oil well enlarged. Burns twelve hours.

The **New Aladdin** has more advantages than any other lamp. If dealer hasn't it, will forward by mail on receipt of price. Send for illustrated circular.

ALADDIN LAMP COMPANY,

518 BROAD STREET,   107 CHAMBERS STREET,
NEWARK, N. J.   NEW YORK CITY.

runs cars back and forth between Bartow and City Island along pleasant roads, and by fields and shores in the park which form delightful picnicking places for a summer day's jaunt. City Island has little to attract the rambler, unless he is especially interested in marine matters and traditions. It has always been famous for oyster planting, fishing, and sailing. Some of the fastest yachts of this country have been built there, and many larger craft. Its houses and gardens show hundreds of relics of dismantled ships, utilized architecturally or ornamentally. The dining-room of a house near the bridge is the cabin of the old war-ship *St. Mary's*. The bridge itself is made wholly of the timbers of one of our early "seventy-fours," the frigate *North Carolina*, a sister-ship of the *New Hampshire*, which is still in use. It was constructed thirty years ago, and the draw is that formerly used in the old Harlem bridge. The large island northeast of City Island is Hart's, which contains the City Lunatic Asylum and the vast Potter's Field, where the pauper dead are buried. It is reached by a ferry from East Twenty-sixth Street (Bellevue Hospital) daily, at 11.00 A. M. The lighthouse opposite is Stepping Stones, and the promontory on the Long Island shore Hewlett's Point, at the extremity of Great Neck. Read Irving's "Knickerbocker History" for the traditions of these names.

Beyond Bartow, which is ensconced in large woods, comes another bit of salt-meadow, where, to the right, we catch a distant view of Long Island Sound ; and after that a rising stretch, where the riding is not more than passable among park improvements, until we reach the stone-pillared entrance to Hunter Island, now a part of the Park, but not long ago the homestead of an old family, who had here a finely cultivated estate. The two islets in front of it, and connected by bridge, have always been a favorite resort with picnickers. Here we enjoy a pleasing view of the fine summer home and athletic grounds of the New York Athletic Club, on Travers Island (2 m. = 16 m.). Beyond it rise the stone parapets of the miniature castle on Starin's Glen Island, the popular summer resort ; more to the eastward is the tall brick chimney on David's Island, a United States Military post, and still beyond stretch the waters of the Sound to the far-away bluish brink of Long Island.

The road now bends to the left down into a little dell, then around and up a slight hill to and past Pelham Priory, deep among the trees, opposite which is the entrance to Travers Island.

☞ The fine road just beyond the Priory leads north to Pelham Manor, and on by good connecting roads to Pelhamville and Mount Vernon. The small ivy-grown church facing this road, just beyond the Priory, is the Bolton Memorial chapel, so called in memory of the Rev. Robert Bolton, the historian of Westchester County, who was for many years rector of this parish.

The road now improves, skirts the rock-bound inlet around *Glen Island*, and soon brings us to Neptune Street, which leads down to the shore and out upon a small island, where is the landing of the ferry to Glen Island, the Government dock, and the ferry to David's Island. To this point come the street cars from New Rochelle, turning down Neptune Street to the ferry landings. Keeping straight on beside the tracks, with a pleasant view across the inlet to Davenport Neck, and over it to the buildings on David's Island, we follow the road half a mile or more to Center Street, where we turn to the left with the cars and run on half a mile farther to Main Street, in New Rochelle (2⅜ m. = 18⅜ m.).

New Rochelle is a very old, beautiful, and wealthy town, and has as summer residents many noted families. It is a great yachting resort. The streets are in good condition, and an hour or two can be well spent in riding about the city, and in visiting Hudson Park, on the harbor east of Davenport Neck; electric cars reach this park. Two excellent roads lead northward — one (Winyah Avenue), via Pelhamville to Mount Vernon, along which an electric railroad is now operated; and North Street, a macadamized road leading straight to White Plains. A stage runs out this road to some extensive nurseries; and about two miles out stands the monument to John Howard Payne, and an interesting old stone house built in 1728. The Windsor Hotel and restaurant on Bridge Street, facing the depot, is a new and well-conducted house.

Leaving New Rochelle we wheel out Main Street and down into the meadows bordering Echo Bay — a charming little harbor. Far away across the sail-flecked expanse of water rise the purplish woodlands and yellowish cliffs of Cow Neck, on Long Island, with the lighthouse on Sand's Point sparkling in the sun. To the northward, guarding the harbor, is the low, rocky headland of Premium's Point, set off by the stately summer residence of C. Oliver Iselin, while several rocky islets are bedecked with the houses of yacht or boat clubs. We pass a road leading down over the marshes to Larchmont, and have another view of the distant Sound. Just above it is Springmyer's Road-house.

☞ The cross-road just beyond here leads from the station on the left to Larchmont Manor, a popular summer colony and yachting resort. It occupies a point of land projecting into the Sound, indented by the small Horseshoe Harbor and forming the southwestern shelter of DeLancey's Cove, or Larchmont Harbor. This "neck" is covered with a network of shady, macadamized avenues, communicating with elegant summer hotels and the residences of wealthy men.

....Janney Pedals

Men's Rat Trap Pedal.

As riders are becoming more and more educated about bicycles they are extremely particular in regard to the equipments. This partly explains the popularity of our pedals.

Impossible for them to bind or tighten.

Hence, you can rely on them for long rides without fear of walking because of an imperfect pedal.

If you were buying a carriage, would you want the king-bolt made of tin? When you purchase your wheel are you careful to see that you have the best of all good things on it? Don't be content with ordinary pedals unless you enjoy walking home when ten miles or more from nowhere.

How small it is; yet the most important part of the wheel.

Retains the Oil. Absolutely Dust and Water Proof.

Men's Combination Pedal.

Our Catalogue gives particulars— tells you **why.** Write for it.

Cycle Improvement Co.

Westboro, Mass. U. S. A.

Ladies' Rubber Pedal.

We next roll along level macadam until DeLancey's Cove comes into view, and beyond it DeLancey's Neck, or Orienta (2⅝ m.= 21¼ m.).

☞ A pleasant detour here goes out Weaver Street, from the great brick school-house on the left to Griffin Avenue, at the Griffin Farm. This is all good macadam, and gives a superb view of the Sound, Long Island shore, and Mamaroneck, to which we return along Grand Park Avenue.

The regular post-road, however, leads straight into *Mamaroneck* (1⅜ m.=22⅝ m.), past the DeLancey mansion on Heathcote Hill. On the left, as we enter the town, is the handsome St. Thomas' Episcopal Church. The New York hotel and restaurant, on the north side of Mamaroneck Avenue, just off of the post-road, is the local hotel ($1.50, L. A. W. $1). Crossing the bridge over the river, we mount a slight incline, just beyond Barry Avenue, bear to the right and cross Stony Brook, just above the road leading on the left to Harrison. The road is rolling, and leads past a succession of grand country houses, and presently brings us to *Rye*.

☞ *The road to Rye Beach* (Rye Beach Avenue) leads off at the right, down to the shore, which is growing in popularity as a seaside resort and bathing place. Beck's is the favorite hotel. This trip can be made a delightful detour by following Forest Avenue or Grace Church Street back to the post-road at Rye, or keeping along the latter into Portchester.

The post-road, just beyond Rye Beach Avenue, bears to the right, passing several old colonial houses, and runs down to a bridge over Mill Brook, and into the square of Rye before the Presbyterian Church (3⅜ m.=26 m.).

☞ Two routes to Portchester may be followed from here, equal in merit. One turns to the right up the little street by the church, and then to the left into Grace Church Street, and goes direct to the business portion of Portchester and the railroad station.

☞ *The left fork*, at the Boston Road-house, leads to Rye station, then into Ridge Street, which runs over the hills back of Portchester, crosses Purchase and Westchester avenues, intersects King Street at the Connecticut line, traverses Glenville and turns south to its termination in Greenwich — partly macadam — rest fair riding but hilly, with fine views of Sound and intermediate country. The first turn on the left, as we go toward the station, is Forest Avenue, which runs into North Street and gives a fair road to White Plains.

We take the right fork at the Boston Road-house ($2), go up over the railroad bridge, and along an almost perfect roadbed. From the top of a rise we see the houses of Portchester, ere we roll down under the railroad bridge, and then to the left into Main Street on to the square. A prominent hotel is Young's, 138 Westchester Avenue ($2, L. A. W. $1.50). (2¼ m.—28¼ m.)

☞ Pleasant side trips may be made from here, notably:

To Stamford. — Straight east along the post-road, which is macadamized all the way, and always interesting. It passes through Greenwich and Cos Cob, and reaches Stamford in 6¼ miles.

To the Byram Valley. — For this, turn sharply to the left after crossing the bridge out Main Street, and go direct through Pemberwick to Glenville. The road is good and replete with fine scenery. At Glenville turn to the left, and then take the south fork into King Street, on which you turn to the left again on a fine macadamized road and return down hill to Portchester.

Westchester Avenue leads directly to White Plains. (See p. 22.) *Purchase Street*, which intersects Westchester Avenue some two miles above the town, is also a broad macadamized avenue, leading from Rye on the south to the old Quaker town of Purchase (now called Harrison).

King Street, leading north from the railway station, is an old highway to the north, along the Connecticut line into the eastern section of Westchester County. From the town to Harrison Avenue it is macadamized, and from there on is of hard dirt, connecting near Armonk with Route 2 (p. 23).

The *southeastern section* of Westchester County, bordering Connecticut, is exceedingly wild and rugged. The roads are miserable, hilly, sandy, and stony. The towns are small, scattering settlements, affording no accommodations in the way of road-houses or hotels, or even boarding-houses, but the farmers will usually entertain the hungry or belated bicycler. The scenery in places is very beautiful — in a savage and mountainous way. From some points the Sound and the intervening territory of Connecticut are within range of the eye, but the general contour of the country is a monotony of rolling hills, rocks, and trees. Trinity Lake, lying between Poundridge and Lewisboro, is the only water of note, and hardly pays for the toil required to reach it.

Cross Routes.

Yonkers to Mount Vernon and New Rochelle.— Leaving Yonkers at Getty Square, we turn to the right on Main Street to Yonkers Avenue, then to the left, following the line of the trolley cars up the hill of asphalt, and taking the right fork where the road branches. (The left is Nepperhan Avenue — See route on p. 35.) As we bear to the right on up the hill, we see down on the left the Nepperhan or Sawmill River — here carried over the aqueduct by an elevated conduit, and then spreading out into the mill-pond below — its shores lined with grimy factories. Toiling on up the slope, bedded with smooth macadam, we pass under the brow of the hill, whose fine old trees are fast giving place to ugly brick tenements, then race down the hill through a shady, rock-bound cut into the valley watered by Tibbetts Brook, with a charming view of the wooded heights of *Dunwoodie* before us. As we dash down to this little station on the New York & Putnam Railroad, the valley stretches in broad savannas to the south, traversed by the stream and the shining rails; the heights rise in gentle slopes on either side, dotted with villas and studded with shapely copses of aged trees. We cross the railway and bear to the right, following the tracks of the trolley line up a long ascent, prettily wooded, passing on the left, as we cross Central Avenue, the historical ground of *Valentine's Hill*, where the Continental Army was encamped under Washington, before the British drove him west of the Hudson, and which was afterward the scene of several skirmishes. The way leads down from this height, and around through a sylvan dale to *West Mount Vernon*, where we intersect Route 2 to the north. Crossing the railroad, we have a short climb over block pavement, then a run of good macadam to Stevens Avenue. Here we turn to the left by the drug store, just this side of the bridge spanning the sunken tracks of the New Haven Railroad, and take Stevens Avenue, parallel with the railroad, direct to Fourth Avenue, **Mount Vernon**.

Turning to the right, by the Mount Vernon Hotel, we cross the tracks and continue out South Fourth Avenue, the main business street of the city and smoothly asphalted, two blocks to Third Street, and then turn to the left.

☞ From this point a somewhat shorter, but less interesting, route may be taken to New Rochelle, by following the electric-car tracks to the "White House," at the intersection of the Pelhamville road, which leads from Pelham Manor and Travers Island on the south to Pelhamville on the north. (See Route 3.) From the White House keep straight on over the hill, and turn to the left at its junction with the old post-road direct to New Rochelle. This road is macadamized all the way.

From *Fourth Avenue* we turn to the left one block on Third Street to Third Avenue, and then turn to the right on that broad, shaded avenue of splendid macadam, which is bordered with fine residences, and continues beyond the city line as the old *Eastchester road*. As we enter this ancient highway it bends to the right under the shadow of the hill, with the cool, blue tops of the highlands, toward the Sound, showing through the green foliage at the left. Now we swing eastward under a gigantic oak. The valley widens, and offers a constant succession of pleasant sights, near or remote, the road winding to the right, by a fine grove of hickory; then through a stretch of broad, cultivated fields, and farther on dipping into an arbor of interwoven branches, where, off to the south, a glimpse is caught of the golden cross on the spire of old St. Pauls. We wheel down through a pathway of trees, with the marshes watered by the Eastchester Creek before us, passing a large country place, half hidden in a cluster of old trees, and across a rustic bridge to the junction of Columbus Avenue, which is only a new local name for this part of the old Kingsbridge road, opened in 1671, and the first stage-route between New York and Boston.

Here, on the left, their grim portals overlooking the tawny salt meadows, are the family burial vaults of **St. Paul's Church**, and, as we turn, we see the church itself, with its semi-covered, blue stone walls and antique red-brick trimmings, seamed and marred by the cannon balls of the Revolution. Its quaint church-yard, full of weather-beaten tombstones, borders the roadside, and are guarded by a file of tall locusts, knotted and gnarled with age. One bears, imbedded in its bark, the iron ring to which, tradition says, culprits were bound and publicly whipped; and here, also, stood the village stocks. This church site was occupied as early as 1699. The present edifice of stone and brick, erected in 1735, is remarkable for the solid character of its masonry and its heavily groined angles and doors. The sweet-toned bell that still rings out the call to service is of silver-bronze, and, according to Bolton, was presented by the Rev. Thomas Standard, in 1758. Together with the sacramental vessels, bible, and prayer-book, it was secreted in a vault in the cellar of the Halsey mansion during the Revolution. One of the vaults beneath contains the ashes of the British incendiary who started the conflagration that destroyed its interior in 1778. In the quaint cemetery are the remains of more than 6,000 of Washington's soldiers; while the ancient tombs, their curious epitaphs, and the quaint rural environments make it a mecca for the lover of history. An atmosphere of antiquity pervades the entire surroundings.

Leaving the aged kirk to its peaceful solitude, we continue out the Eastchester road, through a cluster of small dwellings, a tavern, meeting-house, smithy, and cobbler shop, which constitute the main portion of the old town of *Eastchester*, and reach the white-pillared entrance to another interesting landmark of olden times — the Halsey mansion.

Two gigantic walnuts stand as sentinels at the gate; the stone wall is bordered by a hedge of arborvitæ; and grand old trees grace the lawn and cast their grateful shade over the old manse. This house was built in 1720, by Elkanah Vincent, and although twice enlarged and adorned with broad, low piazzas, the original edifice remains intact. The massive foundations and huge, iron-seasoned oaken timbers are just as they were at the time of erection, nearly two hundred years ago. In the cellar is a stone vault, in which were buried the treasures of St. Paul's Church during the troublesome revolutionary times, where they remained covered by a heap of timbers, masonry, and earth, their resting-place known to but seven trusted patriots until 1791. Since then the property has passed through several hands, and many are the tales and legends associated with its history. For several years it was the residence of Colonel Smith, an officer and politician, who became the son-in-law of President John Quincy Adams, and when, in 1797, the yellow fever raged in Philadelphia, then the seat of government, President Adams and his family made their home here. Isaac Anderson, the proprietor of a noted sporting resort in the city, kept bachelor's hall here for a score of years, surrounded with prodigal luxury, and vivid stories of the bacchanalian revels held in the old house during his ownership are still related. Anderson met with reverses in his precarious career, and staked the property on the turn of a card; the winner was "Kite" Halsey, another "sport," flourishing at Saratoga, in whose family it still remains. From the study of this storied spot we wheel forward into the "New" Boston Pike, which took the place of the older zigzagging highway as a stage-route when traffic became of sufficient importance to call for improvements.

Turning to the left here, we cross Eastchester Creek, or Hutchinson River, and soon enter upon the smooth macadam about Pelham Manor. Keeping straight on, we again have a bit of poor road as we turn to the right down over the bridge over the New Haven Railroad and then bend to the left past Trinity Church into Main Street, **New Rochelle.** (See Route 3.)

Up the Sawmill River Valley.— From Getty Square, Yonkers, we make a long climb up Palisade Avenue to Ashburton Avenue, on which we turn to the right to Nepperhan Avenue — all asphalted. We turn to the north on Nepperhan Avenue, where the asphalt gives way to a smooth level stretch of macadam — the new Yonkers Speedway, a broad boulevard skirting the Nepperhan River for nearly three miles. The ridge rises high, rocky, and wooded on the west; to the right stretch the meadows through which flows the river called "Nepperhan" by the Indians, but christened "Sawmill" by matter-of-fact white settlers. Its banks are lined with trees and bush. Thickets of the white, lace-flowered sambucus intermingle with fragrant wild rose and briar; fields of goldenrod, white **balsams, marguerites, ox-eyed daisies,** and yellow dandelions, with **here and there** clumps of waving **flag and snow-tipped cat-tails** denoting **a bit of** marshland, feed **the eye greedy for nature's beauty. Off to the east rise low,** wooded **hills, on one of which is the cosy, gray-gabled home of the St. Andrews Golf Club, whose links, indicated by small flags,** stretch **away over the slopes. Next we see the streets of Nepara** Park, **and soon reach** *Tompkin's Avenue,* **the present terminus of the** Speedway, **and cross the river into the old Sawmill River road.**

☞ Tompkins **Avenue continues on over the ridge into the Sprain** road, traversing **the valley watered by Sprain Brook, a tributary of the Bronx. It was over this old woodland road, hilly but fair riding, that Washington and his army passed on his retreat to White Plains. Over the opposite ridge lies the Sprain Reservoir, from which Yonkers draws its water supply. The region is pretty and not bad riding, and may be reached either from here or from the Tuckahoe road below. Sprain Brook offers one of the best rambling districts near New York.**

Turning to the north on the Sawmill River road, now a surface of good **dirt and fairly level, we continue up the valley through** a charmingly **varied country until we reach Ardsley.**

☞ **To the left is Ashford Avenue leading on the line of an Indian** trail **to Dobbs Ferry; to the right is Ardsley Avenue up over the** heights **to Scarsdale in the Bronx Valley.**

We **keep straight on through the little settlement of Woodland, to** the west, **the ridge rising in a steep, thickly wooded and rocky bluff,** and every **mile interesting and beautiful. A mountain road leads** over the **hills to the east, and as we bear to the right, two** country lanes lead **off to the west. Across the vale rise the rough slopes** of Beaver **Hill, and we swing around to the north again to** *Elmsford,* anciently Hall's Corners (p. 48). **On our right is the little** meetinghouse erected **in 1790, in whose tiny churchyard lie the** remains of Isaac Van Wart, **one of the captors of Major André, the** modest monument, erected **by the patriotic citizens in 1829,** almost concealed beneath the ivy **Here also repose the ashes of** General Hammond **and Capt.** John Romer, **while many of the moss-covered** tombstones bear **dates as early as 1795. On the corner of the Tarrytown** road is **the Ledger House ($1.50), whose history as a hotel goes back nearly** two centuries. **Several minor conflicts took place in this vicinity during the struggle for American independence, notably the cowardly attack on** three **lads, one of whom, named Vincent, recovered, but was a** cripple for life, **and was accorded a pension, said to be the first** granted by the United States Government. The road now swings around in a crescent, following the course of the valley to *East View*, the East Tarrytown station on the New York & Putnam Railroad. The scenery is grand, rocky, wooded heights towering on either side, and the river traversing the vale between, its banks lined with trees and bushes, while to the westward, through a peak in the Greenburg Range, we can see the bald top of Kaakeout, one of the highest peaks in the country. The road now crosses the river, and bears to the right at the fork.

☞ The left branch of the fork divides again just beyond the station, the south branch leading to McNeil Avenue, a direct road to Tarrytown, and the other skirting Kaakeout Hill, to the Sleepy Hollow and Bedford roads.

We bear to the right, following the western bank of the river, under the brow of the hill, and crossing the stream again just below the upper cross-road, where, in the olden days, Elizabeth Flanagan held forth at her little roadside inn, and regaled the traveler with the first examples of that concoction which has made her famous throughout the land — the American cocktail! Here modestly swung her tiny red sign, bearing on its face in rude white letters the legend: "*Elizabeth Flanagan, Her Hotel.*"

As the road bends to the right, we see towering before us the rockbound heights of old Buttermilk rising abruptly from the river's bank. Passing their shaggy ledges, and bearing to the right, where the road branches just beyond the sawmill, we enter *Unionville* and Route 2.

Tarrytown to White Plains and Portchester. — This route goes out Benedict Avenue, just below the Franklin House, and follows the direct route of the trolley cars as far as *Elmsford station*. This is an extremely pleasant ride over a high region, giving fine landscapes both east and west. From Elmsford (p. 48) follow the car tracks into *White Plains* — an excellent road, but not very entertaining one, passing the Knollwood Golf and Country Clubs' grounds, and the Westchester County Fair grounds. For White Plains see p. 22. Going on up the main street (Railroad Avenue) or better, perhaps, the next street to the left, as far as Broadway, turn to the right at the Soldiers' Monument, go down the hill, and take the left fork — *Westchester Avenue* — for Portchester-on-the-Sound. (A few hundred yards farther this finely macadamized road branches, the right fork being North Street, leading to Rye, Route 3.) We keep well to the left, through the broad, grassy lowlands along the Mamaroneck River. The great brick buildings crowning the hill on the right are those of the Bloomingdale Insane Asylum. We cross the river at the intersection of Harrison Avenue, and keep to the center road, now a level pike, leading down the stream. The meadows are littered with tangled underbrush and flowering weeds, mingled in a rich confusion of color, and water-plants grow luxuriously in the sluggish pools. The half-hidden pillared gateway and keeper's lodge at the entrance to "Ophir Farm," the estate of the Hon. Whitelaw Reid, makes an incident in our ride, and for some distance we skirt the densely-wooded game preserves of this English-like country home. The road presently improves to smooth macadam, and we mount a long, steep hill, cross at the top a country road, and spin down the hill into *Purchase Street*, by the water trough, where the two roads merge for a few hundred yards. The country now assumes a more cultivated appearance; pasture-lands stretch away on either side, and houses dot the distance. We turn to the left as the roads again part (the right branch is Purchase Street, continuing to Rye), cross Blind Brook, and then go up over the hill into *Portchester*.

Along the Croton Valley.—A good run may be made from Sing Sing via Croton and the new Quaker Dam road, up the Croton Valley. This well-built clay turnpike winds around through the hills, with here and there a glimpse of the distant river. Fine old trees, fantastic rocks, shaded glens, and deep gorges succeed one another, and hills rise to the northward into densely wooded heights. When the great work of the New York City water department is completed here, this will be one of the most attractive rides in the country. At Croton Lake, which the road skirts, the surface becomes sandy, and the road often runs inland from the lake and river. Beyond the lake, however, is a fine, interesting country about Somers.

STEAMBOAT AND RAILROAD ROUTES.

Up the Hudson, by Steamboat.

The Hudson River will never cease to be an important means of summer recreation to the people of the metropolis, and will doubtless become more so as time goes on. It is a cause of surprise to strangers that there is no passenger service of fast steamers from the lower part of the city to its upper regions, with landings at Riverside Park, Riverdale, etc., but a growing acquaintance with the peculiar shape and distribution of resident population here forbids that such a service should be profitable to its owners.

It is only necessary here to give some idea of the existing steamboat lines within an excursion distance of the city. In most cases a steamboat of the same or another line can be found to return to the city in the evening; if not, the railroads are always available. The Albany Day Line charges 50 cents and the *Mary Powell* 25 cents, for each bicycle; but on the other boats no charge is made.

1. *To Shady Side, Edgewater, Pleasant Valley, and Fort Lee.*—These are landings on the New Jersey shore, opposite New York (Chapter IV). They are connected by a picturesque old road along the shore; and from Shady Side and Fort Lee roads lead up to the top of Bergen Ridge and over through the woods to the Hackensack Valley. On the point of rocks above Shady Side are the ruins of a blockhouse, which was the scene of a sharp battle in the Revolution between the troops of General Wayne and Tory refugees and woodcutters. From Pleasant Valley trolley cars run to Fort Lee and inland (p. 127). The steamboats leave the foot of West Thirteenth Street at 9.00 a. m. and 1.00 p. m.; single fare, 15 cents; excursion, 25 cents. Time to Fort Lee, ninety minutes. No charge for bicycles. *A ferry* runs half-hourly from 129th Street to Undercliff, the new Fort Lee landing.

To Yonkers. Steamer *Ben Franklin*, from Franklin Street, daily except Sunday, at 3.00 p. m.; fare, 15 cents. The Albany Day Line and the *Mary Powell* also stop there.

To Grassy Point (Haverstraw), *Croton*, and *Peekskill*. Steamers *Peekskill* and *F. Woodall*, from Franklin Street, daily except Sunday, at 3.00 p. m.; Saturday at 2.00 p. m.; fare, 30 to 40 cents; return trip, 50 cents.

To Irvington. Steamer *A. Brearly*, from Jane Street, at 3.00 p. m.; fare, 25 cents.

To Sing Sing and Tarrytown. Steamer *S. A. Jenks*, from Franklin Street, at 3.00 p. m.; fare, 25 cents.

To West Point, Cranston's, Cornwall, and Newburgh. Albany Day Line, from Desbrosses and West Twenty-second streets, daily at 9.00 a. m.; fare, 75 cents. Steamer *Mary Powell*, from Desbrosses and West Twenty-second streets, daily except Sunday, at 4.00 p. m. (Saturday at 1.00 p. m.); fare, 75 cents. Ramsdell Line, from Franklin Street, daily except Sunday, at 9.00 a. m.; fare, 50 cents; calls at West 135th Street.

Railroads in Westchester County.

1. New York Central, Hudson River Division.—Leaving the city at the Grand Central Depot, on Forty-second Street, at Fourth Avenue, the train runs out through the tunnel, crosses the Harlem River, and turns sharply to the left through Motthaven on a course along the eastern bank of the Harlem River. The tracks of the New York & Putnam Railroad (p. 46) are close beside it as far as Kingsbridge, where our main line diverges to the left, bending westward around the curve of the river that embraces Marble Hill, crossing Tibbett's Brook, which may be called the upper part of the Spuyten Duyvil, if you please, and then skirts that classic stream, beneath the rocky heights north of it, to *Spuyten Duyvil station* (11½ miles from the Grand Central Depot).

This is the best place to alight for the delightful walks open to the rambler along the highlands that here come close to the Hudson River. Winding roads lead to the summit, where a magnificent prospect opens. Here batteries were placed during the Revolution, held alternately by the Americans and the British, and there was much skirmishing northward and along the valley in the rear where the old post-road (Broadway) runs. The hill is now covered with beautiful homes, and the broad Spuyten Duyvil Parkway leads northward along its crest to Riverdale.

Having passed the Seton Hospital, surrounded by woods, you presently come to where this leads down to the right to Van Cortlandt Park. Here Riverdale Avenue, a broad, well macadamized road diverges northward and almost immediately passes, on the right, the great, gray stone house, home of the late Waldo Hutchins, which was built by Jacob Van Cortlandt a century and a half ago. "Broad piazzas, a hall of ample width that shows no sign of a stairway, great rooms with high ceilings, thick walls and large windows, recall the old baronial homes of Virginia. . . . The stout, stone farmhouse that another Van Cortlandt built shelters the coachman's family." Many of the great men of the early history of the Republic have been entertained in this beautiful mansion, which is also conspicuous from the roads east of the Mosholu Valley. Beyond its grounds, queer, winding, shady roads and lanes lead down to Broadway and Van Cortlandt Park. Riverdale Avenue—itself like a park road—can be followed north through a delightful region to the Yonkers line, where you can take the electric cars into Yonkers. The distance from Spuyten Duyvil to the Yonkers line, this way, is nearly three miles.

At Spuyten Duyvil the railway line receives, over a long bridge, its branch from West Thirtieth Street, and then turns north through a deep rock-cut, along the verge of the river. Opposite runs the bold escarpment of the Palisades; overhead, on the right, hang rocky and tree-covered cliffs which permit no view of the fine homes on its

THE OLD VAN CORTLANDT SAW MILL IN VAN CORTLANDT PARK.

"NO SNAP" if you use
"ALLERTON'S"

The High-Grade Mica Chain Lubricant "Unlike all others," as it is impervious to Rain, Mud, and Dust, doing away with that "everlasting snapping and grinding" of the chain so annoying to road riders.

IT IS SO NEAT AND CLEAN THAT IT IMMEDIATELY COMMENDS ITSELF TO LADY RIDERS.

Mica does the work. Remember there is only one genuine, and take no substitute.

755 W. 61st St., Chicago, June 11, 1897.

GENTLEMEN: From January 1st to December 31st, 1896, I rode a bicycle 18,225 miles, establishing Illinois State Record for mileage.

During that time I used nothing on the chain but your lubricant, which I found to be the only satisfactory lubricant made for bicycle chains. I am still using your chain lubricant, and take great pleasure in recommending it to all riders who would have their chains run free and clean.

Yours truly,

(Signed) R. E. O'CONNOR, State Centurion,
Century Road Club of America, Illinois Division.

If your dealer does not sell our lubricant and your chain is obstinate, write us; send either 5 or 10 cents for sample, and a little sound advice thrown in.

ADDRESS

ALLERTON LUBRICANT COMPANY,
A1-160 FRANKLIN ST., NEW YORK CITY.

summit. At *Riverdale* (12⅞ m.), and at *Mount St. Vincent* (13⅝ m.), roads ascend by easy gradients from the station, and give access to a beautiful country for rambling or wheeling, as heretofore described. After this the bluff sinks somewhat, and civilization reappears. The new station, *Ludlow*, recalls an old-time family. Then succeeds

Yonkers (15 m.) — The water-front, where the railway, and steamers, and street-cars meet at the central wharf, is solid with warehouses, for here are many important manufacturing establishments. Above these, embowered in trees, rise the shops and houses of 40,000 inhabitants. Yonkers is connected with New York not only by the Hudson River Railroad, but also by the New York & Putnam Railroad, and is a calling place for all lines of steamers. It has a score of churches and a long list of religious, benevolent, and fraternal societies and schools. Electric street-cars run to the suburbs north, east, and south, and pass Getty Square, the City Hall, and hotels. The leading social clubs are the *Ammakassin*, *Park Hill Country Club* (p. 46), and the *City*, on Getty Square — an open space in the center of the city where several streets converge. There is an athletic club (63 Main Street), with good grounds; but the facilities for aquatic sports have given these pre-eminence there, and along the shore, at the northern suburb *Glenwood* — a station on the Hudson River Railroad — are the houses of the Corinthian Yacht Club, Palisades and Yonkers Boat clubs, and the Yonkers Canoe Club. The Bicycle and Photographic clubs should also be mentioned. It is thus apparent that athletic and outdoor sports receive an unusual amount of attention at the hands of its citizens. The National Guard is represented by the Fourth Separate Company, whose armory is on Waverly Street. *Hollywood Inn* is a workingmen's club.

The town has no great pretensions to beauty — though Warburton and Palisade avenues, North Broadway, Park Hill, and some other districts are rapidly acquiring it. Two electric lines run out a mile and a half or more northward, which form pleasant excursions. Another electric line, of little interest, runs southward along Riverdale Avenue to Mount St. Vincent; and another follows Broadway down to Kingsbridge. A fourth line connects Yonkers with Mount Vernon.

Two objects in the city are worthy of attention, as they successfully recall the early history of the locality. These are the *City Hall*, called "Manor Hall" because the building was the home of the Lord of the Manor of Phillipsburgh in colonial times; and *St. John's Protestant Episcopal Church*, a beautiful house of worship, with an interesting story.

Henry Hudson, and the Dutch traders after him, found here a Mohican village, named Nappechemak, at the mouth of a rapid little stream, now spelled Nepperhan. Settlements were made by the Dutch West-India Company in this township as long ago as 1639. These, after a time, passed into the hands of a burgher of Manhattan, Adriaen Van der Donck, who acquired a far wider area than the present city covers, and was, by royal patent, created a Patroon, whose estate was called Colondonck. It has been supposed that " Yonkers" is a corruption of his patronymic, but a better explanation is, that when a village began to grow up at this landing it was called the *Jonk Heer's* (i. e., young lord's), in compliment to the Patroon; whence Jonker's, and gradually (the *j* being sounded like the English *y*) the modern spelling. At that time this village was called Upper Yonkers, and the region now covered by Van Cortlandt Park, in New York City, was Lower Yonkers. The latter was conveyed to the Van Cortlandts, who intermarried with the Van der Doncks; and the upper half was later sold to Frederick Philipse, the first.

The Philipse or Phillips family, which owned extensive lands northward, and whose favorite residence theretofore had been at Tarrytown, at once took possession, and obtained from the English king a patent creating the property into the Manor of Phillipsburgh. Philipse had anticipated this dignity, not perfected until 1693, by erecting, in 1682, the front part of the present City Hall as his manor house; and it was completed by the addition of the back part in 1745. This old house is still elegant, and in its time must have been a very notable place. Having put his house in order, the now reigning lord of the manor, a second Frederick Philipse, bethought him of more heavenly things, and erected a stone church, as he was bound to do by reason of owning the living. It was, of course, of the Established Church of England, was called *St. John's*, and was completed in 1752; but services had been held in the parish ever since 1694. It is upon the foundations of this old edifice that the present beautiful church in Getty Square was erected in 1870.

At this time one of his daughters, *Mary*, born in the manor-house, July 3, 1730, was growing up to be the belle of all the country-side. A few years later (1756) George Washington, then a colonel wearing the laurels which he alone, almost, had brought from the disastrous Braddock campaign, was visiting in New York at the house of Beverly Robinson, a man of wealth and cultivation, who afterward became prominent as a leader of Tories, and especially in connection with the Arnold and André affair. Robinson's wife was the oldest daughter of Philipse, and there Washington met and fell in love with her younger sister, the beautiful Mary Philipse. The affection was not declared, however, and the young Virginian went back to his plantations, confiding his secret to a friend, who wrote him frequently of the social doings of the young lady and her friends. Finally, Washington was informed that a suitor had appeared in the person of Col. Roger Morris, who had been an associate on Braddock's staff, and was advised to make haste to come to New York and contest his claim. He did not do so — why, no one knows — and the belle became the wife of his rival ; but there is no foundation for the tradition that Washington offered himself and was refused.

Yonkers grew apace, and the Nepperhan, which had been trained to work a sawmill, and hence had come to be called Sawmill Creek — even in Van der Donck's time — soon turned the wheels of several mills, and to-day is hidden between factories. When men were taking sides at the approach of the Revolution, the Frederick Philipse of that day — third lord of the manor — endeavored to remain neutral ; but, although Washington stayed more than once under his roof, he fell under suspicion of a leaning toward royalty, and his property was confiscated by act of Legislature in 1779, and was sold by the Commissioners of Forfeiture in 1785 — the year of his death in England. Complications followed, which were cleared up by a sale of the whole thing to John Jacob Astor, from whom the Government had to re-buy it, at a very long advance, in order to confirm the tenants and holders of parts in their titles. The manor-house was occupied as a private residence by various families until 1868, when it was purchased by the village of Yonkers, and finally became the City Hall in 1872.

The *revolutionary history of Yonkers* was full of lively incidents, though no battle of moment occurred near it, except the memorable engagement in the harbor in 1777, between the British frigates *Rose* and *Phenix*, at anchor, and the oared gunboats of the patriots, which were rowed out of the mouth of the Nepperhan, having in tow a large tender, filled with combustibles, intended to be placed alongside of the frigates as a fire-ship. The sailors, however, kept it off by means of spars, and a heavy fire of grape and canister compelled the gunboats and their brave crews to seek shelter near shore. The attempt was witnessed by Generals Heath, Clinton, and others, and came very near succeeding.

During the whole war — after the American army, in 1776, had retreated from its hills, following the disastrous campaign about White Plains — Yonkers was the center of the uncovered " neutral " tract between the British posts at King's Bridge and those of the American army above. This unlucky tract was the foraging ground of both parties, and the rendezvous of the opposing bands of reprobates known as the Skinners and the Cow Boys — the former claiming to act in the service of the Americans, and the latter under the British banner. As far as the quiet folks of the devoted neighborhood were concerned, there was not much choice between the rival bands, since they both served themselves, no matter whether at the cost of friend or of foe. What with the escapades of these fellows, and with the marches and countermarches above and below them, and with now and then a serious skirmish, the "neutral ground" was a busy region at the time, and abounds in such reminiscences of adventure as J. Fenimore Cooper has utilized in his story "The Spy."

Glenwood (16½ m.) is a suburban station of Yonkers. Then comes *Hastings* (19 m.), a village in a glen, with an asphalt company's works by the water and track. Near the station is to be noticed the yellow boat-house of the Tower Ridge Athletic Club, whose grounds for tennis, etc., are elaborately laid out on the hill above. The next station is the pretty and popular **Dobbs Ferry** (20 m.). The village is described on page 11.

The revolutionary fortifications here were mainly by the present railway station — one of the best examples of those *bijous* of architecture in rose granite, red sandstone, and hardwoods with which the New York Central Company is ornamenting the river route from one end to the other — and were intended for the protection of the rowboat ferry. These batteries were a sore vexation to the British ships, which were wont to cruise up the river, and attempt to ravage the shores. In July, 1781, some British frigates that had passed up the river a few days before, took advantage of wind and tide to return to New York, thus exposing themselves to a severe cannonading from these batteries. They returned the fire, but without effect; and Thatcher relates that on board one of them, the *Savage*, a box of powder took fire, whereupon twenty men leaped into the river, only one of whom, an American prisoner, reached the shore. Two years later (May 8, 1783) a British fleet anchored off this shore fired England's first salute to the stars and stripes, following the negotiations of Clinton and Carleton (p. 12) for the evacuation of New York.

Irvington (23 m.) is the next station — a village of comparatively recent growth, inhabited, for the most part, by wealthy New Yorkers, whose estates cover the hills. The large building near the station is occupied by *The Cosmopolitan* (Magazine). Everything here is memorable of Washington Irving, whose home, "Sunnyside," was half a mile north of the station, and can be seen plainly from the trains in passing.

Sunnyside is a many gabled, vine-clad cottage, covered with stucco and shadowed by grand trees. When Irving bought the place, in 1835, the locality was vaguely known as Dearman's, and the farm contained ten acres, and a small stone house called "Wolfert's Roost" (*roost*, rest), from a former owner, Wolfert Acker, who had been one of the Committee of Public Safety in '76, and had come here to set up his Rest and take his ease. Later, eight more acres were added. Irving at once called in the services of a sympathetic artist, George Harvey, who, while he enlarged and modernized the house, kept all the "old-times" air and picturesqueness. Over the entrance to the porch may still be read the inscription *George Harvey, Boumr.*, the last word an abbreviation for "Boumeister," which Mr. Irving had raked up as Dutch for architect. The beautiful growth of English ivy that clothes the front of the cottage has all grown from a slip brought from Melrose Abbey by a friend, Mrs. Renwick, the heroine of several of Robert Burns' songs. The house is reached from Broadway by Sunnyside Avenue.

The approach to **Tarrytown** (25 m.) brings into view many noble properties. As seen from the river, the residences about Tarrytown rise tier upon tier. That on the hill, with the pointed tower, is "Cunningham Castle." Near it are the still stately ruins of the burned home of the painter, *Albert Bierstadt;* and a long list of names of men prominent in the world of business would be found on the door-plates of the mansions ensconced among those umbrageous trees.

Most conspicuous among them, undoubtedly, is the tall square marble tower of the late *Jay Gould's house*, "Lyndehurst," which rises like a bright monument above the green bank of foliage. It is interesting not only as the former residence of the most powerful, and, since the death of Commodore Vanderbilt, the most picturesque business man of the country, but from the fact that it was originally "Paulding Manor," the country house of William Paulding, a nephew of the hero of the André capture, and cousin of Admiral Paulding, U. S. N. He was a prominent merchant of the early decades of this country, and was Mayor of New York at the time of Lafayette's visit in 1824; and his house represents the best type of Tudor architecture. It is best seen from a northerly direction.

The windows of all these mansions look out upon the Tappan Sea, so named because the Tappan Indians were found along its western bank by the Dutchmen. Many a story might be told of its waters and circling shores, some of which Irving has left us in his *Chronicle of Wolfert's Roost*, relating to the revolutionary period, when every farmer had to be upon his guard against the bandits that infested this debatable land between the lines of the opposing armies; and others linger among the legends of the older people.

Tarrytown shows little of its beauty and historical interest about the station, business buildings and trees hiding the pleasant streets and old houses elsewhere referred to (pp. 12, 13). Here, a few rods from the northern end of the station, is a steam ferry to Nyack, which can be seen on the opposite shore, and this is the crossing place of the amateur coaching route between New York and Tuxedo, to which a fine road leads from Nyack. Soon after leaving the station the train emerges from the city upon a bridge crossing the mouth of the river Pocantico. Looking up stream, you see the old

Philipse house and mill; above the pond that feeds the mill are the bridge, church, and road celebrated in Irving's tale of the Headless Horseman, and beyond them the vale of Sleepy Hollow (p. 15).

Continuing, the train cuts across the base of Kingsland's Point, then comes out upon the beach of the Tappan Sea again, passes through *Scarborough* and *Sparta*, and then enters the village of Sing Sing by passing beneath the famous State Penitentiary, a mile south of the station. **Sing Sing** rests upon a series of rocky terraces that overlook, perhaps, the most beautiful landscape the Hudson Valley affords. The river side is occupied to a great extent by factories, among which the old Arcade file works, a patent medicine mill, and an immense shoe factory are conspicuous. (See p. 17).

After leaving Sing Sing the train crosses the estuary of the *Croton River*, whose upper waters are largely diverted through two aqueducts to supply the needs of New York, and where, a little way at the right of the track, the original manor-house of the Van Cortlandts (p. 17) still stands beneath the shade of its venerable trees. The line then cuts across the base of Croton Point, whose tip end is called Teller's Point, and then runs along the shore of *Haverstraw Bay*, where the river is five miles wide, and Haverstraw appears opposite. Here is the little railroad village, *Croton Landing*, the summer "park" town *Oscawanna*, on the slope of Hessian Hill, and then *Cruger's*, at the southern extremity of the Spitzenberg Mountains. The railroad then strikes inland for nearly four miles across Verplank's Point (p. 18), passing *Montrose*, which gives one of the best obtainable views of the river-gap of the Highlands.

Having passed the rural station of Verplank's Point, **Peekskill** (43 m.) is quickly reached. This pleasant city, at the entrance to the Highlands of the Hudson, is characterized elsewhere (p. 19). Its large stove factories clustered about the water-front indicate the principal business, and the conspicuous buildings of the Academy of the Sisters of St. Mary, overlooking the river, contain only one of the several institutions of learning here. Peekskill is the limit of the suburban train service from New York. Eight miles beyond is Garrisons, a lovely region for rambling into the heart of the Highlands, where a steam ferry crosses to *West Point* and *Cranstons*.

New York & Putnam Railroad.

The New York & Putnam Railroad was formerly the New York & Northern, but is now a part of the **New York Central system**, and

PARK HILL

ON THE HUDSON.

The Guide Book of the New York Central & Hudson River Railroad says of this elegant New York suburb:

"There are few places in the world where a view more beautiful can be obtained, and the sightseer and the lover of the beautiful will be richly rewarded by a trip to Park Hill."

"From the summit of Park Hill, there is spread out a panorama of matchless beauty. To the west, the majestic sweep of the Hudson for fifteen miles either way, from Tappan Zee to the Bartholdi statue; to the south the woody knolls and grassy reaches of Van Cortlandt Park; to the east, the silvery glimmer of Long Island Sound, and to the north the historic hills of Westchester. Park Hill has, however, other attractions of equal interest to those seeking a home. It has city advantages, being a part of the city of Yonkers, and shares in the thorough system of sewers, gas, electric lights, police and fire protection, school and church accommodations, of a city of 35,000 people. Many beautiful homes are here and many more will follow. The attention of New York's great army of homeseekers has been turned this way of late and the present population is only the advance guard of the army to follow. In a few years at most, Park Hill will be the center of the New Harlem, and the 'old settler' will soon tell of how he threw away the opportunity of a lifetime by not putting his money into Park Hill lots when he first moved up from the city and Park Hill was only a suburb."

This magnificent suburb is the property of

The American Real Estate Company,
280 BROADWAY, NEW YORK CITY.

A HANDSOMELY ILLUSTRATED SOUVENIR can be had on application.
Send 5 cents in stamps to cover postage.

its tickets, as far as Yonkers, are interchangeable with those on the Hudson River Railroad. Its trains leave from the terminal station of the West Side Elevated railways at Eighth Avenue and 155th Street, and run to Yonkers, and to Brewster's Station, in Putnam County, where they connect with the Harlem Railroad and the New York & New England Railroad for the north and east. This road forms an easy and interesting means of reaching many pleasant places in the northern part of New York City, and in the adjacent parts of Westchester County.

Leaving the *West 155th Street station*, the train crosses the Harlem River upon a lofty bridge, and turns to the left up the Harlem Valley, close under the steep bank. The first station is at the stately *High Bridge*, where stairways lead up to the surface of the old Croton Aqueduct (p. 57). Just beyond, you pass beneath the vast steel arches of the Washington Bridge, and then run along beneath Fordham Heights, upon which the new buildings of the University of the City of New York are rising, past Morris Dock, University Heights, and Fordham Heights stations, opposite which is Fort George, of revolutionary fame, to the ancient settlement of *Kingsbridge*. Thus far (four miles from 155th Street) the track has been beside that of the Hudson River Railroad; but here that line swerves sharply to the left toward Spuyten Duyvil, while this road continues straight north up the valley of Tibbett's (or Mosholu) Brook, parallel with the two aqueducts buried in the high ground at the right. A mile (5 m.) brings us to *Van Cortlandt Park*, where the Van Cortlandt manor (built in 1748) and their mill (whose dam now forms the "lake" beside the track) appear beyond a lane of locust trees ahead on the left; while far away across the meadows towers up the still larger old stone mansion of Jacob Van Cortlandt (p. 40).

Just beyond the bridge, over the outlet of the ancient mill stream, the road divides, the *Rapid Transit Line to Yonkers* leading off to the left along the Parade Ground of Van Cortlandt Park, and past Vault Hill, through an elevated, picturesque park region, having three stations, Mosholu, Lowerre, and Park Hill, and reaching a terminus on Getty Square, in the very center of the city. At Lowerre station are the Yonkers base-ball grounds, and the house of the New Yonkers Driving Park Club. At Park Hill reside many wealthy people in beautiful homes overlooking the Hudson and the park.

The main line continues straight north from Van Cortlandt Park station, through a tree-grown cut past Lincoln Park, and beneath the vine-grown arches of the aqueduct, which here turns sharply through the northern part of Yonkers to the shore of the Hudson, to *Dunwoodie* (8 m.), a station one mile east of Getty Square, Yonkers, on the road and trolley line to Mount Vernon. Continuing, the road makes a detour to the right, over a local water-shed 300 feet above the level of the Hudson. Here is a station called *Summit*, whence brooks flow in all directions. All this region is very charming rambling ground, a thoroughly rural yet far from savage country, with shady old roads, pretty glens, bits of woodland, and breezy outlooks in all directions. Bronxville is not more than two miles east by the Glen road, and it is scarcely more than seven miles across to New Rochelle, all the way through pleasant country byways.

Nepperhan (10½ m.) is the station for the aristocratic northern extension of Yonkers along Broadway. The Nepperhan or Sawmill River, which furnishes water-power to the factories in the gorge at Yonkers, is followed to the Mt. Hope cemeteries. *Ardsley* (14½ m.) is the station for Ashford Avenue, Dobbs Ferry, and for the fine Ardsley Avenue, eastward. *Woodlands* (15½ m.) is another station on the high ground above Dobbs Ferry. The Nepperhan is dammed at the latter station, forming a pretty pond spanned by a long bridge; and here is the old Howland estate and hotel, once famous. A mile farther, the road passes over the deeply-buried new Croton Aqueduct, and, skirting the eastern base of Beaver Mountain, reaches *Elmsford* (18 m.). Here is an electric car line eastward to White Plains, and a road (Benedict Avenue) leading down into Tarrytown —about three miles—along which the trolley is to be extended.

Elmsford, known for a century as Hall's Corners, is an historical center. On the ridge just northeast of the station is located the "Four Corners," where a company of patriots, under Colonel Thompson, was attacked by one thousand British soldiers, in February, 1780, and after losing fifty men, killed and wounded, surrendered. In 1829, citizens of Westchester County erected here, over the remains of Isaac Van Wart, a monument to his memory, as one of the captors of Major André, the British spy. South of the station stands the old Greenburg Dutch Church, the frame of which was raised about 1790. Adjoining is the little burying-ground, where headstones mark the graves of many revolutionary patriots. Just south of the church stood the old Romer homestead, where the British officers used to bring flour, demanding that Mrs. Romer should bake it. She was compelled to do so, but is reputed to have managed that the patriots should get a good share of each baking.

At the next station, *East View* (20½ m.), is the County Farm, whose solid stone buildings are noticeable ; here, also, is a stud farm of very valuable horses, adjoining the historic Van Wart homestead, where the spy, André, spent the first night following his capture. Here the road has swung around the hills to the left, leaving the Nepperhan, and a broad and charming view eastward is disclosed. A mile west it comes to **Tarrytown** (21½ m.), the station having a lovely situation on the heights in the eastern outskirts of the pleasant little city, just above Castle Heights, at the head of Nepara Avenue. The railway then swings around to the east again, and in half a mile or more stops at Sleepy Hollow — the head of the ravine which Washington Irving immortalized by his genial legends. Roads lead down through the quaint old neighborhood to the Dutch Church, etc. (p. 15). *Tarrytown Heights* (23 m.) is even deeper into this weird district, and *Tower Hill* and *Pocantico Hills* are additional stopping places near by. All of this region is very beautiful, and entices the passenger to explore the country lanes and shady brooksides, or climb the hills that diversify the landscape in all directions. Four miles farther comes *Whitson's*, opposite Sing Sing and surrounded by rich farms. *Millwood* (30½ m.), the next station, overlooks a broad valley descending toward Croton Lake, where a curious little conical hill is a prominent landmark. The old stone Merritt House, near by, has been a hotel for almost a century, recalling the days when this was Merritt's Corners, and a place of rural resort. *Kitchawan* (32½ m.), two miles beyond, is on the southern shore of Croton Lake, the source of New York City's water supply. Sing Sing is five miles east, and Mount Kisco four miles west, each reached by capital roads. The road then passes on through Yorktown, Amawalk, and Baldwin Place to Lake Mahopac (by a branch), while the main line turns northeast to Brewsters.

The Harlem Railroad.

The Harlem Railroad affords opportunities for some of the best outings in the neighborhood of New York. Its terminal station is in the Grand Central Depot, the entrance being on the west side (Vanderbilt Avenue) of the building. Its trains run at intervals of only a few minutes as far as White Plains, and every two hours or so to points much farther north, while its through trains give a pleasant route to New England. The tracks of this line diverge from those of the Hudson River line at Motthaven and extend on for four miles over a depressed roadbed, passing the city stations Melrose, Morrisania, and Tremont, and emerging at *Fordham* (nine miles from Grand Central Station). This is a convenient point of departure for bicycling and walking trips, but it is not a good station for Bronx Park, as has been frequently stated, because of its distance (¾ m.) and the hot naked road. The large buildings seen here are St. John's College, a Roman Catholic institution for boys. Bedford Park (10 m.) and *Williamsbridge* (11 m.) are rural stations closely adjacent to Bronx Park, and the latter lies upon the Bronx River, and is the point where in old times the Gunhill road, leaving the Kingsbridge road at the head of the Mosholu marshes, came into the Boston post-road. The Gunhill road may still be followed directly west to the Van Cortlandt Park manor, through a picturesque region. The next station is that for Woodlawn Cemetery (12 m.) a little beyond which the New York & New Haven Railroad, whose tracks have been parallel with those of the Harlem so far, branches off to the right. Here the northern boundary of the city is passed and *Mount Vernon* (13 m.) is reached. The station is in the western outskirts of the town, on the road to Yonkers, which is reached by electric cars via Elmsford and Dunwoodie. Mount Vernon has many rewards for an hour or two of rambling, and electric lines branch out in all directions. A pleasant day's excursion would be to come here in the morning, loiter as long as you please, go over by railroad to New Rochelle, and when done with that pretty route return to New York by the Shore line of railroad to Port Morris and Harlem.

From Mount Vernon on, for many miles, the railroad closely follows the Bronx, and lets the eye of the passenger trace all its pretty curves and get a glimpse of every pool and rapid. The next station, *Bronxville* (15 m.), is set in the midst of residence "parks" where hundreds of cottages fresh with carpentry and paint cover the hillsides. An electric road will soon connect it with Mount Vernon and White Plains.

☞ Just here *Sprain Brook* comes in from the west, through a deep winding vale, offering a delightful tramp across to the heights north and east of Yonkers. Bryn Mawr station on the New York & Putnam Railroad is scarcely 1½ miles distant, or the walk may well be extended another mile to Nepperhan, where you can take the train back to 155th Street.

Tuckahoe (16 m.) is an old village, growing steadily about the marble quarries, which employ hundreds of men and make this a busy town, which lies on the higher ground at the right. Half a mile above it, on the ridge road, is old Tuckahoe, an ancient and pretty settlement. Several "parks" have been platted and put into shape for suburban homes by real estate agencies in this neighborhood, where city men are coming in increasing numbers. The three miles between here and Scarsdale (19 m.) show the dashing stream at its prettiest, and form a delightful rambling ground. The Bronx Aqueduct, or " pipe line," and a good road (p. 19) follow the stream on the western bank, which, above Scarsdale, rises into a line of bold, wooded bluffs that press close upon the river; and here the heavily shaded road is cut like a ledge out of the hillside, and follows every vagary of the swift stream. Scarsdale is the home of several wealthy families, whose estates are among the finest in the county. Very interesting walks may be taken westward, Dobbs Ferry being not too far away for an afternoon's ramble. Passing on to Hartsdale (21 m.) " we enter a very pretty stretch of country, with rolling hills to the right and left, and skirting the track of the silvery Bronx, now broader and deeper than where we left it a few miles below, and wearing more the aspect of a river," we cross a substantial iron bridge, sweep round a grand curve, and halt at **White Plains** (22 m.), which is elsewhere described (p. 22). Proceeding northward charming landscapes await us, for the country becomes more and more rural and hilly. After a fleeting glimpse of Lake Kensico, we reach Kensico station (25 m.), a neat, old-fashioned village. Just north of it is the new Kensico Cemetery, whose grounds contain a traditional revolutionary house, and natural features likely to make this one of the most beautiful of the city burying-grounds of the future. Kensico Park, on the shore of the lake, and New Amsterdam are improved villages of modern houses. Unionville is the next station (29 m.) and at the foot of Buttermilk Hill, from whose summit — nearly the highest in the county — can be seen the spires of New York, the waters of Long Island Sound, and a long stretch of the Hudson River. The line has here bent so far to the westward that it is now scarcely two miles southwest to Eastview (p. 48), and only three miles to Sleepy Hollow. A pleasant round trip for a day would be to come to this point by rail, walk around the northern base of Buttermilk Hill, and on to Tarrytown by the Sleepy Hollow road or by the somewhat shorter Bedford road, then home by the Hudson River or New York & Putnam Railroad. The new houses scattered along the hill slopes at the right of the track in this part of the route belong to Sherman Park, where the new college of the Dominican Fathers is already conspicuous. *Pleasantville*, the next station (31 m.), is a nice little town stretched along a winding, hilly street; and it is an interesting walk to leave the train at the station and follow this main street northward over the ridge and down across the marshy flat beyond, where the Bronx takes its source, into the village of **Chappaqua**. This walk is **only about 2½ miles.** *Chappaqua* is identified not only with **the farming and teaching of Horace Greeley, but with** the Friends, who were formerly so numerous and **are still influential** in Westchester **County.** They have a collegiate **school here. Here, too, is the old Quaker Church, once occupied by sick and wounded soldiers of the Revolution, and on the surrounding slopes lie the bones** of many a hero who fought and died **for liberty. At Chappaqua the** railway begins to rise into the **line of hills which stretches east and** west across the country, and forms **the watershed between the waters draining** southward into the Bronx, **and northward into the Croton. This rugged region having been passed, the thriving town of** *Mount Kisco* **(37 m.) is** reached in **about four miles.**

"Situated," says **one friendly writer, " at a considerable altitude** above the sea level, **Mount Kisco enjoys a pure, brisk air, and rarely** beautiful **natural environments. Like a jewel in its setting, the** village **nestles amid wooded hills, charming valleys, and limpid** streams, **surrounded on all sides by an ever-changing and increasingly-fascinating landscape. A network of country roads, everywhere presenting views that charm the eye, spreads in all directions,** affording a **never-ending combination of drives, whose attractiveness is not soon exhausted. Sharp turns around the base of steep hills, now wending through a deep ravine, then at the very edge of a precipice, give a variety of views that is really kaleidoscopic. A short drive over a picturesque road in a northwesterly direction brings the sight-seer to Croton Lake, a beautiful body of pure drinking water for the denizens of the great metropolis. Here is good** fishing, and **on both sides excellent driveways, while at a little distance** back green **hills present their irregular outlines against the sky.** Two **miles** farther **one is brought face to face with one of the** mightiest engineering **feats in all ages — the new Croton Aqueduct — which can not fail to well** repay **even repeated visits. Just west of the village flows the quiet** Kisco, **from which the place derives its name (meaning " still water"), and in every direction are streams of more** or less magnitude, while springs **of pure, sparkling cold water are almost as numerous as** wells. At the **northwestern limits of the village looms up old Kisco Moun**tain like **a sentinel over the settlement."**

Similar interesting and **healthful villages, in beautiful surroundings, rapidly follow. Bedford station (39 m.) is the next one. Here the surroundings are particularly enticing to the rambler and fishermen, for Croton Lake is only a mile distant. Stages run four miles east to the old country village of Bedford.** *Katonah* **(42 m.) is the** point of departure **for stages through Cross River and South Salem to Boutonville (9½ m.) east) and for stages to Lake Waccabuc (7 m.**

northeast). At Golden's Bridge (44 m.) the branch diverges to Lake Mahopac (51 m.), and the main line keeps on through Purdy's and Croton Falls to Brewster's station, where it forms a junction with the New York & New England Railroad for Connecticut and the East, and where also the New York & Putnam Railroad has its terminus. The Harlem Railroad continues northward to a junction with the Boston & Albany Railroad at Chatham.

The New Haven Railroad.

The New York, New Haven & Hartford Railroad runs eastward from New York, along the shore of Long Island Sound, in two divisions.

1. *The Main Line.* This leaves the Grand Central Depot and follows the line of the Harlem Railroad (p. 49) nearly to *Mount Vernon* (13 m.) where it swings eastward by a depressed way through the heart of that city. Local trains stop at Woodlawn, but nowhere between Woodlawn and the Grand Central Depot. Still curving eastward, the road takes a straight course through a thickly settled district, Pelhamville, on Hutchinson Creek, (so called after Ann Hutchinson, the woman who was expelled from Massachusetts by the Puritans in 1637 because of her religious views, and who lived here) to *New Rochelle* (15½ m.). Here again the tracks are greatly depressed, conducing to safety, but hiding from view this interesting old town (p. 30). Leaving the village, Long Island Sound appears at the right in glimpses separated by rocky hillocks, stretches of old orchards, woods, and fields; and the train winds its way over a rugged, rocky, and beautiful shore country. Larchmont station is the stopping place for Larchmont and the neighboring shore (p. 30), a mile or so distant. A glimpse is caught of De Lancey Cove and Long Beach Point beyond it, a little farther on, and then the large station of *Mamaroneck*, at the mouth of Mamaroneck River, is at hand. The course is now more inland, up the valley of Stony Creek, past Harrison and *Rye*, the latter the station for Rye Neck and Rye Beach, fashionable summer resorts along the Sound shore. Then follow *Portchester*, the last station in New York State; *Greenwich* and *Stamford* (35 m.), in Connecticut, the terminus of the service of local trains.

2. *Harlem Branch.* This branch connects Harlem and New Rochelle along the shore of the East River and Long Island Sound, and is the direct route to Pelham Bay Park and the fishing and

boating places along that very interesting shore. Trains leave from the terminal station of the Third Avenue Elevated Railroad on East 129th Street, at the level of the Elevated platform; thence they cross the bridge and, descending, turn to the right through Morrisania and Port Morris, whose shore, not long ago a beautiful park-like region (Oak Point), is now in the desolate stage of being "improved" into a city. The harbor is still, however, a popular place for fishing, boating, and sailing, but the assemblage met there is decidedly plebeian. The change of this region from a rural community to a densely inhabited part of the city was extraordinarily rapid, and relics of it appear about the mouth of Mill Creek, now the outlet of a sewer, but which was a purling brook flowing down from the grounds of the Cauldwell mansion, within the memory of many persons still living. *Casanovia* station is on Legget Avenue — the old-time road down to Hunt's Point. Immediately to the south is the Port Morris district and the wooded Oak Point — a picnic place. Passing on through a thinly settled region, with old houses exciting one's curiosity here and there, the train enters a rough, wooded-looking country, and halts next at Hunt's Point station. To the right the land reaches out in a promontory between the mouth of Mill Creek and the mouth of the Bronx, which has been cut up into streets, but retains many of its original rural features. This is Hunt's Point. It is completely surrounded by an unfinished shore-line promenade called the Edgewater road, and is a region well worth exploration. Just beyond Hunt's Point station the Bronx comes in sight, sweeping quietly and deviously through broad salt-meadows. On its farther bank (Cornell's Neck) is a beautiful region of rocky woods, among which winding roads, bounded by stone walls and leading past old-fashioned houses and ancient orchards, invite the wayfarer to wander down to the seaside at Classon's Point, which is just opposite College Point, Long Island. Westchester Avenue, the old turnpike that strikes east across this land to Westchester, is crossed, and soon after the train turns to the right, crosses the Bronx, and goes out past a fine old house, now dilapidated, to *West Farms* station, some distance south of the village. Van Nest station is a mile beyond, where the "Bleach road," from Bronxdale south to Unionport, intersects the old Boston post-road, along which the train pursues its way past the Morris Park race track to *Westchester*, the station being on the northern outskirts of that village, which retains little of picturesque interest. Rocky woodlands follow to Baychester, a scattered settlement in the groves on the border of Pelham Bay Park, east of the upper part of Pelham Bay. The Bronx Parkway leads straight here from Bronxdale along the old Pelham road (p. 28), and we see the bridges below us by which it crosses Pelham Bay at a wooded island. The upper end of the bay at the left is broken by grassy and wooded islands, has sparsely tenanted shores, and is extremely picturesque. On the farther bank is Bartow, the station for City Island, which is reached by a tramway, and then follows a run through open woods and old rocky fields, with occasional glimpses of the shore, past Pelham Manor and Woodside into **New Rochelle**.

Suburban Railroads.

The Amsterdam Avenue cable road reaches north to Fort George, giving easy access, by walking, to Washington Heights (Fort Washington) and Inwood.

An electric line will probably be running, by midsummer of 1896, from Third Avenue and 161st Street past Central Bridge (Jerome Avenue), to which it is now in operation, up Sedgwick and Bailey avenues to Kingsbridge, and thence along Broadway to Getty Square, Yonkers.

The East Side Suburban Elevated Railroad runs north on Third Avenue to Tremont, reaching Crotona Park.

Electric lines run from Harlem River at Third Avenue, or (by transfer) from the northern end of Central Bridge to Bedford Park, to Williams Bridge and to Westchester, for one fare; the pleasantest route for the two latter points (and to Bronx Park) is by way of the Southern Boulevard.

An electric line runs from West Farms, through Bronxdale (the best point of approach to Bronx Park), Williamsbridge, and Wakefield to Mount Vernon. Fare, New York to Mount Vernon, 10 cents. (For lines in Mount Vernon and Yonkers, see pages 20, 41, and 50.)

A Rural Walk—Through Bronx and Van Cortlandt Parks.

As an example of the many pleasant walks one may take close to the city, the following route has been selected, for a stroll of about five miles, through the Bronx and Van Cortlandt parks. The electric road will take you from the Harlem River terminus of the Third Avenue Elevated Railroad to West Farms. At West Farms take the road to the left (the old Boston post-road), up the hill, passing the Peabody House and several ancient houses, and in a few moments you are within Bronx Park. Here the roadway is embowered with fine old trees, and bordered by rolling, tree-shaded meadows, which stretch down to a tangle of bushes, weeds, and rock on the river bank to our left. You can walk along the classic stream by paths that come close to the water's edge, winding among the trees and over the rocks in the most irregular way. Chipmunks squeak and scamper across the path, and over there a red creeper (if it be autumn) runs up a pine tree like a living flame. There are girls rowing on the river, and the echo of their voices sounds sharply between the banks. Now and then the lingering sound of some far away city bells falls upon the listening ear, mingling with the chittering of near-by birds. Presently the path leads out to a well-kept road, and crosses by a bridge, below the old bleaching mill, into the hamlet of *Bronxdale*. It was asleep for many years, but the electric road to Mount Vernon has waked it up, and the "Old Homestead" tavern has been reopened. By this electric road you might have ridden from West Farms, but you would have lost the walk through the park. At the old inn you may eat a lunch if you please, and perhaps find some loiterer who can repeat the stories his grandfather had told him of the busy days, a century ago, when this was a famous stopping place of the Boston coaches.

Four roads come in at Bronxdale—the Boston, leading northeasterly through Eastchester and Pelham Manor to New Rochelle and the Sound shore; the Bear Swamp road, partly used by the trolley line, leading east past the Morris Park race course to Westchester; the White Plains road, north to Mount Vernon and White Plains; and Pelham Avenue, leading westward to Fordham station on the Harlem Railroad. It is this last road we follow over the hill to the first fork beyond the smithy at the foot of the hill, where we take the road leading to the right, and back into the Bronx Park. This roadway soon bears to the left, through a bower of trees, and up to the old Lorillard mansion, now occupied by the Department of Parks. Back of the ancient manor house are the ruins of old Pierre Lorillard's original snuff-mill, and behind it some pretty cascades. A shady pathway leads along the water's edge opposite the well-known Hemlock Grove, that haunt of lovers and artists, now appropriated to the use of the New York Botanic Garden, shortly to be begun. We follow this pathway up stream, and take the road passing two bridges. Near the third bridge stands a noted little inn, kept by a genial Frenchman named Lemaire, whose wines

and cookery were far-famed, and became more so after this *al fresco* restaurant had been made the scene of an illustrated magazine story from the creative pen and pencil of Hopkinson Smith. Crossing the bridge, we stroll down the west bank of the river, visit the curious hollow stone called the "Indian's bath-tub," which retains a pool of water after every rainstorm, peer into the "Bear's Cave," and then strike eastward over the hill to Bedford Park station on the Harlem Railroad, whence we may go back to the city by steam or electric car down Third Avenue.

If you care to prolong the walk, however, keep on over the tracks, and turn north on Webster Avenue to the Mosholu Parkway, which you may follow through villa-parks, woods, and meadows, to the entrance to Van Cortlandt Park, where the parkway merges into the old Gunhill road. From the brow of the hill here, where the aqueduct crosses, one has a beautiful view of the shimmering, lily-flecked lake nestling between the hills. Off to the right, over the hillside, stretch the golf links of the Van Cortlandt Golf Club; and an easy down-hill walk brings us to the railway station, back of which lies the manor house and parade ground, with the Kingsbridge road and the heights of Spuyten Duyvil beyond.

A Walk Along the Aqueduct.— The old Croton Aqueduct forms a level and interesting pathway for nearly forty miles north from the Harlem River, giving the pleasant access afoot to the picturesque and historic region along the eastern bank of the Hudson, elsewhere described from the point of view of the cycler and the railway traveler. Many stretches of considerable extent along it are available for wheelmen, also, broken only by the gateways and fences of private estates, which are usually passable by means of a turnstile or steps. An attempt has been made to authorize the construction of a cycle path upon it, but it has not been successful, owing to difficulties connected with city's tenure of the land.

The entrance to the aqueduct is just north of the east end of Washington Bridge, where Aqueduct Avenue connects with Featherbed Lane. This part traverses the old Morris estate, then crosses the old McComb's Dam road and runs at a high elevation, affording an admirable view of the Berkeley Oval, the Harlem River Valley, Fort George, and the heights of Inwood and Spuyten Duyvil. From here on, for some three miles, it passes a residence district, skirts the Claflin estate and the old Jerome Park race course, and emerges upon the hillside just beyond the Gunhill road, which it crosses on a level, overlooking Van Cortlandt Lake and Park. Northward of this point it swings inland to Dunwoodie, where it makes a sharp turn to the west through Yonkers, and turns northward again parallel with Warburton Avenue, giving fine views of the river and Palisades. This part is a popular route for wheelmen, who take Warburton Avenue to its terminus and then run along the aqueduct to Hastings, where they join the post-road again, thus avoiding the steep hills of Yonkers.

From Yonkers, the aqueduct skirts the western side of the ridge at a good elevation, through large estates and nearly always in sight of the river. Pretty glens, bits of wild wood, fantastic rocks, and cultivated gardens follow one another in pleasing contrast, broken at short intervals by small towns, until we reach Tarrytown, when again this pathway swings inland, but at a height that keeps the Hudson within view. All the scenery of this part of the walk is fine. We traverse a section of Sleepy Hollow, cross the pretty Pocantico Vale, and zigzag through large estates toward the Hudson again at Sing Sing, when we cross a deep, rocky, picturesque glen and the old post-road upon a series of massive archways, considered, at the time of building, a stupendous engineering feat. Above Sing Sing, the aqueduct turns inland and closely follows the Croton River to the dam where it originates and derives its water.

East River Steamboats.

Abundant means exist for a trip up the East River, and return the same day; it is always interesting, while in summer this is one of the most cool and refreshing trips on the waters about New York, because there is so much to look at all the way. A complete account of the historical and other objects interesting to an intelligent traveler, and visible from the boats, would require the whole of such a volume as this. To the historian nearly every point of the bold shore on both sides, but especially on that of New York City, speaks of famous men and exploits of past years; and one may still recognize many relics of the country seats of the wealthy New Yorkers of the early half of the century. Every rocky height fronting the river was fortified during the wars of the Revolution and of 1812-14, and a hundred interesting stories might be told of the various "hooks" and "bays" before the steamer passes Blackwell's Island. A most fascinating book in this connection is "A Tour Round New York," by Felix Oldboy (Flavel Mines).

"My Summeracre," he tells us, "fronts upon the East River, near the spot where the waters of Hell Gate begin to seethe and swirl. Standing on the little bluff in which its garden ends . . . one can see the rarest and loveliest of pictures. Across and up the river where Pot Rock once made the waters boil and the Frying Pan was a terror to navigators; where Flood Rock is alternately submerged and exposed by the tides; where the Hog's Back and Nigger's Head yet wreck an occasional vessel; where the shaded river-road of Astoria allows rare glimpses of stately mansions among the trees, and the green ramparts of Ward's Island are wondrous pleasant to the eye and hide other lovely islands beyond that are fruitful of legends as of lobsters, are stretches of scenery than which there is nothing more beautiful on the Atlantic coast line."

Hellgate has now been so deepened and dredged that it has lost the most of its terrors, and, with the building up of its shores, nearly all of its picturesqueness. Its whirlpools lie among the reefs at the upper end of Blackwell's Island. Nearly all steamboats pass to the eastward of this island, along the Astoria shore, and thence emerge into the troubled waters through the narrows between Hallet's Point and Harris' Hook, the latter being where Avenue B ends at Eighty-ninth Street. Then follows Ward's Island, to the right of which is the narrow channel above Hellgate; Sunken Meadow, across which Randall's Island is seen in the mouth of the Harlem, separated from Ward's Island by Little Hellgate, and from the Morrisania shore by Bronx Kills. Rounding Lawrence's Point, at the northern extremity of Astoria, the East River opens widely eastward, broken by islands, of which the largest is Riker's, causing the ship channel to make a curve to the southward. On the right, now, is the inward-curving wooded shore of Bowery Bay (p. 74) ending in Sanford Point, beyond which Flushing Bay deeply indents the Long Island shore, with the estuary of the Bronx making a corresponding bay in the opposite or northern coast. The farther shore of Flushing Bay reaches far out, and is covered with the houses of College Point (p. 74). As Cornell Neck reaches southward to meet it from the shore at the left, the river again narrows until the features of both sides of this beautiful inland sea are plainly visible as one sails past, with the populous bluffs of Whitestone on the south, and the low, green, rural shores of Throg's Neck, at his left hand. Steering between the grim ramparts of Fort Schuyler, and Willet's Point, the vessel's prow suddenly swings around to the left, and enters Long Island Sound. At the right, the Long Island coast falls away in the deep indentation of Little Neck Bay, on the farther side of which Great Neck reaches out into the bold peninsula terminating in Elm and Hewlett's Point. In the midst of the open water here is Stepping Stones Lighthouse, standing upon an islet hardly big enough to hold the foundations of the tower. The prolongation of shallow water behind it is Pelham Bay, whose shores are set apart as Pelham Bay Park (p. 29). Reaching far out on its farther side is City Island, just east of which is Hart's Island. Hewlett's Point is now abeam on the right, and a moment later Manhasset Bay appears between green hills. The water now opens broad and clear of islands. Butler's Point marks the eastern headland of Manhasset Bay, beyond which is the still more out-reaching promontory, Sand's Point. The mainland shore opposite is nearly hidden by islands — Hunter's and The Twins, near Pelham Manor, then David's Island, in the rear of which are Starin's Glen Island, and New Rochelle, and then the rocky little Huckleberry Island. This is about as far as the features of the shore become distinguishable, for beyond Sand's Point, where Cow Bay sets back to Roslyn (p. 76) between sand bluffs crowned with forest, the open sound rolls too broadly to be surveyed from side to side.

The following steamboats run through East River to suburban landings:

1. *To Astoria and Harlem*, steamboats from wharf at northern end of Fulton Fish Market, Fulton Street, at 11.30 a. m. and 3.30 p. m.; fare, 10 cents. There is also a regular ferry from East River Park, at the foot of East 86th Street, across Hellgate to Astoria.

2. *To College Point*, ferry from East Ninety-ninth Street, stopping at North Beach, on Bowery Bay; fare, 10 cents.

3. *To Portchester*, steamer *Glenville*, on Mondays, Wednesdays, and Fridays, from Pike Street wharf; fare 25 cents.

4. *To Mount Vernon* (Eastchester Landing). Steamer *Riverside* from Pier 43, E. R., foot of Rutgers Slip, Mondays, Wednesdays, and Fridays, at 2.00 p. m.; returns on alternate days; fare, 25 cents. No charge for bicycles.

5. *To Glen Island* (and *New Rochelle* by ferry and horse-car). Steamers several times daily from Cortlandt Street. Excursion fare, 40 cents.

6. *To David's Island, Fort Schuyler*, and *Willet's Point*. Government ferry from the Battery. No charge, but a military pass required.

7. Steamer *Idlewild* for Great Neck, Sand's Point, Glen Cove,

Sea Cliff, Glenwood, and Roslyn. This fast and commodious boat leaves from Peck Slip, daily, except Sunday, at 4.00 p. m.; fare, round trip, 50 cents. Calls at East Thirty-first Street.

8. Steamer *Portchester*, to Lloyd's Neck, Oyster Bay, and Cold Spring, daily, from Pike Street; fare, 25 cents.

9. Steamer *Huntington*, to Huntington, on Tuesdays, Thursdays, and Saturdays at 1.00 p. m., from Pike Street wharf; fare, 50 cents.

10. Steamer *Northport*, to Center Island, Bayville, and Northport, Long Island, from Pier 24, Peck Slip; fare, 75 cents.

The steamboats to Norwalk, Bridgeport, New Haven, Hartford, New London, Greenport and Sag Harbor (p. 88), Stonington, Newport, Fall River, and Providence, and the steamships to Boston, Portland, and Martha's Vineyard, go this way and exhibit from their lofty decks all and more than has been described.

II.

ON LONG ISLAND.

Long Island offers a great variety of fields for excursions and out-of-door recreations, her long shore line, and numerous excellent harbors, making her the principal region for sailing, boating, fishing, and other aquatic pleasures; her great extent of macadamized roads inviting bicyclers and drivers, not only to the parks of Brooklyn, but far into the interior; her steam railroads and electric lines giving access to a great number of interesting and pleasant rural localities; and steamboats reaching from New York almost every shore town, while hotels, summer resorts, and pleasure places encircle the thickly settled western end, and occupy every advantageous point at the eastern extremity of the island, which has by far the most attractive seaside within easy reach of New York. An enormous number of persons take daily advantage of these facilities in summer — mainly inhabitants of the great city of Brooklyn, but largely recruited from New York and elsewhere.

Laws relating to bicycles are enforced with varying severity on Long Island. The State law gives no authority for the use of the sidewalks, but leaves its regulation with local authorities. Violation may subject the offender to penalty under both State law and local ordinance. Safety lies in keeping to the roadway, even where the law is not insisted upon by the village police. "In Jamaica and Richmond Hill the laws are enforced, and wheelmen never use the sidewalks in those places. All the towns have regulations requiring the use of a lighted lamp and a bell at night. In Freeport, this latter regulation is rigidly enforced, the penalty being a fine not exceeding $5. In Hempstead, in addition, the speed is limited to ten miles, and the limit of fine is $3. In College Point, Flushing, Whitestone, and in all villages in the town of Newton, the speed limit is seven miles, a lamp and bell is required at night, and the maximum fine is $5. In far Rockaway the speed limit is eight miles an hour, no more than two persons may ride abreast, and a lamp and bell are required at night. Fine, $5. In Milburn, East Rockaway, Fenhurst, Lynbrook, Valley Stream, Woodsburgh, Cedarhurst, Roslyn, Lawrence, and Inwood, there is no special legislation, and the State law applies. The laws, heretofore, have not been enforced against wheelmen in the town of Oyster Bay or North Hempstead, either in the villages or elsewhere. Suffolk County is very liberal in its treatment of wheelmen. Only on the most important streets of the incorporated villages are wheelmen prohibited from using the sidewalks. . . . In all the villages where riding on the sidewalk is permitted by ordinance, it is limited to daytime, and the main streets of the village are excepted."

BICYCLING ROUTES.

1. To Coney Island.

The principal route from New York to Coney Island is as follows:

Leaving Central Park at the Plaza (Fifth Avenue and Fifty-ninth Street), we turn to the east along Fifty-ninth Street (asphalt), to Madison Avenue (asphalt), and descend to East Twenty-sixth Street (asphalt), which is followed east to First Avenue (cobblestones); and thence to Twenty-third Street and the ferry (3 m.), which takes us to the foot of Broadway, *Williamsburg* (Brooklyn, Eastern District). Leaving the ferry in Brooklyn, turn to the right two blocks on Kent Street to South Ninth Street (block pavement) and up to *Bedford Avenue*, where you come upon asphalt, and follow it directly to the Eastern Parkway (3½ m.=6½ m.). Bedford Avenue gives fine level riding, and is the cycling highway of that part of the city; it is lined with handsome residences, and near the Parkway has several stately club houses. On the right is the new armory of the Twenty-third Regiment N. G., Brooklyn's crack corps; and on the left, beyond, is the house of the Kings County Wheelmen, while the high walls of the Kings County Penitentiary (Crow Hill) are seen in the distance. We turn to the right on *Eastern Parkway*—a broad boulevard of macadam taking us straight to the Plaza entrance of *Prospect Park*

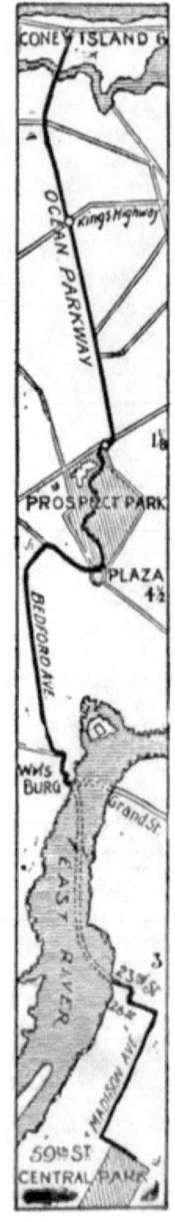

(1 m. = 7½ m.). Turning to the left into the park, we bear around to the right at the next fork, as the driveway winds through Brooklyn's chief pleasure ground, giving an unsurpassed riding surface amid lovely scenes; then to the left again, then around to the right, then a bend to the left skirting the lake, and finally to the right and out at the southern entrance (1½ m. = 9 m.). Prospect Park is properly bounded here by Fort Hamilton Avenue; but beyond it lies the broad champaign of the *Parade Ground*, where cricket, baseball, and other games are played every pleasant day in the year. From this entrance we keep straight on to the **Cycle Pathway** along Ocean Parkway direct to Surf Avenue, the main street of Coney Island (6 m. = 15 m.). This cycle pathway is a level road, ideally constructed for its purpose; and is a result of the efforts of the New York Division of the League of American Wheelmen. It is devoted exclusively to cyclers, and has at its Coney Island terminus a shelter-house, where men and women can rest comfortably in bad weather as well as in good, where wheels may be left under checks, etc. From here one can run, by a road back of the hotels, to Brighton, Manhattan Beach, or the magnificent Oriental Hotel.

Certain Regulations must be observed on this path, and in Prospect Park, as follows:

1. You must ride only upon the park roads—not upon any footpath, or upon the turf. 2. Keep to the right, and wherever practicable, pass such vehicles as you overtake upon the left hand side. 3. Coasting is forbidden; you must keep your feet upon the pedals, you hands upon the handles, and the machine under perfect control. 4. Lamps are strictly required at night. 5. Upon the pathway, anyone who dismounts must move his wheel to the turf at the side, and keep it there until ready to remount. 6. No wheelman shall ride at a rate of speed exceeding eight miles an hour in the park, or ten miles an hour on the parkway, between the park and Coney Island. Racing on the bicycle pathway is prohibited.

☞ A pretty side run may be made via Eighteenth Avenue—leading to the right from the cycle path—just beyond the three-mile post—direct to Avoca Villa, Bath Beach, 3½ miles.

2. To the South Side of Long Island.

This fine run divides itself into two sections:

1. New York or Brooklyn to Freeport, with side trips to Jamaica, and out the Jericho road, and to Rockaway Beach.
2. Freeport to Patchogue and eastward.

Section 1. New York to Freeport.—Leaving Central Park at the Plaza, Fifth Avenue and Fifty-ninth Street, we make our way to

ON LONG ISLAND. 65

Twenty-third Street Ferry, East River, via Madison Avenue, East Twenty-sixth Street, and First Avenue —nearly all asphalt pavement (3 m.). The Ferry (fare 5 cents) carries us to the foot of Broadway, *Williamsburg*. Here we turn to the right on Kent Street, two blocks, to South Ninth Street, and up that street to *Bedford Avenue* — all cobblestone; then straight out Bedford Avenue (asphalt) to the Eastern Parkway (3½ m.=6½ m.). Turning to the left on the macadam of the broad *Eastern Parkway* we make a gradual ascent through a sparsely occupied district until the brow of the hill is reached, where we get an extended view across the archipelago of Jamaica Bay, with Rockaway Beach as a merely hazy outline on the horizon. Before us, in the foreground, are the houses of East New York and Canarsie Landing. Two miles from Bedford Avenue the road is undergoing improvement and is temporarily poor in consequence. We turn to the left on the fork by the Empire Roadhouse into *East New York Avenue*, follow it three-quarters of a mile to the electric car tracks, and then follow the tracks on and to the left over the cobbles of *Liberty Avenue*, cross the steam road to Canarsie Landing, and shortly after run under the structure of the Kings County Elevated Railroad and on to its terminus at the junction of Broadway (5¼ m.= 11¾ m.).

To avoid this tedious ride through Brooklyn take the Kings County Elevated Railroad from Fulton Ferry or the bridge (fare 5 cents), which will carry your cycle at a charge of 15 cents and bring you to this point.

From Liberty Avenue we turn to the left onto the broad, level macadam of *Broadway*, extending east to Jamaica; but, after three-quarters of a mile, we turn to the right on the *Rockaway road*. This broad avenue of smooth macadam traverses a district devoted to truck-gardening, with here and there a pretty bit of woodland. The country is rolling, but the roadbed is so admirably graded that the low hills are but a name. Occasionally we catch a glimpse, away off to the right, of the blue waters of Jamaica Bay, the barren sand dunes of its multitude of little islands glistening in the bright sunlight. We run down a slight incline through a pretty piece of young woods, and bear to the right by the pumping station on the Ridgewood Aqueduct, cross the little bridge, and turn to the left onto *Locust Avenue*, South Jamaica (4⅜ m. from Liberty Avenue, 16½ m. from Central Park). We go directly out Locust Avenue (smooth macadam) through farm lands and villa sites one and a half miles to the intersection of the Merrick road, just beyond the railway station.

☞ **To Jamaica and the Jericho Road.**—The Jericho road is the ancient highway along the center of Long Island from Brooklyn through Jamaica, Garden City, Jericho, Locust Grove, Woodbury, Smithtown, New Village, etc., to Riverhead, where it skirts the northern shore of Peconic Bay to Greenport. It is a turnpike and thoroughly macadamized as far as Jericho. The Brooklyn *Eagle* speaks of it thus:

"The Jericho turnpike can be reached by the route given to reach the Merrick road, if the wheelman, instead of turning off at the Merrick road, will continue on Locust Avenue, turning right into Central Avenue nearly a mile from the Merrick road, keeping to the macadamized road; and then from Central Avenue, after riding a mile and a quarter on that thoroughfare, turn left into Springfield Avenue, passing through Queens to the Jericho pike just beyond the Long Island Railroad. Just before reaching the railroad the road crosses Fulton Street, or the Hempstead plank road, which will carry the wheelman through Elmont and Franklin Square to Hempstead; but a better way to reach the latter place is by turning left at Lynbrook on the Merrick road, or at Rockville Centre, Milburn, or Freeport. The main roads from these villages to the left all lead to Hempstead. A ride along the Jericho road from Jamaica carries the wheelman through Hollis, Queens, where the route from the Merrick road joins it; through Hyde Park, Garden City, Park, Floral, and Mineola, to Jericho, where the road turns to the north and leads to Syosset, Cold Spring Harbor, Huntington, and Northport. The roads beyond this point are rather poor, although ridable for the most part."

Resuming our route to the South Shore by turning from Locust Avenue to the right (south), on to the *Merrick road*, we still have good macadam, for this is the chosen avenue of approach to all points in Southern Suffolk County. Moving on, we swing around to the left, crossing the railroad and then going up a slight grade. Off to the left stretch broad meadows, fringed with low woodlands and furzy coverts, with a border of prettily tree-clad hills, far inland.

Now the road leads down and over the rippling waters of Simonson's Creek into the little hamlet of *Rosedale* or Foster's Meadows—as it was known to the early settlers (3⅝ m.=19¾ m.)—which is at the head of Jamaica Bay. The road runs directly on, past successive patches of meadow and wood, with an occasional pond or tiny stream, through the outskirts of *Valley Stream*, then over another pretty rivulet winding through a shady glade, and a little later up a slight incline. Straight away before us, through an arcade of waving green branches, now appears the tall red spire of the church at *Lynbrook*, and we speedily run into this cosy looking town (3¼ m.= 23 m.).

☞ **To Rockaway Beach.** Lynbrook stands at an important crossroad. Southwest runs the highway (taking the right-hand one of the two roads leading south from the village) to Fenhurst, Woodsburg, Cedarhurst — the home of the Rockaway Hunt Club — Lawrence, and Far Rockaway to Rockaway Beach, riding for the last three miles parallel to the ocean along this far-famed pleasure beach, with its beautiful summer resort called Arverne, half way between Far Rockaway and Rockaway Beach. A bath in the surf is the usual accompaniment of such a ride. The rider can return to the city from Rockaway Beach by taking the steamer back to Canarsie and wheel from that point to Eastern Parkway.

North of Lynbrook, a good, level, but rather crooked, road extends through old Hempstead village, Garden City, and Mineola (where it crosses the great east and west turnpike) northward to Roslyn, approaching which it becomes poorer and more hilly. At Roslyn (about ten miles) it connects with the North Shore route to Long Island City (p. 76), or a steamboat can be taken to New York. From Lynbrook, also, branches off the railroad to *Long Beach*, which, with its big summer hotel, is beyond the reach of cycles.

Keeping to the left out of Lynbrook, we pass the great storage reservoir for Brooklyn's water supply — a pond with a capacity of 414 millions of gallons — catching an alluring view oceanward, and wheel on into *Rockville Center* (1¼ m.=24¼ m.), where a comfortable resting place is offered at the Riverside Hotel ($2). The railway is crossed at Rockville Center, and thenceforth, as far as Oakdale, lies north or inland of our path. Moving on from the hotel, we keep to the left as the road forks, over a surface of smooth macadam; and, as we reach the top of a low hill, with a pretty lake on our left, get a pleasing run over the low moorlands on the right of the blue waters of Hempstead Bay, its many sandy islets dotted with fishermen's huts and summer villas. Then we go down a slight incline and across a pretty stream, from whose bridge we have a

second charming view of the distant bay, and of the settlement of *Milburn*, whose principal houses are prettily clustered in a vale at the left.

☞ Two or three good roads go southward to the shore of the bay on Coe's and Christian hooks here; and there is a good road nearly straight north to Hempstead (5 m.), Garden City, etc.

The next village is *Freeport*, where the eye is attracted by the irregular green-shingled roof of the quaint old "Three Gables" Inn, whose host is well known to wheelmen. This is the home of the Prospect Gun Club (3⅞ m. = 28½ m.).

Section 2. Freeport to Patchogue. — From the Three Gables at Freeport (28½ miles from New York) the road swings southward, and we look across the broad stretch of salt-meadows to the waters of the bay, just a narrow greenish blue streak separated from the southern horizon by a silvery line of shifting sand dunes. The road is now bordered with several handsome summer places, and we cross a limpid stream (Mill Creek) spanned by a rustic bridge, then go up a slight grade, with meadows of waving salt grass stretching bayward on our right, while inland the green moorlands slope to the low bush-clothed hills. Here and there we cross a rivulet rushing eagerly toward the bay, wheel through a long stretch of cedars, interspersed with the brighter green of the oak, chestnut, and maple, and finally cross the broad bush-fringed borders of Massapeaqua Lake, one of the sources of the Brooklyn water supply, beyond which, in the neighborhood of *New Jerusalem* we reach at a cross-road (which gives fair riding north to Farmingdale and Central Park) the end of the macadam road (3⅞ m. = 32 m.).

The roadbed from here on is of sandy loam and gravel, with here and there poor spots. It is always ridable in good weather, but is usually heavy for a day or so after a storm. The side-paths may be taken, *except through the villages*.

Soon we pass upon the right the large Massapeaqua Hotel, a popular summer resort, open only from May

to November ; it is a League hotel, and is famous for its fish dinners.
We cross the waters of Seaford Creek, which expands into a pretty
lake on the left of the roadside, and pass through the little town of
Seaford (5 m.=33⅛ m.).   Then comes the bridge over Massapeaqua
Creek, whose waters broaden as they approach South Oyster Bay,
as the water east of North, Middle, and South Line islands is called
by the baymen.

This water is defended from the ocean by Jones or Seaford Beach,
and a series of islets and shallows stretching from Zach's Inlet east
to Gilgo Inlet ; but it would puzzle anybody but one of the amphibi-
ous natives of this region to say how Hempstead Bay is separated
from South Oyster Bay, or that from the Great South Bay east of it.
East of Gilgo Inlet begins the Oak Island Beach, which fronts the
Atlantic as far as Fire Island Inlet ; and then comes Fire Island
or Great South Beach, extending unbroken eastward to its junction
with the mainland at Quogue — an isthmus beyond which stretches
the similar lagoon called Shinnecock Bay.

We are now on the old Babylon road, and traverse broad
meadows, varied by bits of woodland; dry islets, where cottages
have been built, and pretty streams; and now and then one can
catch fleeting views of the bay through the vista of trees. Now we
cross a bridge, roll through an avenue of drooping willows, and
swing to the right into the quaint town of *Amityville* (4⅛m.=37¼m.).
At the left of the road stands the Russell House ($2), an ancient
hostelry still highly esteemed.

☞ Good roads lead south from here to the shore, populous in
summer, and northward for some distance into the country.

Continuing, the road swings southward, following the contour of
the great South Bay, whose blue sail-dotted waters begin to be seen
in the distance.   Inlets and creeks follow one another in rapid succession, and, as we cross a bridge, having a beautiful lake and residence on the left, we enjoy a pleasing contrast, for off to the right
stretches a wide expanse of salt marsh, indented by a tidal inlet on
whose banks are several humble fishermen's huts.   Their low, dingy
boats roll lazily under bare poles at their moorings near the shore,
and beyond, outlined picturesquely against the blue sky, is a gigantic
fishing net coiled upon its quadrangular reel.   Then follows a space
of woodland, succeeded by an avenue doubly bordered by neat
houses, which conducts us to the shore town of Babylon, whose
advantageous situation on the Great South Bay — the finest of
America's fishing grounds — has brought to it a large number of

wealthy people, whose summer houses are among the finest on Long Island (5⅝ m. = 42⅞ m.).

☞ Two fair roads lead north from here into the interior: One ascends Carll's Brook, beyond the railway tracks, and then takes a northeasterly course, parallel with and close beside the railroad to Farmingdale, affording a route for crossing the island to Oyster Bay on the north shore; the other, a few rods east, leads directly north through Deer Park to Northport. Both are soft but ridable in good weather.

Our route forms the main business street of Babylon, facing which is the Sherman House ($2), patronized by wheelmen. Leaving the village the road crosses over the bridge by the old grist mill, below which the little stream (Sampawam's Brook) broadens into the cosy anchorage of Babylon Cove off to the right. Toiling up a slight incline as the road winds to the right, we gain a charming view of the pretty mill pond, bordered with dense thickets to the water's edge. At its upper end a white bridge of Venetian design spans the waters of the brook and on its eastern shores is a handsome home. Now we run across the marsh lands of another inlet; beyond which the bay shimmers in the sunlight; then through an avenue of spreading branches over a rustic bridge spanning a brook, past a tiny isle-dotted lake bordered with a fringe of deep green cedars, across the point of Appletree Neck—every extension of the shore is called a "neck" and has its name, often from the language of the aborigines—and again we come into view of the bay, now wide, and open, and sending us breezes laden with refreshing briny odors.

Here and there the white top-sails of a fishing boat or trim yacht peep above the trees; and away off across the broad expanse of blue is the dome of the lighthouse on Fire Island, but a speck on the horizon. The road now curves around to the left into Main Street, *Bay Shore* (4¼ m. = 47⅝ m.). This is another example of a fishing, oystering, clamming, and bay-shooting town, transformed into a wealthy, populous, and fashionable summer resort, having in the Olympic Club one of the leading country clubs of the island.

☞ At the eastern edge of the village a road offering fair riding in summer crosses the island via Brentwood (5 m.) and Happauge to Smithtown (10 m.), and thence eastwardly to Stony Brook (6 m.), Setauket (8 m.), East Setauket (10 m.), and Port Jefferson (12 m.). There is now a cycle path from Commac to Smithtown and Smithtown to Happauge.

From Bay Shore the road skirts the irregular outline of Great Cove, and passes through the towns of *Islip* and *East Islip*, which are separated by Champlin's Creek; and on through woodland and rural scenes to the shore of Connetquot River, whose estuary is known as Islip Bay. Here we turn up toward the head of the inlet and take to the smooth side-path, winding in and out among the trees, passing on the right the richly wooded park-like estate of W. Bayard Cutting, then on the left the green-turfed golf-links of the South Side Club — an association of wealthy New Yorkers, summer residents here, who cultivate outdoor sports. The road swings to the right over the railroad tracks, then across the pretty stream that winds down through a wooded glen, and brings us to the gates of the club's grounds (5½ m. = 53½ m.).

☞ **To Lake Ronkonkoma.**—Directly after crossing the railroad, and just before coming to the club gate, a fine road strikes northeast to the village of Bohemia, and then, turning to the left, straight on to Lake Ronkonkoma, which is reached at the village on its southern shore; the distance is about five miles.

At the gates of the *South Side Club* we turn sharply to the right through a fine grove of fragrant pines — a truly delightful bit of riding on a summer's day, and quite the prettiest part of the trip. The road bears again to the right and crosses the railroad once more, just at the vine-clad entrance-lodge to "Oakdale," the beautiful estate of W. K. Vanderbilt. Immediately opposite stands *St. John's Church in Oakdale*, built more than 125 years ago. The road skirts the shady park under the entwined branches of huge trees. On the left we pass the neat railway station and then traverse the large estate of C. R. Roberts. The road gradually inclines southward toward the shore of the bay and passes through the old hamlet of Greenville, with its quaint meeting-house and ancient tombs. From the low hill top here we again see the waters of the bay, and then swing around to the left into *Sayville* (9⅞ m. = 57½ m.) to the Kensington Hotel ($2). Proceeding from the hotel, we choose the right-hand road at the first fork, and go straight on along the main street of *Bayport* whose shore front is Blue Point, which gave its name long ago to the particularly appetizing oysters that were cultivated in this neighborhood. On the first street beyond the post office we turn to the left; this is Bayport Avenue and takes us three-quarters of a mile northward and across the railroad, where we turn to the right on the side-path along the sandy main road, and run straight into **Patchogue** (5⅛ m. = 62⅝ m. from Central Park, New York).

Patchogue has the largest harbor on the Great South Bay, and is the most citified town on Long Island. It is the headquarters of the varied marine industries of the region, a noted resort for fishermen and gunners, and is constantly growing in popularity as a place of summer residence. It abounds in boarding-houses and hotels, among which Roe's ($3 to $4), which long ago established a high reputation, has been recently enlarged and now is more than ever deserving of popularity.

The Century Runs on Long Island have followed this southside course. It is reckoned fifty miles from a point just east of Jamaica to Patchogue. The one that starts from Sag Harbor and comes east to Jamaica, 100 miles of straightaway riding except for the windings of the road in Suffolk County, should also be mentioned. The road is good the entire distance except for 100 yards or so on the Shinnecock Hills, where the deep sand renders wheeling impossible.

The New Cycle Path across Long Island starts from this town and ends at Port Jefferson. It leads north along an old road to a point about a mile north of the main line of the Long Island road, just west of Medford station, then turns to the left (west) for about 1¼ miles along the Horseblock road, and then north again. It crosses the main or 'middle road" east and west at Seldon, passes on through Ferryville, and enters Port Jefferson by the Canal road. The distance is about seventeen miles. The completion of this and of the improvements along the North Shore opens to cyclists a fine round-trip route of about 125 miles from Brooklyn back to Brooklyn.

3. To the North Shore.

Astoria to Roslyn.—Starting at the Plaza, Fifth Avenue and Fifty-ninth Street, New York, we run along the East Drive through Central Park to the Ninetieth Street gate, then up Fifth Avenue to Ninety-second Street and down to *Astoria Ferry* (2¾ m.). These streets are stone paved and very rough, but mostly down grade. The ferry (fare 5 cents) lands us at the foot of Flushing Avenue, *Astoria*, over the cobbles of which we ride for two blocks to *Halsey Street*, on which we turn to the left one block to *Franklin Street*, where we come upon good macadam. Then up a slight hill through the best residential part of the town, which is the oldest and finest part of Long Island City. Turning to the left on *Woolsey Street* we go on direct to the Shore road.

As the *Shore road* swings down to the left we have an excellent view of the waters of Hellgate rushing and seething off the rocky shores of Ward's Island, and can see where the great excavations were made, twenty years ago, into which the bottom of the strait was dropped by the aid of dynamite. The level macadamized road closely follows the contour of the shore, along which, facing the river, is a row of old mansions, each in a highly cultivated park.

These shores were taken possession of by the British immediately after the battle of Long Island, in 1776, and batteries were erected here from which an artillery fire was kept up against the American forts, blockhouses, and camps that lined the heights of Harlem until Washington withdrew his forces to the north. The islands in the river were fortified and held by the English, and one of them (Randall's) was once unsuccessfully attacked by a band of Americans, who were repulsed with severe loss after a sharp fight. The East River, thronged with steamers and sailing vessels and small craft of every sort, makes an ever-changing and ever-pleasing panorama of marine life upon our left as we roll on; and we get glimpses across it not only of islands and bays, but through Bronx Kills of the Harlem River and Port Morris shores.

At the *Casino*, we turn to the right over a sandy dirt road, having a fairly ridable side-path, and undertake a bit of a climb, to be rewarded by a pleasing landscape from the top of the hill. Below us, in the foreground, is a broad stretch of salt-meadow watered by tiny flood-tide rivulets; just off shore lies Berrian's Island, and beyond, dotting the broad expanse of shimmering blue, are the two Brother islands, with the rugged outline of Hunt's Point as a background to the picture. Eastward sweeps the Sound, and in the distance, that way, we discern the outlines of Sanford Point, behind which Flushing Bay deeply indents the coast; and the distant towns of College Point, seen at the left and Flushing at the right, are on the opposite shore of that bay. The descent of the hill leads us into the manufacturing town of *Steinway* (2¾ m. = 5½ m.), where the central industry is that of making pianos. We follow the Shore road across the electric car tracks, and keep directly out till the road bears to the left by the waterworks. The riding is not very good, but by picking one's way along the side-path fair progress can be made. Now up a straight hill as we bear to the left through a

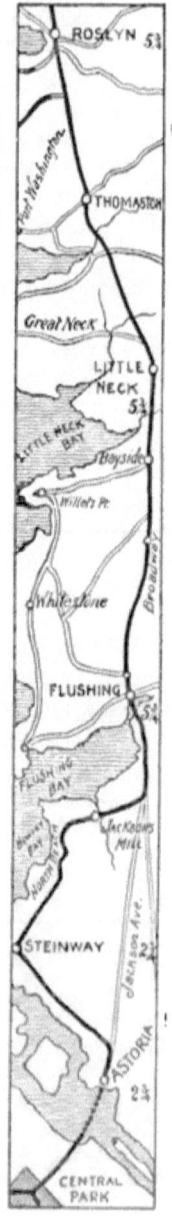

settlement of old houses having a fine view of the Sound, and then a turn to the right again, skirting the water's edge through the summer gardens of *Bowery Bay* and *North Beach*, where the road is lined with beer-shops and small amusement places like those at South Beach or Canarsie; the place is decent enough, and a favorite resort of the tenement-house population of Long Island City and of Harlem, but a grade too plebeian for more refined folks. Electric cars run into Astoria, and the steamers of the ferry between Harlem (East Ninety-ninth Street) and College Point call here. Having passed the pier (at the end of Sanford Point) we bear around to the right, still following the shore, where the road makes a turn back of the hotel through a pretty grove to the trolley-line tracks, when we turn to the left and follow the line over poor road to one of the oldest landmarks on this end of Long Island — *Jackson's Mill*. It was built in 1657, but was long ago remodeled on the original frame and put to use as a roadside tavern. It is a delightful place for an hour's rest on a warm day. We cross the bridge over Jackson's Creek and follow the trolley wires direct to Jackson Avenue, where the poor road ends. Turning to the left we speed along the smooth macadam across the salt-meadows bordering Flushing Bay, and presently rise into Broadway and bring up at the public square of Flushing (5¾ m.=11¼ m.) where stands the Flushing Hotel ($2.50, L. A. W. $2).

Flushing is a charming town with an individuality of its own. "Its long business street has the look of a city thoroughfare in spite of the trees that almost arch it, for there are stores, banks, hotels, restaurants, agencies, and newspaper offices, and on the clean and shaded side streets, and avenues, are churches and schools, and many homes that bespeak the possession of comfortable bank accounts, as well as of taste and moderate leisure. Some of the houses are sufficiently quaint and ancient to take on an Old World aspect. There is a park in the business center, and famous nurseries on the skirts of the town."

Leaving Flushing we go directly out Broadway — a broad macadamized avenue, arched with grand old trees, and bordered by fine residences, which runs straight east. It carries us up a slight hill, known as Flushing Heights, to the speculators in suburban lots, who are doing all they can to spoil this fine old village.

☞ **Whitestone, College Point,** and **Willet's Point** are reached by a fine road striking off to the left from here. These are shore villages on the East River, about one and a quarter miles northward. *College Point* (which is connected with Flushing by an electric road, and good wagon road, along the shore of Flushing Bay) is a manufacturing place, and the terminus of a ferry line to Ninety-second Street, New York. *Whitestone* lies a mile east of it, and is a pretty village opposite Throgs Neck, the nearest land being Old Ferry Point, at the mouth (east side) of Westchester Creek; it has a lighthouse, and is a favorite summer residence. It is a calling place for the Roslyn and New York steamboats. East of it is the indentation called Little Bay, beyond which is the projection, between the East River and Little Neck Bay, called Willet's Point. This is immediately opposite Fort Schuyler (p. 26), and is familiar to river travelers by the great sign on the beach—TORPEDOES: DON'T ANCHOR.

Willet's Point is a United States military reservation containing 117 acres, admirably located, and highly cultivated. It is the permanent headquarters of Companies A, B, and C, of the Engineer Battalion of the United States Army; Company D being permanently at the Military Academy at West Point. The strength of the battalion is 500 enlisted men, while the entire number of persons usually at the post, including men, women, and children, is about 700. A school is maintained at the post for the instruction of young officers in engineering work, and the drilling of the enlisted men in the building of fortifications, handling torpedoes, and many other departments of technical military work. The fortifications date from 1862; and during the Civil War it was the seat of a great military hospital, long since burned. Three barracks, the post office-buildings and laboratories, and the residences of the officers, constitute the structures about the parade ground. The fort, alluded to above, faces the water, and is entered through a long tunnel, which descends gradually for several hundred feet. This work is considered obsolete, and remains unfinished. Other works, which comply with the requirements of modern warfare, are being constructed ; and this station, whose high-power guns will be supplemented by new batteries at Fort Schuyler, in conjunction with submarine mines operated from each shore, will, when completed, effectually close East River against entrance by an enemy's ships of war, and constitute the principal defense of the metropolis on that side.

From Flushing Heights a steady descent is made to *Bayside* (4 m. = 15¼ m.), followed by a swift run across the broad meadows at the head of Little Neck Bay, of which we have a full view, and a gradual ascent again through Douglaston and Little Neck, keeping to the right as the road forks, and always on a surface of fine macadam. All these villages overlook an inlet of the Sound, Little Neck Bay—the home of the original "Little Neck clam." The peninsula, east of this bay, is known as *Great Neck*, and we cross it through high-rolling farm lands, which carry the hard shady road up hill and down dale, and form many pretty bits of rural scenery to divert the eye. Then comes a long descent, at the bottom of which is a sharp turn to the left, then a swing to the right at the Centennial

Hotel, and so down over the bridge. To the right lies a pretty little pond, surrounded by hills, while on the left its overflow tumbles over rocks and stumps, down a wild ravine to Manhasset Bay, which sparkles in the distance through a curtain of foliage. East of the bridge the road rises through the secluded village of *Manhasset*, noticeable for its ancient church and burying-ground. We are now upon Cow Neck, which juts out into the Sound and terminates in Sand's Point, whose lighthouse is straight across from New Rochelle.

☞ *The Shore road*, from Manhasset to the left (north), leads to Port Washington, a quaint village of fishermen and oyster planters, whence a small steamboat runs to New York every day.

A charming bit of country lies ahead, with hills easy to ride over, pleasant to look at, and exposing from their summits variable and always delightful landscapes. This part of Long Island is very old, and bears not only the marks of long and careful cultivation, but the added elegancies produced by the scattered homes of city men, who make it their home in summer in great numbers, and to some extent all the year round. Presently we see ahead of, and below us, the Ward Memorial Clock-tower in Roslyn, and settle ourselves in the saddle for a long run down hill, which ends at the Mansion House ($2), 11½ miles from Flushing, and 22¾ from the Central Park Plaza, in New York. **Roslyn** is at the head of Cow Bay, and is the terminus of a daily steamboat line to New York, the boats stopping also at Glen Cove and Sea Cliff, which are on the eastern shore of the same bay (p. 84). Fairly good roads, though rather sandy, may be followed around the bay to Glen Head, Sea Cliff, Glen Cove, and Locust Valley (about 7 m.), but the wheeling along the north shore of Long Island, east of Roslyn is, in general, too bad to be recommended. A good road is now under construction, but there is little hope of its being available for cyclers before the spring of 1897. (For further local particulars, see p. 83.)

DRIVES ON LONG ISLAND.

Though the roads on Long Island are inclined to be sandy, so large a proportion of them have been turnpiked, paved, or otherwise improved, that many excellent drives exist. This is especially true near Brooklyn, where Prospect Park, and the various outlying parks, parkways, and suburban roads, offer delightful routes. In Prospect Park the drives are exceedingly picturesque. The East Drive passes

THE LAKE, PROSPECT PARK, BROOKLYN.

through *Battle Pass*, the scene of the most terrific struggle of the battle of Long Island, which fact is commemorated by a tablet on the left of the road, and then winds through the most cultivated parts, and around the lake shore to the Ocean Parkway entrance. A drive through Prospect Park, down Ocean Avenue to Sheepshead Bay over a road straight as the crow flies, will bring one to the rear of Manhattan Beach in an hour. Another drive is through the park to Franklin Avenue on the east side, and then, still going east, down Clarkson Street, in Flatbush, past the county buildings, to Flatlands Neck, and Canarsie, on Jamaica Bay. None of these drives need occupy more than three hours.

Another pleasant drive, the Brooklyn *Eagle* tells us, is out Twenty-second Avenue (Bay Parkway), which branches from the Ocean Parkway, passing through Bensonhurst and ending at Bath Beach. At Bath Beach one may turn to the east and ride along the oldest road in the county, if not in the State—for the King's Highway was established two centuries ago, under grant from the Georges of England, and was a post-road before the Revolution. It runs through a picturesque country, lined by houses almost as old as itself, for three miles, and into the village of Flatlands, where it terminates in Flatbush Avenue, by which road, running now to the west, the driver may reach the city again. Flatbush Avenue is a pleasant drive, going through the original country towns of Kings County, sheltered by huge and ancient elms. Another drive much used is a continuation of the Eastern Parkway into Fulton Street, out through the Twenty-eighth Ward, on to Jamaica, and so along the south side of Long Island as far as may be desired. Summer tourists occasionally make trips with horse and wagon, starting along this road and making a tour of the island, returning by the north side, through Flushing, and across to Jamaica again. This circuit of the island usually occupies a fortnight. A study of the bicycle routes given herein will be of advantage to the driver proposing such a trip. Excellent roads are to be found at the eastern end of Long Island, through Southold, Greenport, Orient Point, etc., on Shelter Island; and from Sag Harbor to Amagansett, Easthampton, etc.

The drive along Fort Hamilton Avenue is from the rear entrance of Prospect Park. It is about three miles long, and connects with the Shore Drive which is being constructed along the edge of the lower bay as far as Fort Hamilton. Those who traverse it usually go through Prospect Park to Fort Hamilton Avenue; thence along

Fort Hamilton Avenue to Ovington Avenue; thence to the right to Bay Ridge Avenue, the direction being to the shore of the upper bay. This shore they follow to the south, enjoying the lovely views of Staten Island, the Jersey Hills, the Narrows, forts, and Liberty Statue. Shipping animates the harbor, and incoming and outgoing steamers are in constant view. The drive has historic interest, as well as natural beauty, and is interrupted by Fort Hamilton, with dismantled Fort Lafayette on an island just off shore, famous as the prison of those held for treason during the War of the Rebellion. The grass-grown works of Fort Hamilton are at the left, the guns of Fort Wadsworth frown across the Narrows, while farther out may be seen the hospitals and houses of detention at upper and lower quarantine, and Sandy Hook, with the Atlantic Highlands, far to the south; the road then continues along the shore to Bath Beach, Bensonhurst, and other villages, until it ends at the creek that separates Coney Island from the mainland.

The completion of the projected Shore Drive or boulevard (an extension of the park system), along the shore of New York Bay, from near Sixty-fifth Street (Bay Ridge), will be welcomed. This shore is high, and affords a continuous and far-reaching view of the harbor and the Staten Island shore. This extension also contemplates additional parks and boulevards, so that, when the plan is completed, there will be a chain of parks about the city, and carriages may drive from one to the other over park roads for a distance of fifty miles. Doubtless, the near future will see a ferry connection between Pelham Bay Park and Long Island, connecting these drives with those in upper New York City.

Several suburban parks outside of the present more thickly settled parts of Brooklyn should be mentioned. The finest is the *Brooklyn Forest*. This is a natural woodland park, extending from the boundary of the present Ridgewood Park as far as Richmond Hill. It contains about 540 acres, and is intended to provide a playground and breathing spot for the people of the Eastern District. It is easily reached from all parts of the city by trolley roads; is filled with forest trees and shrubbery; and from its high points are obtained views of the Atlantic Ocean, Jamaica Bay, and Long Island Sound. Cooper Park is in the Eighteenth Ward, and it covers two blocks without improvement. Irving Square is in the Twenty-eighth Ward. Saratoga Square is on Halsey Street, in the Twenty-fifth Ward. Lincoln Terrace, on the Eastern Parkway, is at the junction of several existing and proposed boulevards, and preserves a magnificent sea and landscape view.

Dyker Beach Park is the largest of the seaside parks. It contains 144 acres and cost $229,942. It adjoins the Government property at Fort Hamilton, and will make the finest seaside park in the world, providing, in addition to the usual park pleasures, fishing, boating, and bathing. Canarsie Beach Park, the next in size, containing forty acres, is upon the shores of Jamaica Bay. Bensonhurst Beach, opposite Norton's Point, is a local park for Gravesend and New Utrecht. It possesses a fine beach, and, prior to its purchase by the county, was used as a park by the people in the neighborhood. New Lots Playground is located in the part of the Twenty-sixth Ward known as Brownsville.

RAILROAD AND STEAMBOAT ROUTES.

Long Island Railroad.

1. **Main Line.**—Trains leave Long Island City (Thirty-fourth Street ferry from New York) and Brooklyn (Flatbush Avenue station) for all points. The main line passes directly east along the center of the island through *Jamaica*, Queens (the station for the shooting-ranges of Creedmoor), Mineola (and Garden City, close by), Hicksville, etc. The last few stations are on the great Hempstead plains — a level region in the center of the island, traversed in all directions by excellent roads for bicycling. At Mineola the Queens County Fair Grounds attract farmers and a curious lot of other people to the autumnal agricultural shows and races. "At a short distance from *Westbury* is located the famous Meadow Brook [fox-hunting] Club, an organization of well-known New York gentlemen. Central Park and Farmingdale are thriving villages, where much of the produce is raised that finds its way to the city markets. A large portion of the farm products that are supplied to Brooklyn come from Long Island, and a still larger quantity finds its way to New York. These villages all offer quiet retreats for the summer vacationist. Passing through West Deer Park, Deer Park, and Edgewood, *Brentwood* is reached." This is on a good cycle road extending across the island and is at the edge of the pine woods, and several hotels here invite patrons to reside in them as a combined health and pleasure resort, like those of New Jersey. The conditions of geography and climate are substantially the same as at Lakewood. *Ronkonkoma*

is the station for Lake Ronkonkoma, a mile or so to the southward. This lake is about three miles in circumference, is sixty-five feet deep in places, and is closely surrounded by heavy pine woods, among which a great many houses and hotels are set. It is an attractive spot; and is connected with the South shore by a good bicycle road (p. 71). Beyond Ronkonkoma are Waverly, *Medford* near the crossing of the cycle path (p. 72), *Yaphank*, Manor, and Baiting Hollow, all healthy places, surrounded by a good farming section, with fish and game in abundance. West of Manor is Panamoko Park, a tract of two thousand acres of woodlands which is to be converted into a winter and summer health retreat. At Yaphank is a model farm connected with the county almshouse. From *Manor* a connecting line goes south to Eastport. The shire town of Suffolk County is *Riverhead*. It is centrally located, and an active village of two thousand inhabitants. It takes its name from the Peconic River, which empties into a bay of that name a short distance away. Riverhead has many advantages as a summer resort. A half-hour's drive will take one to Peconic Bay, and a ride of eight miles to the ocean, and it is less than that distance to the Sound. The village is handsomely laid out and has many fine residences. It is a bustling town, and during Fair week and Court time is crowded with strangers.

East of Riverhead the railroad runs along the north shore of Peconic Bay. *Jamesport* has become a very popular summer resort of late years, and like the other towns on this excellent bit of inclosed water, has admirable facilities for boating, fishing, crabbing, and still-water bathing. Mattituck, Cutchogue, and New Suffolk are delightful old villages, thronged in summer by city people. Opposite this point, and distant a few minutes' sail, is *Robbins Island*, a famous hunting preserve, owned by the Robbins Island Gun Club, an organization composed of prominent Brooklyn gentlemen. The island contains 469 acres of land. It is diversified with hills, cliffs, forests, fertile fields, and sand beaches. Adjacent to Cutchogue on the east is Peconic, a rich and beautiful section of productive farms and rural homes. Next east comes *Southold*, one of the oldest and most attractive villages on Long Island, whose history goes back to the earliest coming of white men, and whose surroundings are very delightful. This brings the traveler to the terminus at **Greenport**, a large and flourishing town and seaport, the favorite harbor of yachtsmen, and the ferry station for **Shelter Island**, landing at both the fashionable Manhansett House and the almost equally large and comfortable Prospect House. Steamboats make daily trips between this town, Sag Harbor, New London, Conn., and New York. A mile to the east is Orient Point, and Plumb Island, famous for water-fowl and shore-birds in the shooting season. Good roads connect these towns and neighboring villages, so that the horseman, or bicycler, or rambler, will find himself here in a country favorable to his leisurely pleasures in every respect; while the beautiful, historic, healthful bluffs, groves, beaches, and fishing waters of Shelter Island are only "across the creek." There is probably no region within easy access of New York which presents such varied and satisfactory attractions to the summer wanderer as the shores and islands of Peconic Bay.

2. **To the South Shore.**—It is unnecessary to dwell here upon the numerous short lines which take trains from both Long Island City and Brooklyn to Manhattan Beach, Rockaway, and Long Beach. Two lines of railroad carry passengers to the farther "South Shore" of the island, uniting at Babylon. One runs by way of Jamaica, Floral Park, Garden City, and Hempstead across the plain; the other keeps to the southward from Jamaica, and follows substantially the route described on pp. 64 to 72. Beyond *Babylon*, where there is a connecting steamboat for Fire Island (7 m.) during the season when the Surf Hotel is open, the route is close beside the main road (see Bicycle Route 2, p. 69) to *Patchogue*, where it enters upon new and interesting ground. *Bellport*, Brookhaven, and Mastic are favorite summer resorts, the first-named having large hotels and fashionable patrons. This is a locality of ancient settlement and much revolutionary interest. Then follow *Moriches* with its many hotels, of which the finest is the great Hotel Brooklyn; *Eastport*, where the line from Manor comes in and where the Long Island Country Club has its property; Speonk, and Union Place. All these are villages in the woods on the shore of East Bay, whose inhabitants live through the winter by faith and fishing, spend the spring in shooting and plowing, make their harvest from city boarders in summer, and take a vacation and oysters in the autumn.

Westhampton begins a new line of still more pleasant and more truly seaside towns, since they are right upon the ocean beach, or within access of it without the help of a boat. Country roads, good for driving and fair for wheeling, when not too sandy, connect them, wandering under the shadow of time-honored windmills, and past the gates of ancestral farms, tenanted by a people who are, perhaps, more expert with the oar than with the plow, and noxiously mingle their industry by nourishing the harvest of the land with the harvest of the sea, to the great offense of sensitive noses. Joining Westhampton is *Quogue*, which has exceptionally fine opportunities for fishing and for surf bathing. East of Quogue lies another lagoon, *Shinnecock Bay*, which has been made a household word among artists of late years, the stations upon which are: Atlanticville; Good Ground (Ponquogue Point); Canoe Place, where there used to be a "carry" over into Peconic Bay, and now a canal has been dug; and Shinnecock Hills, where the sand dunes are dotted with hotels and cottages, and with artists' tents and easels in a way wonderful to see. Here, commanding a far-reaching view of the hills, the sea, and the waters of Peconic Bay, stands the handsome home of the Shinnecock Golf Club. Beyond them lie the better agricultural lands about the ancient village of *Southampton*. Bridgehampton, where the Sag Harbor branch diverges from the Montauk line, is a few miles beyond; and a little farther on is *Easthampton*, then Amagansett, and after that the wave-beaten and wind-swept sand bluffs of Montauk Point, where only those venture who are enamored of solitude and the sea. The neighborhood of historic old Easthampton, beloved of painters and writers, and of sea-faring, breezy Amagansett, is the most delightful part; and good roads lead north to the shore of Peconic Bay and the flourishing and beautiful town of *Sag Harbor*. From Sag Harbor there is ferriage to Shelter Island and thence to Greenport, and a daily steamboat service to Greenport, New London, Conn., and New York.

3. **To the North Shore.**—The northern coast of Long Island is a pile of glacial drift, deeply cut by outflowing rivers and the inroads of the Sound, much diversified by hills and valleys, and thickly covered with forest wherever the axe of mankind has been stayed. It is a district of old settlements, and much picturesque and historical interest, both along shore and in the rural interior, while flourishing villages are scattered about at short intervals. The northern or coastal face of the hills presents steep and often precipitous bluffs of gravel that occasionally rise one hundred feet above the water. At the foot of these bluffs are beaches, narrow, and strewn with bowlders, where the surf is always light, and boating safe and easy, while every inlet presents a safe anchorage for yachts, and the whole foreshore is planted with oysters and clams. The shores of the inlets

are formed by the steep slopes of hills, most of which are clothed with forest and dotted with new and substantial villas and summer homes. The highest point is Harbor Hill, near Roslyn, about 350 feet in altitude. Like all the heights in this range, it commands a splendid view of the green fields and forests to the east and south, the shining Sound below, and the cultivated shores of Westchester and Connecticut to the northwest and north. The hills known as "the back-bone of the island" run along from three to seven miles inland, and are distinct ridges. In the pine and oak regions the hunter or the traveler might easily imagine himself in the fastnesses of an Adirondack wilderness, were it not for the lack of peaks in the field of vision. The writer of an excellent pamphlet entitled "Out on Long Island," from which many of these particulars are borrowed, assures us that these hills are rapidly passing into the hands of persons from the city in search of summer homes.

The railroad reaches this North Shore by three lines.

The first is hardly more than local, running from Long Island City to *Flushing*, and thence branching north to Whitestone and east to *Great Neck*.

The second carries passengers from either Long Island City, or Brooklyn, via Jamaica and Mineola to the shore towns on Cow Neck, over the "Oyster Bay Branch." It has stations at Roslyn, Sea Cliff, Glen Cove, Locust Valley, and Oyster Bay—a terminus on the Sound shore, by way of which were formerly run through trains to Boston, ferried across from this point to South Norwalk, Conn.

"To fully appreciate the beauties of this region," remarks the discerning writer of *Out on Long Island*, "one must leave the railroad and travel along the woodland roads, and from the hills and high bluffs view the numerous bays, inlets, and delightful vistas of blue waters, with the sails of vessels going up and down the Sound

. Who has not heard of *Roslyn?* At the old toll-house at the summit of the hill, at the foot of which is Roslyn, one gets the first glimpse of the little town which is memorable as containing the home where the poet Bryant lived, and the grave where his ashes rest. The village is in the valley, divided by an inlet from Hempstead Harbor, which runs backward to the hills, and across which is a narrow causeway, over which the railroad winds. Northward is a little stretch of marsh, which the tides keep sweet and clean, and beyond is the harbor, white with the sails of oystermen. In the distance, across the Sound, are the hills of Connecticut, and bounding the harbor on either side are great hills, thick with foliage, in which great estates and castles rise among the branches, and look off upon the waters of the bay. Half a mile or more on the road which lies eastward of the harbor is 'Cedarmere,' the home of Bryant. Here he wrote some of his best poems, and here he came when in mood of inspiration. The house is large and rambling, the frame being at least a century old. There are broad piazzas, quiet nooks and coverts, extensions and subextensions, and the house is high enough above the waters to get the effect of intervening lawns, yet not too far to hear the music of the waves. There is a great variety of trees about the place, with ivy and clambering vines, truly a poet's home, where in spring it learns to

'Wear the green coronal of leaves,
And a thousand suns could not add aught,
Of splendor in the grass.'

"The grave of Bryant is in the village cemetery, about a mile away.

"The highest elevation on Long Island is the summit [Harbor Hill], back of the village, and from the observatory which surmounts it can be seen the surrounding country for miles about. Roslyn has a paper mill, the oldest in the State, a flouring mill, a good hotel, and is a very popular place in summer. See also p. 76.

"Beyond are Glen Head, a picturesque and growing resort, and Sea Cliff, possessing one of the most superb locations in Long Island.

. . . *Sea Cliff* is a very lively place in summer, and several hotels and numerous boarding-houses are taxed to their utmost . . . The village was originally owned by the Sea Cliff Grove and Metropolitan Camp-Meeting Association, and after several years of vicissitudes the land passed out of the control of the Association, and the only camp-meetings now held are by the Methodists. It is needless to add that the boating and bathing are excellent."

Glen Cove, a short distance east, is a prosperous little town mainly supported by an immense starch factory. Two miles away is the island of Dosoris, where Charles A. Dana, editor of the New York *Sun*, has a residence in the midst of a highly cultivated park, the whole island being inclosed by a vine-clad sea-wall. The next property, facing the Sound, was the estate of the late Charles Pratt, founder of the Pratt Institute in Brooklyn; and there 150 acres have been set aside for the agricultural department of the Institute. A course in practical and theoretical agriculture is given, during the summer months of July and August, to young men engaged in school work. Everywhere here are excellent facilities for boating, bathing, and fishing; and men are always at hand with excellent sail-boats for hire. Locust Valley is a quiet village between the hills, which has changed little from its ancient appearance. Among the older landmarks is the Friends' Academy, erected 125 years ago, and still profiting by Gideon Frost's endowment.

Oyster Bay is another quiet, rural, exclusive sort of village, very attractive in many respects and having surroundings inviting to a rambler. " It is the headquarters of several prominent yacht clubs, and regattas and rowing races are frequently held during the season. The Seawanhaka Yacht Club of New York have a fine club house and grounds on Center Island opposite Oyster Bay. The drives are numerous and delightful. The place is noted for its many fine residences. There are several old homesteads which played important parts in the early history of the country, and many relics of colonial times are to be found. At one time the Quakers had a footing here, as they did in the region for miles around."

Until the new North Shore road is completed, drivers and wheelmen must put up with bad going in this part of the island. The roads are hilly, sandy, and ill-kept, but they offer delightful walking and saddle routes.

To reach this farther part of the coast by rail, trains leave the main line at Hicksville (p. 79), and move northeast through Syosset, and the station for *Cold Spring*, which is reached by stages, as it is three miles distant at the head of Oyster Bay. This picturesque village contains one of the State's fish-hatcheries, in connection with which is maintained the laboratory and seaside school of biology of the Brooklyn Institute, where, in summer, a corps of teachers and students gather for the study of the marine life of these waters. The village has a hotel and boarding-houses, but is not very attractive. The next railway station is for Huntington, beyond which is the old-fashioned shore village and shipyards of Northport. Between these places are the headlands of Lloyd's Neck and Eaton's Point, an out-of-the-way region, with colonial relics and traditions, and much to repay the rambler. About *Huntington*, in particular, occurred revolutionary incidents, and here, as well as at Centerport and *Northport*, New Yorkers are settling in increasing numbers. Northport has sufficient remains of its old ship-building and maritime industries to make it very attractive as a sketching-ground. *King's Park*, next beyond, is largely occupied by benevolent institutions, in the midst of great farms. This whole region remains " truly rural," yet it is slowly, but surely, being invaded by the city men and turned to the uses of health and recreation. At *Smithtown* the Brooklyn Gun Club have a preserve of 700 acres, with leased rights over 5,000 acres surrounding it. The shores are fronted with precipitous cliffs, and many fresh-water streams and ponds are scattered through the woods and fields. Stony Brook and *Setauket* are pleasant villages beyond here, resorted to largely by summer boarders. To those who delight in anti-revolutionary relics, two quaint old shingled churches, with burying-grounds containing moss-covered gravestones, will prove of interest. It is said that when Washington visited this portion of Long Island he spent a night at Setauket, stopping at an inn kept by a zealous Tory.

Two miles to the east is *Port Jefferson*, the terminus of the railroad. The main portion of the village is in a valley. The streets are irregular, and houses and stores have been built with slight regard to street lines and architectural grace. It is a curious and odd town, but strikingly interesting. The greatest charm is the harbor, one of the finest on the north shore; and a steamboat plies between this port and Bridgeport, Conn., during the summer months, connecting with a daily stage to Patchogue. Upon both sides are lofty hills covered with trees, with a commanding view of the Sound and the Connecticut shore. A few old hulls and numerous shipyards give evidence of the activity that once existed and made Port Jefferson known as a ship-building port the world over. It has long been popular as a summer home, and is a favorite yachting harbor. Northwest of Port Jefferson harbor is *Oldfield Point*, a quiet place, and to the east, beyond the railroad, are Mount Sinai, Miller's Place, Rocky Point, and Middle Island, retired country settlements.

Local Suburban Lines.

Electric and elevated lines of railroad not only form a network over Brooklyn and Long Island City, but reach far into the country, but few of them offer much inducement to the pleasure traveler.

The Kings County Elevated Railroad runs to Liberty Avenue, near Jamaica, and carries bicycles at a uniform charge of 15 cents. From its terminus an electric line continues on Liberty Avenue to Hempstead.

The Brooklyn Elevated Railroad has one line to Ridgewood, where surface cars (steam or electric) can be taken to *Jamaica*, through Richmond Hill, giving a very pleasant ride for 10 cents.

An electric line of cars goes from the New York ferry landing (Ninety-second Street) in Astoria out to Steinway and North Beach on Bowery Bay, and there connects with a line running down to Williamsburg through Corona and Maspeth. Neither can be recommended for a pleasure ride, though cool on a summer day.

A line to Flushing runs straight from Hunters Point (Thirty-fourth Street ferry), Long Island City, through the desolate back regions of that half-built town to Flushing and College Point, but no one ought to take the journey as an amusement. It connects at Corona with the line north to Jackson's Mill and North Beach, and south to Newton, Maspeth, and Williamsburg.

Several lines go to Coney Island, Manhattan, and Bath beaches.

Steamboats to Long Island Ports.

1. Brooklyn Ferries.—See "Handy Guide to New York."

2. To Thirty-ninth Street, Brooklyn.— From Whitehall Street (South Ferry), eight miles, fare 5 cents, time forty minutes.

3. To Bay Ridge.—From Whitehall Street (South Ferry), ten miles, fare 10 cents, time forty minutes.

4. To Coney Island.—See "Handy Guide to New York" and daily newspapers. All these boats leave from the Battery, and some also from uptown wharves.

5. To Rockaway.—See daily newspapers for place and time of departure. These boats give a long sail upon the open sea, which, in effect, is entered upon as soon as one has passed through the Narrows. This is the strait between the Long Island and Staten Island shores, forming the entrance from the lower bay into the upper bay or harbor. On the right (going down) are the fortifications at Fort Wadsworth (p. 96), on the Staten Island heights; on the left Fort Lafayette at the water's edge, and Fort Hamilton on top of the bank. As the great lower bay expands before you the Brooklyn shore recedes rapidly along Bath Beach to the inlet behind the western end of Coney Island (Norton's Point), whose crowded buildings presently come into clear view on the left. As the steamer's prow turns gradually toward the sea (eastward) the deep bight of Raritan Bay, between Staten Island and the Jersey coast, lies astern, broken by the two islands occupied by the quarantine service; the high Monmouth shore of New Jersey, culminating in Atlantic Highlands (p. 171), is off at the right, and the channel entrance ahead, nearly closed by Sandy Hook. A good idea of all there is to see at Sandy Hook can be obtained as you pass it and reach the open sea. Coney Island, West Brighton, Brighton Beach, Manhattan Beach, and the Oriental Hotel are passed in succession at a moderate distance, and then the steamer draws shoreward into the outlet of Jamaica Bay, with Barren Island on the left and the extremity of Rockaway Beach on the right, where a landing is made in the quiet waters of the inlet about four miles from the sea. The hotels, amusement places, railway stations, and bathing beach are close at hand. A good bicycle route (p. 67) connects Rockaway Beach with Brooklyn.

6. *To the North Shore.* See p. 68.

7. *To the Eastern End of Long Island.*— Steamboats of the Montauk Steamboat Company run daily (except Sunday) to the eastern end of Long Island, calling at Greenport, Shelter Island, Southold, and Sag Harbor, each way. The trip is made in the night, but early rising will enable one to see, in summer, the beauties of Gardiners and Peconic bays, as the boat enters around Orient Point and sails up the southern shore and then around Shelter Island to its terminal port. For this region see pages 80 and 82. The boats are new and first class, and give a very comfortable and enjoyable trip, free from the dust which is the bane of all land travel on Long Island. Fare $1; stateroom $1 extra.

Note as to Bicycle Riding in Brooklyn.—The rules for the season of 1897, made and enforced by the Brooklyn Park Commissioners, are as follows:

Riding more than two abreast on the cycle paths is prohibited.

Cyclists must use the west path going toward Coney Island and the east path in returning.

Cyclists must not mount or dismount except on the extreme right of the paths.

Cyclists must not exceed a speed of eight miles an hour in the park and twelve miles an hour on the cycle pathways.

Racing on the bicycle pathways is prohibited.

Horses, carriages, wagons, and pedestrians must not use the bicycle pathways.

III.

ON STATEN ISLAND.

Staten Island is a somewhat triangular body of hilly land, forming the southern boundary of New York harbor and distant five miles from the city. Its eastern elbow, ending in abrupt highlands, extends out to meet the jutting highlands of Long Island, and forms the Narrows — the strait between the upper and lower bays. On the western side, Staten Island is separated from New Jersey by the Kill von Kull, which forms the water passage between New York harbor and Newark Bay; by Newark Bay; and by the longer and narrower tidal channel, winding through extensive salt marshes and receiving many creeks, which is called nowadays Staten Island Sound, but whose older name is Arthur Kill, a corruption of the early Dutch Achter Kill, or "Back River." This is the route of the steamboats *New Brunswick* and *Meta* (see below).

Staten Island, so named by the Dutch in honor of the States General or Congress of independent Holland, was bought from the Indians by Lovelace, one of the earliest English governors, about 1670, but it was almost one hundred years later before intercourse with the city would justify a regular sloop-ferry twice a week. It was settled by farmers and fishermen, many of whom came from New Jersey; and, at the opening of the eighteenth century, by Huguenot and Waldense refugees from religious persecution in France. The southern side of the island still retains many residents of French descent. Geographically the island seems a natural part of New Jersey, but it was owned by New York as a colony, and passed into the Union with it, becoming Richmond County. This is one of the smallest and weakest counties of New York State, having only 58½ square miles, but its population approaches 60,000, and its taxable wealth is very large. It is included within the plan of the Greater

New York, a circumstance due rather to the large number of persons who now reside there and do business in New York than to its proximity. These persons have overcome a deeply-rooted prejudice against the island as a place of residence, which alleges malaria, mosquitoes, and inaccessibility as objectionable features. Whatever force these objections formerly had is gradually disappearing, and the northern parts of the island are steadily increasing in suburban population and attractions, while certain new places have sprung up within recent years and are flourishing. One of the foremost and most successful of these is Prohibition Park, on some pretty hills above Port Richmond, and connected with it by an electric railway. For this prejudice and slowness of development the natives and property-holders of the island are largely responsible, for they have shown themselves, beyond any other community in the neighborhood of the metropolis, slow to understand and grasp their advantages. In many parts of the island this unbending old-fashioned conservatism still holds sway, and has kept, for the amusement of the present generation, the buildings, furniture, and to a great extent the speech and manners, of a century ago. Every Staten Island village has several men who have not had animation enough to go to New York in twenty years, and grown youths who have never been to the city, though they can see its spires from the hilltops. This primitive class, and the relics of interesting bygone times which they have kept about them; the quaint old farmhouses, fishing ports, tidemills, and country churches hidden along the shores, creeks, and byroads; the historical associations and romantic scenery, often with the noble expanse of the bay or the ocean in the distance — all these things make Staten Island very attractive to the citizen in search of a ramble in his wagon, on a wheel, or afoot, or in the trolley cars, which are rapidly extending into the interior; and no part of the suburban district can now be more easily reached by such wanderers.

Access.—The Staten Island Rapid Transit ferry, replacing the several rivals of former days, is between the Battery, New York, and St. George, the port of Tompkinsville. Boats run at intervals of about twenty minutes from daylight until midnight, and the fare is 10 cents, including fare to any shore point on the Rapid Transit Railroad lines, which extend along the north shore to Erastina, and along the south shore to South Beach. Conversely a ticket bought for 10 cents, at any Rapid Transit station, carries the passenger to any other station or to New York. Trains run promptly in connection with the boats.

St. George is the terminus of the Baltimore & Ohio Railroad's Staten Island Branch, which is connected with its lines in New Jersey by a great bridge across the Arthur Kill at Elizabethport. Over this bridge and along the north shore are run trains of freight cars to be placed upon floats at St. George and ferried to New York. The hotel, conspicuous upon the hilltop facing the landing, is The Castleton, occupying a site famous in the social and military annals of the island, and much patronized as a summer home by city people. The hotel is open all the year round.

Staten Island may also be reached by ferries from Constable Hook (to New Brighton); from Bergen Point (to Port Richmond); from Perth Amboy (to Tottenville); and by the new ferry to Elizabethport, at Howland Hook, connecting the electric car system of New Jersey with that of the island.

Bicycle Tours.

Staten Island is not the most attractive of suburban regions to the bicycler, though not without interest and good qualities. The usual country roads are inclined to be hilly, and are nearly always sandy. Still there is fair riding in the northern part of the island; and near the shore the roads that connect the towns, from Fort Wadsworth around to Erastina, are well-paved, level, and usually shady. There is also a fair route across the center of the island either by the Richmond turnpike from St. George, or across by Rockland Avenue, or by Richmond from New Dorp, and then to Port Richmond on the Port Richmond road. The Manor road is another favorite.

Tour of the South Shore.—The regular touring route on Staten Island is as follows: From the upper part of New York City go down, carrying the wheel (15 cents) on a Belt Line street-car, to the Battery; or, if you ride your wheel, take Eighth Avenue from Central Park (all asphalt) direct to West Fourteenth Street, then bear to the right to Hudson Street, and descend that street to West Broadway, and keep on down that street and Greenwich Street to Dey; cross through to Washington Street and go down to Battery Place, and then around through State Street to the Staten Island ferry, at the edge of Battery Park. Nearly all this below Fourteenth Street is block pavement, and the distance from Central Park is 5½ miles. Staten Island ferry-boats run every twenty minutes; the fare is 10 cents, and there is no charge for wheels, which may be left on the lower deck while the rider goes upstairs to enjoy the view of the harbor. The distance to St. George is about five miles. Leaving the ferry we turn to the left, mount a slight incline, and, turning to the left again, follow the trolley line into Bay Street — an avenue of good macadam, as is, in fact, the entire road to Tottenville, excepting a small piece near Gifford's, which is rapidly being converted from sand to telford pavement. Pretty villas line the roadway, and now and then we catch glimpses of the harbor. Leaving the trolley-line we turn to the left into *Tompkinsville*, and then to the right to the square (½ m.). Here we turn left again, resuming the guidance of the trolley-line on Bay Street through *Stapleton* (¾ m.=1¼ m.) and passing, on the right, the United States Marine Hospital, we turn to the right into Vanderbilt Avenue (½ m.=1¾ m.), and go over a long hill giving an excellent view of the interior heights of the island; then a turn to the left as the road merges into the old Richmond pike through the outskirts of *Concord* (hotels). The route now swings to the right as it meets the Fingerboard road (good), leading off to the left to *Fort Wadsworth*, Arrochar, and *South Beach* (p. 98) on the bay side; and we get a beautiful view through the foliage of the Lower Bay ahead on the left. The road now winds down a slight hill bordered by country estates, passes a tavern near Garretsons station, and gives a sight of the big hotels, elevator tower, and other high structures on Coney Island; at the right are green hills. Now we spin past the arbor-restaurants of *Grant City*, where Red Lane turns off to Midland Beach, and on to the historic Black Horse Tavern, at *New Dorp* (4½ m.=6¼ m.). Here we take the road to the left.

☞ *The right fork leads to Richmond*, the county-seat, a mile and a half west, a queer isolated old town, whence another road, fairly good, leads northwestward nearly two miles to a paved road into Port Richmond.

The country now takes a more rural aspect; small farms, pasture lands, and meadows line the way, with here and there a bit of woodland. A mile beyond New Dorp we come to the only stretch of poor riding on the route—red sandy loam for some two miles, with poor sidepaths. We wind around at Bauer's Hotel through chestnut groves, and do not again strike a good telford surface until we near *Gifford's* (2½ m.=8¾ m.), where is Carroll's Hotel at the right, near the railway station. Next comes a stretch of woodland known as the Woods of Arden, and we pass in succession the villages of Annandale and Huguenot, then cross the railroad and bear to the left through *Prince's Bay* direct to *Pleasant Plains*, and, after various windings, enter *Richmond Valley*, where we catch a view, through a break in the hills at the right, of Perth Amboy across the saltmeadows bordering Mill Creek. A few moments more brings us to **Tottenville** (6¼ m.), fifteen miles from St. George, and about twenty-five from Central Park. Floeroch's Excelsior Hotel, near the Amboy ferry (L. A. W. $1.50), furnishes all accommodations.

A Returning Route is along the western and northern shores of the island. The first stage is through Kriescherville and Rossville to *Fresh Kills*—good road along the shore of Staten Island Sound; then follows about three miles of poor road, now being paved, leading northward on South Broadway or the old turnpike to *New Springville*. Chelsea is a little port on the Sound, off at the left.

☞*Eastward from New Springville* runs a pretty good road—Jones or Rockland Avenue to New Dorp. At the distance of a mile it intersects Willow Brook road, which is rather hilly and crooked, but fair riding north to the old Richmond turnpike (1¾ m.), and then good straight on to Graniteville and Port Richmond. Half a mile farther Rockland Avenue forks; the right-hand branch goes on to New Dorp, the left-hand branch becomes the Bradley road north to Port Richmond or West New Brighton, intersecting the Richmond turnpike half a mile west of Castleton Corners, and passing through Prohibition Park.

From New Springville north you have good telford pavement along the Port Richmond road. At the end of a mile you come to the old Richmond turnpike at the crossing of Willow Brook. To the left (southwest) the road leads down Long Neck to Linoleumville, opposite the mouth of the Rahway River, New Jersey where in colonial days there was a ferry, which was the scene of many military movements during the troublous days of 1776-1783, but that road is now very poor.

☞ *The Richmond Turnpike* is the ancient road across the island from Tompkinsville to the Sound, at the mouth of Fresh Kills, where, in old times, stood the Blazing Star Tavern, whose signboard had a picture of a comet. This, about 1830, was the principal stage route to Philadelphia. The road is now fairly good eastward through Castleton Corners (whence the paved Manor road and trolley line leads to West New Brighton), on over the far-viewing hills to St. George. A mile east of Castleton Corners it intersects the Clove road, ridable northward to New Brighton, and southward to Concord and Fort Wadsworth. Trolley lines also use these roads.

One and a half miles northeast of the crossing of the Richmond turnpike brings you to *Graniteville*.

☞ *An interesting side-trip* to Old Place, near the mouth of Old Place Creek, two miles west, may be made from here. It is a farming settlement of quaint old houses and an ancient mill, and is full of historical traditions as well as picturesque value. A good road leads from the head of this creek straight to the north shore at Arlington station, the terminus of the Rapid Transit Line, whence you have macadam eastward; the shore road leads north to trolley cars.

From Graniteville the Morning Star road (macadam) goes straight north to Elm Park, or a jog to the right will take you into Richmond Avenue and straight down to Port Richmond. The new *Prohibition Park* is about a mile eastward, through a beautiful region threaded by Cherry Lane, and thence you can follow the trolley-line tracks to Port Richmond, where a ferry will carry you (5 cents) to Bergen Point and the Hudson County (N. J.) boulevard.

The North Shore of Staten Island is bordered by a magnificent, winding, level road from Howland Hook, opposite Elizabethport, eastward, through the newer villages of Arlington and Erastina, opposite Newark Bay, to the populous and continuous towns of Port Richmond, West New Brighton, New Brighton (between which stands the free Sailor's Snug Harbor), and Tompkinsville. This latter part of the road is called "Richmond Terrace," and is one of the handsomest boulevards in the vicinity of New York. This road and that next described form delightful walking places.

Southward from St. George, the shore is lined with old towns closely connected down almost to Fort Wadsworth. Passing around the railway station you come to the wharf-front of *Tompkinsville*, where the most notable thing is the station of the United States Lighthouse Service, where the steamers in use for the inspection and supplying of lighthouses and lightships, and a large amount of spare buoys, buoy anchors, an extra lightship, and other materials connected with that beneficent service is stored. The cove beyond is a favorite

place for anchorage of small craft, and is further made picturesque by the stranded wrecks and queer structures along the shore. This is a good loitering place for the man with the sketch book. Insensibly you pass into the streets of Stapleton (hotels), which is an uninteresting water-side town, largely devoted to beer and green groceries for ships, and to the wharves of two or three wrecking companies, where strange gear may be seen; and then move on to Clifton, by any of several streets which grow more interesting as you proceed. The principal connecting thoroughfare is Center Street, a quarter of a mile back from the water, which continues straight southward, along the terrace to Arrochar, but is called Tompkins Avenue in its southern extension. Clifton was in early days chosen as a home by French people, and, probably for this reason, attracted long ago many Italian families. It was here, therefore, that Garibaldi made his home, when he came as a political refugee to America, and dwelt quietly here as a small farmer for several years. The southern edge of Clifton merges into the village of Avondale or Rosebank.

Rosebank is one of the oldest and pleasantest of the east-side shore villages, and abounds in storied houses and traditions. One of these was pulled down a few years ago which had 1644 graven on the cornerstone, which has been preserved. The most remarkable of the old places is that known as the Austen House, near the water's edge at the foot of Pennsylvania Avenue, which sweeps down to the shore at that point. It is a low, stone cottage, still occupied and now standing in the midst of finely improved grounds, with three dormer windows that command a wide view of the Narrows. Its structure partakes of the solidity and durability of most colonial buildings; but the date of its founding is unknown. Its recorded history begins in 1710. During the Revolutionary War it was occupied by British officers, one of whom is said to have hung himself, because of a disappointment in his suit of an island maiden, in the large south room. In this room there is still the vast old fireplace, having ancient brass andirons, and bordered by Dutch tiles painted with grotesque biblical illustrations. Over the fireplace now lie a link and bolt of the chain which was stretched across the river at West Point in 1778 to prevent the passage of British ships up the Hudson; this chain was forged by Peter Townsend at the Stirling Iron Works in Orange County, N. Y. The great grandchildren of Peter Townsend are the present occupants of the house; and his brass door-knocker hangs near the link of the great chain; but the other brass knocker, on the front door, came from a French chateau near Ruen. These are only a few of the interesting objects in this very interesting old house, which is filled with colonial furniture, and instinct with memories and suggestions of long ago.

The Quarantine Station for the port of New York is in the

southern part of Rosebank, at the edge of the water. It now consists only of the offices and residences of the health officer of the port and his immediate staff, and the wharves where the steam tugs, in which the boarding officers do their work, land and tie up when off duty. In the early days New York's quarantine station was on Bedloe's, and afterward on Nutten (Governor's) Island; but after the yellow-fever visitations, of the latter part of the last century, the citizens thought it better to move it farther down the bay. This site was selected by commissioners, and the legislature gave authority to condemn the land. Here were not only the boarding station, but extensive hospitals for the reception of patients removed from ships, whether their diseases were contagious or not. There was great local opposition, which increased, when it was found that again and again the neighborhood was infected with yellow fever and other pests; and at last the Staten Islanders arose, moved the sick out of the hospitals, and then burned and razed to the ground the whole establishment. This happened in 1858, after which the pest-hospitals, etc., were moved to two little islands in the midst of the Lower Bay, and only the harmless offices of the administration were re-erected here.

☞ From Quarantine station *the Fingerboard road* winds inland over the hills through Grassmere to the Richmond road below Concord, giving good wheeling all the way. New York Avenue, however, continues straight on down the shore to and beyond Fort Wadsworth, and is followed by the trolley cars.

Fort Wadsworth is the name applied in general to the military reservation and its neighborhood, on the heights overlooking the Narrows; though only the fort down at the water's edge is properly so called. The reservation is surrounded by a high wall and fence, and contains the residences of the officers of the garrison, barracks, and much additional land. It is grown up with large trees and is beautiful. A sentry is met at the gate, but no one is challenged at suitable hours, though strict decorum is enforced. The visitor goes on toward the shore between two rows of officers' residences and up to the turn in the roadway where the headquarters office stands. Obsolete guns, solid shot and shell, the latter of the old "fish kettle" mold, adorn the turns of the roadways or find place in ornamental pyramids. These things, with the artillerymen flitting about, give a stimulating military appearance to the pretty scene.

The hills rise abruptly from the water here to the height of, perhaps, 300 feet, and command a long view down toward Sandy Hook

and in all other directions. Here, as early as 1640, the Dutch merchants planted a flag-pole and paid a watcher to signal to them the earliest approach of a vessel entering from the ocean. They also planted a battery here, which the English enlarged, so that this commanding point has been a defensive station since the earliest occupation of the shores by civilized men. The top of the hill is now occupied with a huge fortification. This is Fort Tompkins, and its spacious interior forms a parade ground where guard-mounting and dress-parades are held daily in good weather, and which forms the barracks of the men who make their homes in the casemates, and have their mess-rooms, reading-room, billiard-room, and school-room. Formidable as was this fort and its armament, in the days when it was constructed, to meet attacks and resist a fire from smooth-bore cannon and wooden ships, its walls would have to be greatly thickened and strengthened in order to adapt them to modern requirements. Instead of doing this the engineers, who have slowly been modernizing the defenses of the harbor here, have built new works outside Fort Tompkins and just to the south of it. Here new emplacements for a large battery of 8-inch rifles, with disappearing carriages, have already been constructed.

In front of Fort Tompkins is a lofty earth parapet, along the top of which, reached by a narrow stairway, runs a path which forms one of the most delightful summer walks near the metropolis. The whole Lower Bay, the Narrows, and the greater part of the harbor, with the picturesque Long Island shore, lies under your eye. Fort Lafayette, at the water's edge, and the parapets of Fort Hamilton on the Brooklyn shore, are immediately opposite, supplementing the harbor defenses from their side of the channel. As you stand on this parapet and look down, you see below you, on the narrow flat near the water, the walls of Fort Wadsworth, proper, whose guns would fire point-blank on passing ships. From its deep embrasures old-time cannon frown upon the passing ships. They are toothless dogs of war. South of it along the water-front lies South Cliff Battery, with big old guns on old-fashioned carriages; it is extended on southward by dismantled fortifications for cannons and mortars. One of these was known as the Smith mortar battery. The grass-grown parapets and emplacements look farm-like. North of Fort Wadsworth another line of old guns, called the North Cliff Battery, peer out over the water. Some distance to the north of this a small iron-roofed brick house near the shore, sheltered from an enemy's guns by a tall embankment, forms the headquarters of the submarine torpedo station for the defense of the harbor.

It is a very pleasant drive or walk on to the south end of New York Avenue, past fine old estates. There you may go straight southwest along Richmond Avenue to Linden Park and Garretsons (2 m.), or turn quickly to the left through narrow roads and on to South Beach, 1½ miles from the fort. Trolley cars now run to the southern end of New York Avenue.

Railroads and Steamboats.

Rapid Transit Lines.—These trains, as has been said, run in connection with the New York ferryboats, charging a uniform fare of 10 cents between all stations, including ferriage to or from New York. One line runs *west from St. George* along the north shore, stopping at New Brighton, Snug Harbor, Livingston, West New Brighton, Port Richmond (station for Bergen Point by ferry and Prohibition Park by electric car), Tower Hill, Erastina, and Arlington. This road uses the regular freight tracks of the Baltimore & Ohio Railroad; and by following them to the edges of the marshes and climbing down to the road, it becomes a short walk to Old Place (p. 94). This is an extremely pleasant little trip on a summer day, and there is a great variety of picturesque and amusing life to be seen along the shore. All the villages have their hotels and restaurants; but a better way is to cross to Bergen Point and dine at one of the really good waterside restaurants there.

The South Shore Line leads through the lower parts of Tompkinsville, Stapleton, and Clifton, with good views of the bay, through Rosebank, Fort Wadsworth (¾ m. inland from the fort, of which nothing can be seen from the train), and Arrochar, to the terminus at South Beach. The latter part of the way is almost wholly through deep cuttings that permit little outlook upon the country. *South Beach* is a seaside summer place on the shore of the Lower Bay. It consists of one long street facing the beach, and is much like the west end of Coney Island on a cheap scale. There are two or three fairly good Italian and German restaurants there, and as the place, though plebeian, is rarely if ever disorderly, one might find a much worse place to while away an hour and get dinner. There is a long pier where steamboats land; boats may be hired for rowing or fishing, and the bathing facilities are up to the average. A pleasant inland walk from here would be to take the road leading north from the station, west of the railway, which leads to the Fingerboard road, and then to Rosebank, or to Concord, or further west by the Richmond turnpike.

The Tottenville Line follows substantially the line of the old turnpike and south shore bicycle route from St. George to Tottenville (p. 93). Its stations southward are St. George, Stapleton, Clifton, Grassmere (Concord), Garretsons, Grant City, New Dorp (station for Richmond, by stage), Oakwood, Giffords (Great Kills), Ellingville

(Woods of Arden), Annandale, Huguenot, Prince's Bay, Pleasant Plains, (Redbank and Prince's Bay Lighthouse), Richmond Valley, and Tottenville. These trains run frequently, and the trip forms a very pretty excursion, costing 60 cents, while a charming day's ramble can be put in almost anywhere in this southern part of the island, which is full of relics of the past, grown quaint and beautiful with age and the weather. Great Kills and Prince's Bay are famous fishing grounds.

Electric Railways have recently made great advancement on Staten Island, and further extensions are in progress, so that before the close of 1896 all of the lines following will be in operation:

1. *St. George to South Beach.*—These cars leave the New York railroad and ferry station, take a winding course to the head of Bay Street in Tompkinsville, and then follow along the shore and New York Avenue to the southern gate of Fort Wadsworth reservation, when they turn to the right and make their way through various streets to South Beach. This is a very pleasant ride. Fare, 5 cents.

2. *St. George to Elizabeth Ferry.*—This route follows a circuitous course to the south of the hills of Tompkinsville, around through Jersey Street to the Richmond Terrace in New Brighton, and then along the Terrace past Sailors Snug Harbor, and through West New Brighton and Port Richmond to the new steam ferry from Howland Hook to the foot of Jersey Street, in Elizabethport, N. J. It is intended to extend the New Jersey electric-car system to this ferry, and make arrangements for excursions to the Staten Island beaches. At present, horse cars run from the ferry to the Union Depot; the electric cars are one block distant.

3. *Broadway and Castleton Corners.*—This line starts at the foot of Broadway, on the Terrace in West New Brighton, goes south to Castleton Avenue, then west to Columbia Street, and out to Prospect Street, where it makes a short turn, and then continues south for a mile and a half along Manor road to some distance beyond *Castleton Corners*. This penetrates a pretty country, and would make an excellent starting-point for a walk into the interior of the island. Fare, 5 cents. A transfer is given to South Beach, etc.

4. *Prohibition Park and Turnpike Line.*—This line starts from the Bergen Point ferry, passes the railway station, and runs up Division Avenue or the Pond road on the western side of the water course called The Clove. Something over a mile from the railway station it reaches *Prohibition Park*, a new residence town founded on temperance principles, and having a large auditorium where summer lec-

tures and entertainments are given throughout each season. It then continues on half a mile to the Richmond turnpike, and turning east follows that historic road—the King's Highway of colonial days—to Tompkinsville and St. George. Fare, 5 cents. Transfers are exchanged between routes 1 and 2, and between 3 and 4; but not between the last two and the first two.

Midland Beach is an enterprise connected with an extension of this line along the Clove road down to the Richmond road in Concord, then along that road to Grant City and down Red Lane to the shore, where a seaside picnic ground and bathing resort, catering to patrons of refinement, is to be opened during the summer of 1896. This bids fair to be a highly successful attempt at making a first-class seaside resort on Staten Island. Various other extensions of the trolley system are also planned, and these cars already add greatly to the availability of the island as a recreation ground.

A Steamboat Journey of great interest is that around Staten Island, filling a leisurely day with pleasure; but this service is intermittent, and information in respect to it must be sought in official transportation guides and the newspapers. The steamer *New Brunswick* makes a daily trip, at 3.00 p. m., from the Harrison Street wharf, New York, through the Kills and Staten Island Sound, stopping at various landings, to Tottenville, Perth, and South Amboy, and then goes up the Raritan River to New Brunswick, N. J., which is reached before 7.00 p. m. The fare to Tottenville and the Amboys is 25 cents; to New Brunswick, 50 cents; and the trip has much to recommend it.

The Steamer Meta runs daily, at 3.00 p. m., from Franklin Street, to all landings in Arthur Kills and Staten Island Sound.

South Beach is reached by steamboat from pier 1 North River, twice daily. See advertisements.

IV.
SUBURBAN NEW JERSEY.

For the purposes of this chapter "Suburban New Jersey" may be considered as all that part of the State north of a line from Newark to Morristown. This is the most densely populated district outside of the metropolis, a large area in "the Oranges" and thence to Passaic and Paterson, being, in effect, almost a continuous city of residences, which are supplied with provisions and other simple necessities by groups of shops and stores clustered about some railway station or cross-roads, whose early name is usually kept as a means of designating the present indefinitely bounded neighborhood. As might be expected under these circumstances, the majority of the roads in Northern New Jersey are excellent for driving or wheeling, hundreds of miles of excellent macadam or telford pavement forming a network of highways everywhere east of the Watchung or Orange Mountains, and extending its principal lines along many far-reaching country roads. Railways, both steam and electric, make every point accessible; and the latter now afford great opportunities for cheap pleasure trips, since several of them run for long distances through rural districts, and reach excellent points to begin a ramble. The attention of the reader is particularly invited to this point; and a close study of the map is earnestly recommended.

BICYCLING ROUTES.
1. To Englewood and Nyack.

Leaving **New York** take the ferry at the foot of West Forty-second Street to Weehawken (fare 5 cents), then up the heights by riding a long hill, and across to the Hudson County Boulevard. Turning to the right on the boulevard, which is fine, hard macadam, we gain a broad view of the Hackensack Valley, and wheel rapidly northward

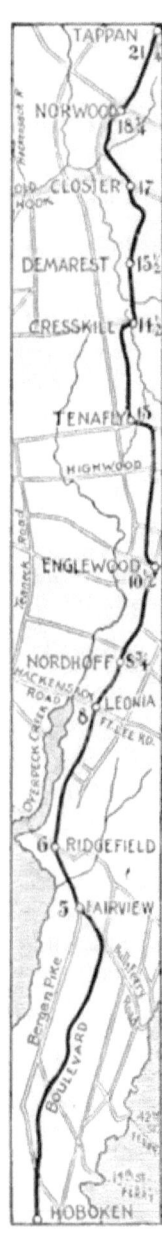

through the broken blocks and squalid tenements of West Hoboken, Union Hill, and Guttenberg. After passing the race-track, we bear to the right as the road forks, and then turn around to the left onto the old *Bull's Ferry road*, an ancient wagon road diagonally across Bergen Ridge — as the whole length of this highland from Jersey City to Fort Lee is called — that formed the colonial highway of the farmers and woodcutters between the Hackensack settlements and New York. This old thoroughfare was the scene of many armed marches and stirring fights during the Revolution, and evidences of its antiquity present themselves to our eyes, even yet, as we follow it northwestward, until presently we come out on the bluff of North Bergen, and overlook the broad green prairies and tidal lagoons of the Hackensack and Overpeck valleys. With a firm hand on the brake we roll down the curving hill to *Fairview* (5 m.), a scattered village at the edge of the marshes, where lately the new tunnel and bridge of the New York, Susquehanna & Western Railroad have been built, doing more harm than good to what was formerly a nice, picturesque little town.

Here we turn to the right upon the broad and busy *Bergen Pike*.

This was one of the earliest highways in this part of the State improved and set apart as a turnpiked toll and stage road. It extended at first from Hoboken to Paterson, coming down the hill from the top of the Ridge at Hoboken, along the course now followed by the Paterson electric cars to where the Secaucus road (later the Paterson plank road) diverged at what is now called Homestead, then turning northward past the famous old Three Pigeons Tavern (destroyed in 1893) and through New Durham, where it reached the level edge of the marshes and continued to this point. As it had been from the earliest times the main road in this direction, which attracted the earliest settlers, the historian will notice all along it relics of colonial days and ways in the shape of ancient stone farmhouses and other interesting mementoes of the past.

The ancient mill and pond, and the mossy tollgate here at Fairview, attract our attention as we hasten on to *Ridgefield* (1 m. = 6 m.), marked by an old-fashioned church in a graveyard.

☞ The road crossed here comes over the hill from Edgewater, on the Hudson River, opposite Manhattanville, and leads to the left past the church, then by a bridge across the Overpeck Creek, and on through Little Ferry to Hackensack. It is ridable, but not good as far as Little Ferry (p. 129), where a bridge across the Hackensack carries you to the macadamized road from Carlstadt to and beyond Hackensack. This is a part of the turnpike; and it was this way, in part, that the old Albany mail-stages ran, on the route west of the Hudson.

Keeping straight on by the pretty home of the Bergen County Wheelmen, we take the left fork of the road into Grand Avenue (the old Tappan road under a new name), and follow the bank of Overpeck Creek through the new town-made settlement of Palisades Park, over a rise and down along the shady main street of *Leonia*, (2 m. = 8 m.)—one of the most flourishing of the newer boroughs.

☞ The cross-roads above the railway station should be noted. To the *right* the road (rough and hilly, but ridable most of the way) leads straight over to Fort Lee (2 m.). To the left the road goes down past the station and across a bridge over the meadows, where fishermen and crabbers are usually to be seen, and up over the hill of Ridgefield Park to Bogota, a suburb of Hackensack. This road is rather soft and hilly, but is picturesque all the way from Fort Lee to Hackensack. An electric railroad from the Fort Lee ferry to Hackensack will soon occupy it.

Nordhoff is nearly a mile beyond Leonia, along a road bordered continuously with village houses, among which, here and there, is seen a relic of the past. Until quite recently this stretch of farms, all the way from Fairview to Englewood, was known as the English Neighborhood, by which name it appears in the history of the constantly recurring fights that took place along this road between expeditions and outposts of the American and British armies. It was really not until the railway was built that separate village centers became segregated, and were given separate names in conformity with post office and railway convenience.

☞ *A pleasant detour at Nordhoff* is to turn to the left, cross the railway near the station, and then turn to the right into "Tea Neck," the extensive park-like estate of the late William Walter Phelps, whose winding and beautifully paved roads are open to well-disposed ramblers. You can then go on, by pretty country roads, to Englewood, and usually find good side-paths for your leisurely wheel.

Beyond Nordhoff, Grand Avenue leads straight on between highly cultivated rural homes into Englewood (4½ m. = 10½ m.).

The electric line, now under construction, takes the parallel street (Broad Avenue) on the hillside.

The main street of this, one of the most beautiful of metropolitan suburban villages, runs at right angles to the valley, and forms the wide, heavily shaded, hard-surfaced Palisade Avenue. It extends from the marshes at the foot of the town, eastward, up the hill to the summit of the Palisades, where a small park has been reserved on the brink of the cliffs, from which a magnificent view of the river, the city, and the harbor is obtained. This is immediately opposite Riverdale. It is not beyond the powers of the ordinary rider to make the ascent, if he does not hurry too much; and the return trip is one long coast. Costly and beautiful residences, in the midst of large and long cultivated grounds, border this fine avenue nearly from end to end; but the lower end, near the railway crossing (which occupies almost the site of the ancient Liberty Pole Tavern that figured so largely in the story of the earlier years of the Revolution), is devoted to business houses. Here is the comfortable Palisade House ($2.50), and more than one shop where an injured cycle may be mended " while you wait."

An hour or more may be well spent in rambling about Englewood, which has profited greatly by having had, since the first days of its modern development, an energetic Village Improvement Society. Several very fine churches, of which the First Presbyterian is probably the most conspicuous, will be noticed; and attention should be given to the handsome Lyceum, known by its clock tower. This artistic edifice contains the Public Library, the rooms of the Gentlemen's Club, and a bank.

☞ The continuation of Palisade Avenue west, across the bridge, offers an interesting route to Hackensack, by way of *New Bridge* (p. 131) and thence down the valley on the western bank of that river; or up the Hackensack Valley, following fine roads through a country that abounds in pretty scenes and interesting relics of the past, many houses surviving from the colonial times when the Dutch were the rulers and occupiers of all this part of New Jersey.

Leaving Englewood, northward bound, we keep straight out Engle Street, which is smooth, level, and planted with fine shade trees. Large country houses are all about us, and excellent landscapes greet us at every rise in the undulating road. We pass the thoroughly appointed grounds of the Englewood Field Club, and then dip down into a pretty ravine through which flows the tiny head of the Overpeck Creek, and rise again to the level of Highwood village, and then roll straight on into *Tenafly* (2½ m. = 13 m.). This is a flourishing village, rising upon Teaneck Ridge, mainly inhabited by New York business men. Then to the right, at the hotel, we pass the station, and take the right fork by the Town Hall, to the next turn, where we turn to the left through a rural bit of country, and turn again to the left at the second fork into *Cresskill* (1½ m. = 14½ m.).

☞ A well macadamized and interesting road runs straight west across the romantic valley of the Tienekill, and over the hill to the curious old Dutch village of Schraalenburgh, and on to the fair roads along the Hackensack River.

At Cresskill we turn to the right on Railroad Avenue, parallel with the tracks, and over a poor, sandy surface for about three-quarters of a mile, after which the road improves as we enter *Demarest* (1 m. = 15½ m.). Passing through this pretty village, with its charming background of hills, we keep to the left as the road forks beyond the stone bridge, over a fair bit of road, inclining to the right up a gradual ascent, from the top of which we get a pleasing view of the broadening valley and the little town of *Closter*, then turn to the left into the midst of the village (1½ m. = 17 m.).

☞ Closter is an old Dutch settlement, on the old road from the Hudson River landing of Alpine, opposite Yonkers, and about three miles distant (southeast), to the upper Hackensack and Saddle River valleys. A mile west of Closter this road crosses the Hackensack at the point where Pascack Brook and the Tienekill join it, and it curves about an elbow known for perhaps two centuries as Old Hook. There is much to attract thither the artist, historian, and rambler afoot, but the wheelman will find the roads rather slow and sandy.

Beyond Closter we cross the railway tracks and bear to the right as the road forks, up the hill and then to the right again over a poor sandy road with fair side-path. The country is very wild and pretty, dense thickets line the way, and tall trees cast welcome shadows. We bear to the left as the road forks, cross two bridges over small tributaries of the Tienekill, and turn to the right directly into *Norwood* (1¾ m. = 18¾ m.). Here we turn to the left by the tennis courts onto Central Avenue of good macadam; but alas! at the third turn we swing to the right into the old Tappan road, whose surface is sandy, with occasional bits of side-path, to the ancient village of **Tappan** (2½ m. = 21¼ m.). One feels like halting for a long exploration and noting down many facts of interesting history here. An ancient center of Dutch civilization here, since it stood at the crossing of the principal north-and-south and east-and-west highways, Tappan became an important strategic point during all the revolutionary operations in the Hudson Valley. Two miles and a half east is Sneden's Landing, where Dobb's ferryboat used to land its passengers; and westward the road strikes across Rockland County to Spring Valley, Suffern, and farther towns. This town and this old highway were much used by the patriot armies; and you may still visit the house occupied by Washington and his generals, and climb to the ridge on the left where Major André was hung. For the particulars of this sad incident consult Ingersoll's "Hudson River Guide" (Rand, McNally & Co., 1896).

At Egger's Hotel ($1.50) we turn to the left to the next road, and then to the right onto the Rockland County road. It is of good macadam, and leads up hill at first, then down hill to *Sparkill* (1¼ m. = 22½ m.). We keep straight on through the town, turn to the left at the grocery store, then make a sharp turn to the right as we reach the railroad tracks, and then to the left down the valley of the river which flows in a deep vale. Below us on the right, as we reach the foot of the hill, we have a fine view of its mouth with the broad Hudson and its distant eastern shore beyond. We turn to the left by the Exchange Hotel onto Piermont Avenue, level and of good macadam, following the outline of the shore, through Piermont, where the river broadens into the Tappan Zee. Across this sparkling bay we see the houses and heights of Tarrytown, and, as the eye sweeps northward, even the white prison buildings and terraced heights of Sing Sing.

Rugged masses of red rock, half concealed beneath turf and shrubbery, and here and there upholding neat residences, rise high above our heads at the left, so that we wonder how some of the buildings manage to stick on. The road shows us constantly renewed beauties of broad landscape and picturesque detail. Handsome houses dot each elevation, and landscape gardeners have taken advantage of the varied slopes, crags, and precipitous ravines, to improve upon nature's crudities with artistic skill. The last gentle hill shows us the riverside shoemaking city of **Nyack** (4¼ m. = 27¼ m.), and we run smoothly down to the main street and halt at the Hotel St. George ($2.50), an inn with a foreign flavor that has made it very popular with uncommercial travelers. Two large hotels, facing the river, are open here in summer for city guests. They are the Prospect and Tappan Zee, $4 each.

This is the end of the ride. A good plan for returning would be to cross the ferry (25 cents) to Tarrytown, and then run to New York (25 m.) over the Broadway route (p. 9). See also p. 113.

2. To Hackensack and Paramus.

Take the route of the Englewood tour (p. 102) as far as *Ridgefield*. Here two courses are open to Hackensack. The more direct one is to turn to the left at Ridgefield Corners, go down across the railway at the station, and out past the old church. Half a mile beyond, this road (which is only fair) ends at a very quaint bridge set at right angles to the line of the road in order to cross Overpeck Creek. Down stream are seen the bridges at Little Ferry; and at their left a long willow-grown causeway crossing the marsh, which is the remains of the old stage-road. From the other end of the bridge the road leads along the northern verge of the stream a mile or more to *Little Ferry* (p. 129). Here one can, if he wishes, turn northward along old roads through Ridgefield Park and Bogota to Hackensack; but all these, though pleasant, are rather hilly and rough. The better way is, go on across the Hackensack here and turn north on the old Bergen pike or Albany post-road, which the Hackensack people now call the Little Ferry road. This is a broad, level, smoothly macadamized avenue, mathematically straight into the square of the ancient Jersey town (4 m. from Ridgefield=10 m. from New York).

☞ *Another route* from Ridgefield is, go north along Grand Avenue to Nordhoff and then turn to the left through the Phelps estate and on along the Cedar road—a hard and shady, though moderately hilly, thoroughfare, giving fine views—to Anderson Street Bridge, a mile or more north of the square in Hackensack. This is the usual route taken by those who come across from Fort Lee.

Hackensack is one of the oldest and most beautiful villages near New York. Settled by the Dutch at the earliest colonization of this region, it remained almost wholly Dutch until long after the Revolution, when it formed more than once the headquarters of the sorely tried armies of the cause of Independence. The old Mansion House on the square goes back to that time when it was already a well-known tavern, and rooms are shown in it which Washington occupied. The old Dutch Church on the same square is even much older, and its history includes all the simple annals of the community, for the life of such a town in those days centered in the church. It will be worth while to devote a little time to its churchyard. Many other quaint and ancient relics of colonial times remain in the town, one of which is occupied by a club devoted to outdoor sports as well as indoor enjoyments. That part of the town lying along the river north of Main Street and the square is the pleasantest, since the streets are overshadowed for miles by magnificent elms, and the citizens have everywhere taken pains to beautify their dooryards. The village abounds in wheelmen, whom the police keep well within the regulations, but they have an exceptionally fine series of smooth streets and hard country roads in every direction upon which to take their graceful exercise.

☞ *Rides north of Hackensack* may extend on macadamized roads as far as Cherry Hill (about 2 m.), on the west bank of the Hackensack River, where you may cross on the historic old bridge (p. 133), and return on the other side. Wheeling above that point varies with the weather, but the roads are fair, as a rule.

Southward a fair road (Terrace Avenue) runs along the dry bank of Berry's Creek to Rutherford (4 m.) where the system of macadamized roads in the Passaic Valley is entered.

Essex Street leads west via Dundee to Paterson, but is not to be recommended.

To Saddle River and Paterson, the best road is Passaic Avenue, leading west from one block south of the Anderson Street bridge. This is a macadam road and perfectly straight through the Maywood suburban district on the Susquehanna Railroad until it crosses Sprout Brook, when it bends around to the right until it reaches and crosses the Saddle River at *Arcola* (4 m. from Main Street). Here you turn north to Paramus.

☞ *To Paramus* two roads lead straight up the course of Saddle River (that upon the west side being the better), threading a valley which retains more than the usual traces of the simple-minded Dutch colonists, who began to farm here more than two centuries ago. The old *Paramus Church*, four miles above Arcola, is still a worthy object of historical pilgrimage, although a committee of the church has furbished almost out of existence the venerable building and its graveyard, where many revolutionary soldiers were buried beside their fathers and grandfathers. This church and settlement are identified with the campaigns of 1777 and following years, for this cross-road was a strategic point often struggled for; and here culminated the romance of one of its most brilliant leaders—Col. **Aaron Burr**—when he was married in this church, at the close of the war, to Mrs. Prevost, the widow of a British officer, whom he had again and again risked his life to visit in this region, where half the people were Tories. The surroundings of Paramus and the whole Saddle River Valley, which has no railroad, are extremely pretty and peaceful. From Paramus the old colonial road is ridable northwest to Suffern via Hohokus (p. 113), and eastward to Oradell, the latter

EAST SIDE PARK, PATERSON, N. J.

The Fire Ball

THE GREATEST NOVELTY IN CYCLE LAMPS.

One piece of highly polished nickel, with no reflector, lens, or oil well to get out of order.

A front light and danger signal in one.

Showing white front light, green sides, and red back. Burns ten hours; can't blow out, and is an ornament to any wheel.

Lightest lamp on the market.

....COSTS BUT $2.00

If dealer does not have it, we will send it, charges prepaid, on receipt of price.

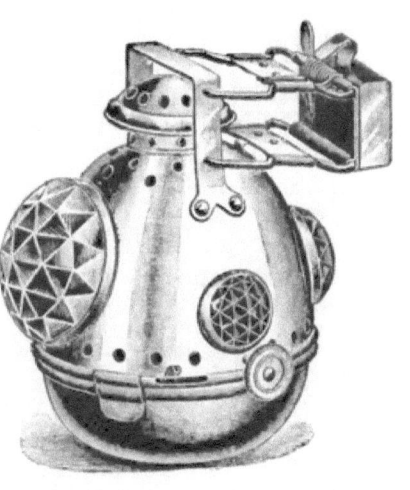

SEND FOR CIRCULAR.

Cycle Danger Signal Co.

107 Chambers St., NEW YORK.

affording a pleasant return journey down the Hackensack and across to Englewood.

From Arcola to Paterson you cross the Saddle River and take the left-hand road at the fork. It is good, and runs straight down to the Passaic (2 m.), crossing the Erie Railway at Warren Point station about half-way. The bridge here is at the eastern end of Broadway, Paterson, and takes you straight into the city.

3. Up the Ramapo Valley to Suffern.

A rather long but very interesting trip is that up the Ramapo Valley to Suffern, N. Y., whence you may return by a different route through New Jersey, or across Rockland County, New York, to Nyack and Tarrytown.

The real starting point is Paterson, which may be reached from Fort Lee or Hoboken via Hackensack, as already described; from Jersey City or Hoboken over the Paterson plank road through Secaucus, Rutherford, and Passaic, following the trolley line (p. 142); or across the Aqueduct road to Belleville, and then up the river. For the route from New York to Belleville, via Weehawken, see Route 6.

From Newark you would travel up the river to Belleville to the Erie Railway station.

From Belleville to Paterson take the road south of the station and turn to the left through the village, and on to the bridge over the little Yantecaw or Third River (2½ m. from Belleville). Just beyond it turn to the right, cross the railroad tracks (Boonton branch, D., L. & W. Ry.), turn again to the left a third of a mile beyond, and follow the river road to Passaic Bridge (2 m. =4½ m.). Here you pass beneath the Erie Railway tracks, and then keep on into Passaic (1 m. =5½ m.). At the railway station take the road on the east side and follow the river (here called Dundee Lake, where the water broadens quietly out above the dam) for three miles (8½ m.), then turn to the left into Paterson, turning first to the right into Madison Street and then to the left along Park Avenue to Market Street, which is to be followed until it ends about 1½ miles out (10 m.) at Passaic Falls. A restaurant will be found at Dundee Lake.

Leaving Paterson you take the Little Falls road up the river, following the electric-car tracks, and soon come to the entrance to the little park about the Great or Passaic Falls of the Passaic. These falls, formerly regarded as a spectacle of the first class, are still worth seeing, though their surroundings have been stripped of trees, and otherwise so vulgarized as nearly to ruin the picturesque interest of the spot. The river drops fifty feet into a narrow and irregular chasm in the rocks, whence it struggles out into a large pool surrounded by cliffs, which are heightened by large buildings, and where there are swimming baths, etc.

Resuming your wheel at the road-gate, you continue up the south side of the river, following the trolley-car tracks until you have passed under the D., L. & W. Railroad bridge (1¾ m. from Market Street, Paterson). The road forks an eighth of a mile beyond, but you keep always to the right along the river-road until you come to Little Falls (2¼ m.=4 m.).

☞ Here it would be feasible to turn south on fair roads and run down the valley between the Watchung Mountains to **Montclair** (5 m.), or to Orange, via Eagle Rock and Llewellyn **Park** (10 m.), or to return eastward through Great **Notch** and Richfield to **Passaic**.

The further route leads on to the right and around the bend of the river to *Singac* (1¼ m.=5½ m.), where you turn to the right at the first cross-roads beyond the railway station, go over the river, and straight out to Mountain View.

This is the *Pompton turnpike*, which affords a straight and excellent road to this point from Montclair, as it leaves Bloomfield Avenue, the main thoroughfare of that city, just to the west of where it crosses the mountain. The distance from the crest of the Watchung or First Mountain to the Passaic is four miles.

As you run along this Pompton turnpike from Singac northwestward, you have the New York & Greenwood Lake Railway beside the road on the left, and the Morris Canal and Boonton branch of the Lackawanna Railroad on the right. These roads pass straight across the level lowlands of a brook that comes down from Preakness; and at the left stretch the Great Piece Meadows, through which the Passaic finds a sluggish and winding course, and where it is joined by the Pompton — one of its largest and most important northern tributaries. As *Mountain View* (2¼ m.=8 m.) is approached, the Pompton appears on the left, with comparatively dry banks, and a low winding ridge stands across the path; this ridge is S-shaped northeast and southwest, is of sandstone, and is abrupt at the left, where the Passaic approaches its base, but is everywhere cultivated and dotted with comfortable farm-houses and bountiful orchards and fields. The hills sink down to the meadow level, where the Pompton has cut its way through, draining, in times long past, the basin northward now called Pompton Plains, the marshy depressions in which are now many feet lower than the level of any of the neighboring valleys. It is exactly in this gateway through the ridge that the

POMPTON PLAINS, N. J.

hamlet of Mountain View lies; and through the gap go both the railways above mentioned and the canal. The Greenwood Lake road continues northward; the Lackawanna road strikes westward, crossing the river a mile beyond. The canal is carried westward upon an aqueduct over the river right here, and skirts the northern base of the ridge toward the west, accompanied by wagon roads. Another road climbs the ridge at the right, which finally reaches an altitude of 468 feet, and commands a beautiful landscape toward both the Passaic and Pompton valleys.

☞ For the ride from Mountain View to Boonton and Morristown see page 113.

Leaving Mountain View, take the road north over the little swell of ground, and gently ascend to Wayne — a hamlet and station on the Greenwood Lake Railroad—and pass straight on, something over a mile farther, to the bridge crossing the canal-feeder and the Pompton River. Here the road forks.

☞ The right-hand road is good, and follows the eastern bank of the river to the foot of Pompton Lake, about 3½ miles. A mile and a half from this fork there comes into it from the east the *Preakness road*, a straight, macadamized avenue, leading directly east to Haledon Avenue, Paterson, about seven miles. This gives an opportunity for a pretty round trip of some twenty miles out of Paterson.

Turning to the left you cross the bridge, go for half a mile through low grounds and across the railroad at Pequannock station, to the main road north, which usually affords good riding. A mile and a half after turning to the right you come to the village center of *Pompton Plains* (4¼ m. = 12¼ m.), where a good road leads to the right across the river to the Preakness road, and straight east to Paterson (see above).

Pompton Plains is one of the garden spots of New Jersey, and a picture of quiet, rural beauty, where many artists have lived and painted, of whom the best known, perhaps, is Julian Rix. The Preakness range defends it on the east, and westward stands a broad mass of rugged hills, whose highest visible peak, called Bald Hill, is 964 feet high. Several trout brooks chatter down their ravines, to be lost in the swamps and wet meadows along the base of the range, which is the lower, ill-defined extremity of the Ramapo Mountains, that extend, more and more range-like northeastward, almost to the Highlands of the Hudson. Hidden in their woods are several iron mines, reached by rough roads.

Two miles (=14¼ m.) beyond the village of Pompton Plains this road comes to the Pequannock River, which flows down from the west, a fair road ascending its valley to the left and penetrating to the Wawayanda Mountains.

☞ *For Greenwood Lake* keep on across the Pequannock, and follow the railroad and Wanaque River all the way. The distance is about fifteen miles (to Coopers), and the roads are in most places only fair, while some stretches are very poor. On the whole, wheelmen are shy of the journey.

Turning to the right upon the Pequannock Valley road, which is good, you cross the railroad, then the river, and a little farther on the Wanaque River, which is the outlet of Greenwood Lake, and empties into the Pequannock about a mile below; then, bearing to the right, you cross by two bridges the Ramapo River, at the lower extremity of Pompton Lake (1½ m. = 15¾ m.).

Pompton Lake is an expansion of the Ramapo River, which rises in Rockland County, New York, close to the sources of the Hackensack, and flows southwestward along the eastern base of the Ramapo Mountains. Some persons apply the name to the stream all the way down to its end in the Passaic, below Mountain View, but the best authorities make the Pequannock, Wanaque, and Ramapo, which come together at Pompton, as has been said, end at their confluence, and call the united river below, the Pompton. A road leads southeast from the lake to the Preakness road to Paterson.

The route now leads along the eastern shore of Pompton Lake, at a sufficient height to give a good view across it to the steep hills beyond it. The railway track along the farther side of the valley is that of the New York, Susquehanna & Western Company. The road bends about to accommodate itself to the uneven ground, and soon after leaving the lake swerves to the right, and then, above a tiny pond, crosses a ravine and strikes northeast across a nearly level plateau to the station at *Oakland* (3 m. = 18¾ m.). Keeping on, a very interesting run carries you for several miles along the romantic Ramapo, often close to its bright and rapid current. At your right are wooded hills, while on the left, beyond the valley, rise the wooded summits of the Ramapo range, some of which rise 800 feet above the valley. They are broken, about 2½ miles north of Oakland, by a cleft in which a road is visible that makes its way over to the Wanaque Valley at Midvale station, on the Greenwood Lake Railroad. Four miles from Oakland you cross a bridge, where a mountain road turns up into the hills nowhere in particular. A mile farther brings you to a second stream and road which come in from the east at a point where the valley broadens out; this is the *Darlington road* (5¾ m. = 24½ m.).

☞ *An interesting route back to New York* is to be found by following this road southward through Darlington to Ramseys, a station on the Erie Railway frequented by New Yorkers in summer. As this is within the suburban limit, accommodation trains to New York are frequent, if you care to return from here by rail. Leaving Ramseys you turn to the right (south) along the highway west of the railroad, and follow around the hill, bearing to the left to Allendale (2¼ m.—28¼ m.), another pretty summer village on the railway, and on the banks of Hohokus Creek, which is a curious string of small ponds connected by a rapid brook. All this part of the route is crooked, but fair riding. The next stage is across the railroad, and then to the right straight down the valley to Hohokus (2 m.). Leaving Hohokus, which is only across the valley from Paramus, you run south half a mile, turn to the right and cross the creek, and go straight down to Ridgewood (1¾ m.—32 m.). From Ridgewood excellent roads lead directly east to Paramus (p. 108), and on through New Milford to Cresskill or Tenafly and southward; or south along the Saddle River Valley from Paramus to Hackensack, Englewood, and so to Fort Lee (about 15 m.); or straight on through Hawthorne into Paterson, about five miles. This gives a round trip of about thirty-seven miles out and back to Paterson.

From the Darlington road it is only three miles, straight up the Ramapo Valley to **Suffern** (=28 m.), a station on the Erie Railway, the terminus of a large part of the local service, and therefore a convenient place to return from by rail to the city. It is a pretty village, having now few marks of its colonial existence and stirring revolutionary history, when it was the center of so much campaigning. High, rugged, wooded hills ensconce it, and the Ramapo expands into quiet shadowy reaches delightful for boating. Many new houses are building, for city folks are finding out its beauties, and in summer the farmhouses of the vicinity are filled with boarders. Two or three small hotels open their doors to the traveler, of which the best is *not* that labeled "L. A. W."

Suffern is in the extreme western corner of Rockland County, New York, and a good road leads on up the valley some seven miles to Tuxedo Park. Eastward runs the old highway, straight across the center of Rockland County to Nyack (about 20 m.), whence you may ride back to New York through Tappan and Englewood or cross to Tarrytown and go down through Westchester County.

4. To Morristown, via Paterson and Boonton.

An excursion of great interest is that by way of Boonton to Morristown. Follow the course outlined for the Ramapo Valley trip as far as *Mountain View* (18 m. from Belleville), cross the Pompton

River on the bridge just below the Morris Canal Aqueduct, and follow the canal-bank along the base of the hill to *Lincoln Park* (2½ m.=20½ m.). This is a railway station and farming center overlooking the fine orchards and fields of the Pompton Plains northward. Recrossing the canal, continue along the flank of the hill straight west to *White Hall* (2 m.=22½ m.), a little village where roads lead north and south into rude hills. Continue southwest along the railroad, cross the tracks and go straight on, recrossing, after a time, both the railroad and the canal, and follow the winding road into *Montville* (1¾ m.=24¼ m.), a village right among the green hills. A mountain brook comes southward here, on its way to the Rockaway River; and there are the pleasantest of rural scenes on all sides. The brooks are spanned by quaint stone bridges, old trees shade the road, and antique farmhouses, with old, red barns, alternate with modern cottages. From Montville keep straight along the main road between the railway and the canal, bearing gradually to the south until you reach the city of **Boonton** (2¼ m.=26½ m.). Turn to the right over the bridge above the railroad, and pass up the main street to the top of the hill, where stands the excellent Mansion House ($2), where, if you have begun your journey in the morning, you will find it advisable to dine.

Boonton is a town of about 4,000 people, having a mayor and council, piped-mountain water, electric lights, good schools, several churches, a public library and free reading-room, an opera house, and other conveniences of an enterprising town. It stands in the midst of beautiful hills, and surmounts one whose summit is 630 feet above the sea. It is a station on the Boonton branch of the Delaware, Lackawanna & Western Railroad, which extends on through to a connection with the main line at Washington, N. J., and has many daily trains back and forth to New York, where a number of persons go to business daily. Many families make it a summer residence. The station is in the valley beside the rushing Rockaway River, whose wooded banks have been reserved as a park by the people; this beautiful river is a rapid, tortuous, hill-girt stream, which joins the Whippany and Passaic in the great Hatfield Swamp. In its valley here are a large paper-mill, an extensive rolling-mill, and a silk mill—the last preparing " yarn " or thread for weaving into cloth elsewhere. The town was formerly very prominent as a center for iron manufacturing. Main Street runs nearly east and west, overlooking the valley, and has upon it a simple but striking soldiers' monument, erected to the volunteers of the Civil War by Old Pequannock—the name by which all this region was known before being divided into the present townships. In the cemetery is a monument to the Hon. John Hill, who is best remembered by the public as the originator of the postal card and other improvements in the postal service; but locally he was most famous as a Sunday-school leader, and this monument was erected by the children of Morris County. The side streets, higher up, contain many handsome residences, and others are scattered about on the near hill-slopes, especially to the northward, above the railway station. The higher points of the town command a fine landscape; and a mile north is Sheep Hill, 935 feet high, reached by a wood-road, which overlooks a wide and extremely pretty region toward the Pompton and Passaic valleys. One can also drive through Main Street to Powerville (one mile distant), and by winding paths reach the summit of Tor — another lofty view-point. Here a tower has been erected from which one sees Morristown, Madison, Caldwell, and peaceful valleys surrounded by rolling hills and mountains. Descending, one drives through West Boonton and Boonton Park, the Rockaway River dividing the town from these suburbs. The park was laid out by Vaux, the architect, thirty years ago, with charming drives, shaded by native oaks, chestnuts, elms, maples, hemlocks, and pines. A lake at the foot of West Boonton empties itself over the Boonton Falls, tumbling over precipitous rocks until it reaches again the Rockaway River that feeds the factories at the lower end of the gorge.

North and west of Boonton is a wild, mountainous, thinly-settled region, watered by streams full of fish — even brook trout for those that are skillful — and inclosing several large ponds. Small game abounds, but in most cases the owners of the land forbid shooting (by posting notices to that effect), except by their designated friends. Roads, good enough for driving but only passable for sturdy wheelmen in good weather, reach Dixon's, Splitrock, Denmark, and Green Pond. The last is the largest, most distant (about 10 m.), and best for sport and picnicking. It lies northwest of Boonton, and is an oval lakelet of deep, pure water, 2½ miles long by nearly half a mile wide. It lies 1,050 feet above the sea, and is surrounded by steep hills — those upon the east constituting the Green Pond Mountains, and those on the west Copperas Mountains, along which are scattered many iron mines. This lake contains an abundance of bass and other fish, and excellent spots for camping can be found; there is also a small hotel at the outlet, where meals are given and boats may be hired. It is possible also to reach within a mile of Green Pond by rail, on mining roads connecting with the Lackawanna at Rockaway station and at Dover, or with the New York, Susquehanna & Western at Chambersburg. The line of the latter gives the readiest access to the wildest parts of this hill country.

This is a fascinating region for exploration, and one instinct with memories of colonial New Jersey and the darkest days of the American struggle for independence. Deep among those hills, at Hibernia, and Mount Hope, and elsewhere, were foundries for casting the cannon and cannon-balls which the Americans could not buy, and mills for making the powder they so sorely needed. No British grenadier or Hessian horseman ever penetrated their fastnesses or destroyed these primitive factories of war material, and their traces may still be found. The Mount Hope works were particularly useful, and were owned by Col. Jacob Ford, whose big stone mansion in the meadows there, built just before the Revolution, is still standing; it was his descendants who owned the Headquarters in Morristown (p. 123), now turned into a colonial museum.

From Boonton to Morristown pleasant runs may be made by three routes:

1. The shortest route (8 m.) is as follows: Cross the D., L. & W. tracks at the station in Boonton, and keep to the left through the park without turning; cross the D., L. & W. tracks again at Ball's Crossing, following the same road until you come to the stone bridge over Troy Brook. Here turn to the right, and again to the left at the next corner, by the schoolhouse; from here on, the road is straight through Littleton and Morris Plains to Morristown Square (8 m.). This road is fairly good at all seasons, and good in summer, though the first three miles are rather hilly; between Morristown and Morris Plains it is macadamized.

2. A longer but more level route (12 m.) is as follows: Go out from Boonton over the new Washington Street, or Hanover, bridge over Rockaway River — an iron structure 475 feet long and 70 feet high — and straight south through Old Boonton to Parsippany (3 m.), an ancient settlement along Troy Brook. Thence keep straight on south to Whippany (3 m. = 6 m.) on the Whippany River. Thus far it is good road. Thence cross the river, turn to the left, and follow the main valley road (macadamized) through the cross-roads (about half-way) called Monroe, and thence into Morristown, passing the Headquarters and the railway station (6 m. = 12 m.).

3. This is a level route, which takes the same road as No. 2 to and through Parsippany; then, at the next turn, goes to the right and follows the straight road through Littleton and Morris Plains (see No. 1) to Morristown (10 m.).

5. New York to Lake Hopatcong.

This long and attractive ride practically begins at *Bloomfield*, N. J., which may be reached via Newark or from Weehawken via the Paterson plank road, Rutherford, and Belleville.

LAKE HOPATCONG, NEW JERSEY.

Leaving Bloomfield at the square we go directly out the macadamized Bloomfield Avenue to *Montclair* (2 m.) and ascend First Mountain — the easternmost of the two ridges of the Watchung, or Orange, Mountains; and as we pause to rest on its brow, an exceptionally broad and interesting view is opened to the eastward. The roads concentrate here at a convenient gap 509 feet above the level of the Hudson, and the summit of the ridges north and south, to which side-trips may easily be made, is more than 100 feet higher. The valley of the Passaic lies spread before us for many miles. It has all been highly cultivated, and, indeed, is practically a continuous city; yet so numerous are the trees and so dense the foliage that were it not for the spires and tall buildings overtopping them at frequent intervals, one might easily imagine himself looking upon a forest. Immediately below are the homes and spires of Montclair; beyond them lies Bloomfield; to the southeast the Oranges, and behind them the smoking chimneys of Newark, outlined against the sparkling waters of Newark Bay; while upon the horizon is the dim, irregular outline of the towering edifices of the lower part of New York City, blue with a haze of smoke and steam. In the far south are the cool gray hills of Staten Island, and northward the eye sweeps along the crest of the Palisades. (Compare Eagle Rock, p. 152). Bearing to the left by the Mountain House, under the brow of a frowning ledge of rock, we plunge down through the valley into the little town of *Verona* (2 m.=4 m.; Verona Hotel, $2).

☞ "This is in the valley between First and Second mountains, and good level roads extend north and south. Northward 1½ miles and then east one mile will carry you back over the mountain into Upper Montclair; or one mile farther and one mile east, back into Montclair Heights; or 4½ miles will take you to Great Notch, where two miles east will take you over the mountain into Richfield on the road to Passaic (about four miles from Great Notch); or turning to the left at Great Notch a mile and a half will take you to Little Falls, whence it is a pleasant run down the Passaic (about 4 m.) to Paterson. Southward from Verona, 1¾ miles takes you to the cross-road from Montclair through the Eagle Rock Gap to Pleasantdale, Roseland, and the west; turn to the right for Eagle Rock (¾ m., p. 152) and the electric cars to Orange; a mile beyond this cross-road are St. Cloud and the cable incline, west of which are highly picturesque roads west and south to Morristown (p. 124), Short Hills, etc.

From Verona westward comes first a long but easy climb up Second Mountain, taking us to the charming little hamlet of Caldwell (2 m.=6 m.), now destined to immortality as the birthplace of President Grover Cleveland. We keep to the right where the road forks near the hotel, still on the macadam of the old Bloomfield turnpike, and enjoy a charming glimpse of Boonton, in the distance northward, across a richly rolling landscape of farms and country homes. The road now descends, and bearing to the left we have a level run through Franklin and the Hatfield swamp. "On each side," writes a correspondent, "stretch low marshlands, clothed in a wild confusion of brush and weeds. Here and there winds the river, now broadening into a miniature lake, now narrowing, sometimes shaded by a grove or thicket, sometimes lost under a growth of flowering aquatic plants. Many places are not unlike tropical lagoons; and one half anticipates seeing the saw-toothed jaws of an alligator protrude from this or that dark and stagnant pool."

In the midst of this great area of half submerged swamp and meadow, the Rockaway and Whippany rivers struggle through tortuous courses to a junction with the Passaic, whose whole course is curiously circuitous among these hills. There are many minor tributaries also, well known to fishermen, who find now and then trout, and always fishes of less dignity, in their currents, and to painters who revel in the picturesqueness of their neglected ravines.

The road now crosses the Passaic where its marshes are narrowest, a mile or two below the confluence of the Whippany, traverses the little settlement of Pine Brook (3 m.=9 m.), and turns to the left up a low hill, and, still bearing to the left, reaches and crosses the Rockaway River.

☞ The road branching northward, just before you cross the bridge, would lead into the hilly, picturesque country half a dozen miles northward, where are Montville, Whitehall, and other stations along the Morris Canal and the Boonton Branch of the Delaware, Lackawanna & Western Railroad. See pages 114 and 143.

The way now traverses the northern verge of the Troy Meadows, that extend southward to the Whippany River, then passes through the little town of Parsippany (4½ m.=13½ m.; no tavern), and increases in badness, being clay, sandy in spots, but ridable in good weather, until we reach the Denville House, where we turn to the right onto good telford, which we keep direct to *Rockaway*. The road is here about 300 feet above the sea, and the hills on the left from 350 to 400; but northward the heights, around which the Rockaway makes its great bend, exceed 700 feet in altitude. It goes without saying, that the scenery is highly picturesque. Rockaway (6 m.=19½ m.; Central, $2) is perched upon a hillside overlooking the rapid river, and is a town of considerable importance.

Leaving Rockaway we cross the railroad (D., L. & W. Rd.) tracks, climb the hill, and turn to the left at the post office, then keep to the left, as the road forks, parallel with the canal. The road skirts a ridge, with the river on the left below, and beyond it green hills. Now we cross the canal and gradually mount still higher, amusing our minds as we go, slowly here, by the quaint incidents of canal-life displayed in the vale beneath us. Great quantities of coal are brought to New York in this slow and primitive but cheap manner. Soon we roll down an incline, again cross the canal, turn to the right and follow the road skirting the river into the trim and busy town of *Dover* (3½ m. = 23 m.). We enter via Blackwell Street and draw up at the Mansion House ($2.50; L. A. W. $2). This is largely a mining town, iron, copper, zinc, etc., being obtained near by.

Leaving Dover we continue out Blackwell Street, cross the railroad, and then have a long climb over Mine Hill with a corresponding descent to Kenville (4 m. = 27 m.). The scenery here is very interesting indeed, for at every turn some new landscape is presented of the Succasinna and the mountains toward Lake Hopatcong.

☞ The first road to the right out of Kenville, beyond the railroad, leads directly through the hills to Mount Arlington and Nolan's Point; it has a fair surface, but is one continual climb.

We cross the railway and keep straight on, parallel with the canal, to *Drakesville* (1½ m. = 28½ m.), then turn to the right into the main street, passing the Ledgewood House ($2), then go up a slight hill, and bear to the right where the road forks (the left-hand one passing under the canal). Then we cross over the canal and keep to the left direct to the Lake End Hotel ($2), then turn to the right over the bridge to the steamboat landing (2 m. = 30½ m.) at the lower end of **Lake Hopatcong**, whence steamboats run to all other landings. All of this route from Dover is fairly level and of good telford pavement.

☞ To Mount Arlington (3 m.) and Nolan's Point (5 m.) turn to the right at the crossing of the bridge, by the post office, take the first road to the left, and bear to the left over the main road direct to destination. The road is hilly, but affords fair to good riding.

6. Through the Oranges to Morristown.

One of the longer, but among the most pleasant, of suburban rides for the cyclist is that to Morristown, N. J., which may be extended to Lake Hopatcong, or even to the Delaware Water Gap, if you please. The route recommended is as follows, but it may be admitted, at the start, that it is best ridden from Morristown to New York than outward bound:

Leave New York by the Weehawken (Forty-second or Jay Street ferries). From the ferry we have a long climb to the top of the heights, but the view of New York is magnificent. At the top of the hill turn to the left into Fulton Street, and go along it direct to the Hudson County Boulevard, where you turn to the left and proceed as far as Higgins' saloon. Here you turn to the right, down the hill. The roadway is rough cobbles, and the descent requires caution. At the Marble Works bear to the left as far as the old Paterson plank road; here we get the first view of the broad meadows of the Hackensack — always interesting, varying with the seasons, and each day showing some new beauty to the close observer. At the foot of the hill is the ancient hamlet of *Homestead*, under its aged willows, not far from which, at the left, is the great Schuetzen Park, where so many German summer festivals are held. Through Homestead passes the New Jersey Northern Railroad; and hither might easily be brought the cycles of those who preferred to come that way, avoiding the ride through Hoboken, and beginning their trip here. Less than a mile north, on the old Bergen road, is the site of the Three Pigeons Tavern, famous in revolutionary annals, and close to the old-time hamlet of New Durham.

From Homestead the way lies along the Paterson plank road, across the meadows, following the recently instituted trolley line.

This is a very old road, having been laid out as early as 1718, as far, at least, as Secaucus Island. The causeway rests upon an invisible ridge, separating the waters of Pinhorne Creek, which flows southward to the Hackensack below Snake Hill, and of the Cromakill which drains sluggishly northward into the same river. These shore marshes were the scene of an experiment in farming which ruined a prosperous family many years ago. Prominent men in the early years of the century were Samuel and Robert Swartwout; and they imagined that these meadows might be reclaimed and made very profitable as market-gardens. They built ten miles of embankment, and sank some hundreds of thousands of dollars in a fruitless attempt, so far as they were concerned, though others have since profited to some extent by their labors. "When in summer," remarks Felix Oldboy, "the train dashes across the miles of swamp land beyond Hoboken, and the long salt grass, jeweled with wild flowers of brilliant hue, sways and tosses to the breath of the

wind, it seems to me, as I look out from the car window, as if the wild roses and the meadow grasses were growing over the graves of those buried hopes." Secaucus Island was one of the earliest settled country districts near New York; and as the farmers were all Tories, they were frequently raided by the Americans, who wanted their cattle and horses. The community is now mainly a squalid lot of goose farms and market gardens, and we hasten on along the Paterson plank road, which was built by private enterprise early in the century, and passed under county control many years ago. It crosses the Hackensack, passes a road leading northward on somewhat firm ground to Moonachie, Little Ferry, and Hackensack, crosses the Boiling Spring marshes along Berry's Creek, and reaches the real shore again at *Carlstadt*. Crossing here the New Jersey & New York Railroad, we bear to the left up the hill, to Park Avenue, where we turn to the left and proceed straight on to *Rutherford* (8¼ m. from Weehawken). Crossing the Erie Railway, we keep straight on along Park Avenue, up a gradual ascent lined with pretty houses, and then down a long hill, which gives pleasant views abroad, pass under the tracks of the Boonton branch of the Lackawanna Railroad, and then turn to the left by an old stone farmhouse. This is the village of Kingsland, a memento of an eminent colonist and wide owner here almost 200 years ago. The next turn is to the right, and over a bridge spanning the Passaic River into *Avondale*, where we turn to the left on the river road. All of the way, so far, is fair macadam.

Proceeding down the river we pass the Newark waterworks and run along an exceedingly pretty road, close by the water side, where stately trees shade both the road and the quiet current. Four and a half miles brings us into *Belleville* (12¾ m.), by its main street.

This region in the last century belonged to the Schuyler family; and their ancient copper mines, where the first steam engine in this part of the country was set up, were in the adjacent rocky heights, the old shafts being now partly filled with water and partly with snakes. The main street of the village shows many colonial houses, and the local hotel is a noted building. It was built in 1683, and was temporarily occupied by Washington and his staff during his campaign in this State in 1776. A mantel in one of the upper rooms bears an imprint said to have been made by a British cannon-ball, and another mantel (in the sitting-room, downstairs) is valued at over $2,000 on account of its age and sculpturing.

We turn to the right at this venerable hostelry, cross Washington Avenue, the highway to Newark, and follow up Second River, ascending a straight incline, passing on the left the site of a mill that disappeared long ago, but whose dam remains, forming a miniature lake and cataract, embowered in trees. The road then sweeps around to the right, a pretty glen, amid sandstone rocks, dropping at the left, then crosses the stream, bears leftward along the Morris Canal, and we soon turn to the right, recross Second River, and then to the left upon Montgomery Street. At the church we turn to the left into Washington Avenue, and wheel to the village square of *Bloomfield* (3 m. = 15¾ m.). The American House (L. A. W. $2.50) on the square, and the Essex Hotel and restaurant, are the houses of entertainment. All the above section of the route is macadamized.

From Bloomfield Square we turn by Baker's grocery into Glenwood Avenue, and bearing left where the road forks, follow the electric-car tracks to East Orange (1 m. = 16¾ m.); then straight out Prospect Street to *Brick Church* (1¼ m. = 18 m.). The road is level, macadamized, and bordered by beautiful residences. At the Brick Church we turn to the right on Main Street (p. 150), wheel two blocks to Harrison Street, and follow this street into the Hamilton road, and, bearing right, down a long hill into South Orange (3 m. = 21 m.). At the South Orange Hotel ($2) we turn to the left on the Valley Road, which is good, level macadam, and run along the foot of the mountains, through lovely village districts, to Maplewood Hotel, where we turn to the right and mount a slight hill, whence *Millburn* is seen nestling in the side of the gap. Wide and interesting views attract the eye in every direction, and fortunately the expert wheelman may enjoy them ; for it is a smooth and easy run down to the village (3¾ = 24¾ m.). Millburn Hotel, $2.

Leaving Millburn we go straight out the Morristown Pike, over a fair macadam, through a pastoral valley rising in cultivated terraces to the mountains on the right. We keep to the right as the road forks by the Farmers' Hotel, traverse a bit of woodland, pass a massive stone arch, carrying the Morris & Essex Railway, and then undertake a long but gradual climb, to be rewarded at the top by one of the most charming landscape views in New Jersey. As we descend, one loveliness after another follows in quick and varied succession. The valley broadens out toward the west, new hills appear in the distance, and our roadway becomes a level, maple-bowered avenue, as we enter *Chatham* (4½ m. = 29¼ m.; Fairview House, $2). Leaving Chatham via Main Street we wheel on direct to *Madison* (2¼ m. = 31½ m.; American House, $2). At the borough office we turn to the left and go up hill, over the railway tracks, passing on the left the handsome grounds and buildings of Drew Seminary. We bear to the left again at the next fork, and then around to the right through small, pretty villages and past a charming glen reaching down on the left. The road now is lined for over two miles with fine and costly residences, in the midst of which is the large field and cottage club-house of the Morris County Golf Club. The homes of city people become gradually closer together and finally coalesce into the compact and beautiful little city of Morristown, which is entered along South Street, leading straight to the square ($4\frac{3}{4}$m.$=36\frac{1}{4}$m.).

Morristown, clustered upon the hills that make Morris County the mother of rivers, and that slope down to the Whippany, is one of the most delightful and most interesting of the Jersey cities. It was settled as early as 1710 by New Englanders, who went thither on account of the iron mines in the neighboring hills, and, later, named the town and county after Lewis Morris, who was the colonial Governor from 1738 to 1746. At the time of the Revolution it was a town of 250 people, having a court house, jail, and, after hostilities began, the principal powder magazine of the patriot forces, and a powder mill. At present the most prominent structure in the place is the beautiful new white stone Presbyterian Church on the square.

This is the second successor of the original church on that site, which was erected in 1738. The tall-spired Baptist Church on the same square has an ancestry almost as old; and both the buildings which preceded the present structures were used as hospitals by the troops encamped here during the terrible winter of 1777, when smallpox was rife in the American army. The whole district abounds in buildings and sites which go back to those early and stirring times, and have connected with them entertaining and instructive historical legends. Morristown was a central point on the roads of that period, and had a high strategic value. Washington therefore chose it as the center of the aggressive operations which he began immediately after his success at the battle of Princeton, bringing his official headquarters to the town in January, 1777, and again in later years, as is related further on.

The Morristown of the present is a large and flourishing city inhabited by people of wealth and culture, and is thronged in summer with visitors. The Mansion House ($3, L. A. W. $2.50) and the United States ($2) are both good hotels open all the year. Several other summer hotels and boarding-houses offer excellent seasonal accommodation. The streets, of which South, Washington, Mount

Kemble, and Morris are the principal, are excellently paved and beautifully shaded; and charming view-points are easily reached by the cycler or pedestrian, while good runs can be made in all directions, excellent roads leading down the Whippany to Boonton (p. 114), southward to Scotch Plains, Plainfield, etc., (p. 156), and westward to the Delaware River. There are few places in the State where the rambler acquainted with history or fond of nature can take more delight than about here. Within the town itself the special object of attention should be the historical museum at

The Washington Headquarters. The preservation and intelligent use of this historic building is the first and best fruit of the formation here, in 1874, of the Washington Association of New Jersey. Previously this property, which was to be sold by the heirs of the Ford family, to which it had belonged since long before the Revolutionary War, had been bought by a few patriotic gentlemen of the town, who became the founders of the association, to which the property was deeded.

The object of this association in acquiring this building was and is to "maintain it through future generations as a memorial of George Washington, and also commemorative of his associate officers, and the heroism and fortitude of the army with which they (the Continental troops) withstood the severe hardships and suffering of the winters of 1777, 1779-80, 1780-81, while encamped in and about Morristown; and also for the collection and preservation of papers, documents, relics, and objects of interest connected with the Revolutionary War." The funds have been raised mainly by subscription to the stock, and the State has bound itself to give an annual subsidy, so long as the property is devoted to these uses; and admission to it is free to everyone.

Within the house, which "remains in all points of structure as it was then," has been gathered a very valuable and notable collection of revolutionary relics, exceeding in interest, indeed, that at Mount Vernon or at the headquarters in Newburgh. Besides a great number of papers, letters, engravings, and portraits, and a large collection of early pottery, pewter ware, kitchen utensils, etc., there is an unrivaled collection of arms and accouterments, including several captured cannons, filling the whole upper hall, and a roomful of costumes, dress-goods, cloths, and needlework of a century ago. Among objects of especial interest are the original commission of Washington as Commander-in-Chief of the continental forces; the suit of clothes owned by Washington and worn by him on the day of his first inauguration as President of the United States, with a silver-hilted dress sword and buckles worn with it; a unique marble bust of Washington, by Houdon; the silk Masonic sash worn by Washington; and one of the few autograph letters of his wife. No historical collection in the country is better worth examination.

Another favorite route to or from Morristown is up the Mountain Railway, as follows. Go out through the Oranges as before to Highland Avenue, and up to Chestnut Avenue, near Highland Avenue railway station. Here an inclined cable railway will haul you and your cycle to the top of First Mountain at *St. Cloud*. From here follow the main road (Northfield Avenue) southwest across the Rahway and around the head of the Orange Reservoir, where, just after the turn to the left, west of the bridge, the road forks.

☞ The *left-hand* branch is Cherry Lane, which goes straight south to the South Orange road, and thence back to South Orange and Newark, or on to Millburn and the Morris turnpike.

Taking the *right-hand* branch you presently swing to the right, but keep to the left at the next fork, where Cedar Street strikes off to Livingston, and go on to *Northfield*. From Northfield the route goes around the southern end of Mine Hill to West Livingston. Here you may turn north over the Cheapside road to the Hanover road, and then to the left to Whippany and Morristown, as on page 116; or you may turn south three-quarters of a mile to Cheapside. This is at the head of South Orange Avenue, which continues west as the Columbia turnpike. A mile from Cheapside Corners the Passaic is crossed by Columbia Bridge, which carries you from Passaic into Morris County, and a mile farther brings you to *Afton*, a hamlet, where a road strikes south to Madison and another north to Hanover. From Afton a straight run of five miles along the turnpike, level at first, but rising into Morris Avenue as the town is approached, carries you into Morristown, past the Headquarters and the railroad station.

The roads on this line of travel are not of the best, but it is a favorite outward-bound route, because of the help the inclined railway gives, and because wheelmen enjoy better the route of Route 6 when reversed—that is as a return ride from Morristown.

RAILROAD ROUTES IN NORTHERN NEW JERSEY.

1. Electric Lines Along the Palisades.

It is only within a year that the beautiful wild region along the summit of the Palisades of the Hudson, north of Weehawken, has become accessible to the excursionist without so much toil, discomfort, and loss of time as practically to bar it out of the citizen's list of places for outings; yet no district in the vicinity of the city can compare with it in attractiveness in certain respects, and it is now within ten cents and twenty minutes of all the central part of New York. An electric line of the North Hudson County Railroad Company penetrates this region from the south, and the new line of the Bergen County Company crosses it from Fort Lee westward.

1. *The North and South Line.* This is based upon the old "Palisades Railroad," operated by steam locomotives, and which ran from the elevator at the West Shore Railroad ferry in Weehawken to the Guttenberg race track of evil memory. It has now been extended to Coytesville, three-fourths of a mile north of the village of Fort Lee, and is wholly operated by electricity (trolleys). The elevator at the ferry is no longer run, since the closing of the former amusement resort "El Dorado" on the brow of the hill; and the cars start from the ferry station and climb the hill to a point immediately over the West Shore Railroad tunnel, where a magnificent picture of North River and the City of New York is spread before the eye. Here the car turns inland a short distance, and touches another electric line which comes up from Fourteenth Street ferry, Hoboken, ascends the hill by the ancient Weehawken road, through the long ravine which has been used as a thoroughfare since the earliest colonial days, and proceeds north to this point, and then out to the Guttenberg race track by a more westerly street. Transfers are exchanged between these lines, and between the Fourteenth Street and other lines in Hoboken, so that a person can reach the Palisades road for one fare from any of the Hoboken or Jersey City ferries by one or two changes of cars.

From this junction-point the Palisades line takes a direct northward course through Union Hill and Guttenberg, thinly built up with small houses, until it intersects the old Bull's Ferry road, which came up from the foot of a ravine opposite Ninety-sixth Street, where, in colonial times, and until long afterward, a ferry was operated to New York. It still retains here many of the characteristics of a country road, and a quarter of a mile west, in North Bergen, is the terminus of the Fourteenth Street (Hoboken) electric line spoken of above; this, doubtless, will soon be extended to Fairview and beyond, opening a pretty locality to the suburban tourist. The settlement on this road near the race track is called North Bergen; but the eastern part of the road on the brow of the Palisades overlooking the Hudson is known as *Hudson Heights*, and contains many old as well as new houses situated along retired roads.

To this point (Hudson Heights) the fare is 5 cents, and cars run every fifteen minutes or less. Beyond this the cars run at longer intervals (once an hour in winter), and an additional fare is charged of 5 cents to Edgewater and 10 cents to the terminus—total, 20 cents from New York. The line takes an almost straight course, irrespective of streets or roads (which are very few), and in a mile reaches *Edgewater*, whose inhabitants, however, are mainly down on the river at the foot of the cross-road, which westward leads to Ridgefield (p. 102). Cutting its way through the rough rocks and woods of the crest of this Bergen Ridge, which is almost covered with woods of small growth, the line proceeds thence nearly straight northward to **Fort Lee**, whose main street (the Fort Lee road to Hackensack) is crossed about a quarter of a mile west of the center of the village on the brow of the hill. Here the Bergen County trolley line, next to be mentioned, crosses the tracks. The cars then proceed northward through the woods to Coytesville, or Linwood, as it is more often labeled upon the maps.

Nearly the whole of this line north of the Bull's Ferry road is through a wilderness which has never been invaded by streets or leveled for farms or houses, being too rocky for tillage, and opens the wildest and most natural hunting ground for the botanist, naturalist, or wood-rambler in the vicinity of the metropolis. This state of things, however, will soon pass away, for land companies are rapidly moving toward the "development" of the region, and laying out residence tracts in all directions. Meanwhile this line offers one of the prettiest and coolest summer excursions out of the city.

2. *The Fort Lee Road Line to Englewood, etc.*—The former ferry to Fort Lee was from the foot of West 129th Street, landing at the foot of the Fort Lee hill and road. A steamboat still plies between that landing and West Thirteenth Street in summer, landing at Pleasant Valley, Edgewater, and Shadyside, which are on the road from Weehawken to Fort Lee along the edge of the river. The Bergen County Traction Company bought the Fort Lee Ferry in 1896, and built a handsome new landing and ferry house at Undercliff (formerly Pleasant Valley), immediately opposite 129th Street, and about 1½ miles below the old landing, to which a stage (5 cents) runs half-hourly. All boats now run to Undercliff. There an electric line, built with most skillful engineering, zigzags up the face of the rocky cliff, and then strikes off through the rocky woods and along a winding road to the village of Englewood. These woods on top of this cliff are, perhaps, the most wild and natural of any

within half a day's ride of New York, yet they are scarcely ten minutes away from its busy streets. They are filled with mossy rocks, clear streams and ponds, and the cliffs overlook the whole grand picture of the city and its northern and eastern environs from Yonkers to Prospect Park—a magnificent view. The tract along the edge of the cliffs is to be "improved" into a residence park.

Fort Lee Landing and the crags north of it have been for a great many years a summer resort of varying fortunes. The fact that it is the only place for a long distance where a rift in the cliffs enables a wagon-road to ascend from the bank of the river to the surface of the plateau, caused such a road and a boat-landing to be built there long before the Revolution. This was in constant use by the New Jersey farmers long before the Revolution; and when that war broke out, the protection of this landing and road, as well as the natural defensibility of the crags, caused the patriots to build forts upon the heights here, whose ruins can still be traced. When the disasters on Manhattan Island in the autumn of 1776, and the consequent flank movement of the British, who, under Lord Cornwallis, were enabled to put a large force across the river at what is now called Alpine Landing, five miles above, and attack Forts Greene and Lee in the rear, the instant abandonment of this position became necessary; and it was along this country road, which now forms the main street of the little village, that Washington skillfully led his fleeing but unbeaten little army. A series of articles by Ernest Ingersoll in the *Outing* magazine, for 1894, gives a circumstantial description of this old road, and many other roads, villages, and historical sites and incidents in this interesting and highly picturesque region. Latterly for many years there have been extensive picnic grounds and beer-gardens on the heights at Fort Lee, but they have never risen above a plebeian character and often were the scenes of rowdyism. It is hoped that, with the new effort toward making the place easily accessible and developing its advantages for residence, a better state of things will arise for this region, which ought to be one of the preferred districts for suburban residence.

At Fort Lee village the cars turn west along this old road to the top of the hill (Taylorsville), at the foot of which is Leonia.

Descending the hill to Broad Avenue, the Englewood line turns northward along Broad Avenue to Englewood, where it turns to the left as far as the center of the village. It is probable that this line will soon be extended to New Bridge, and southward through Fairmount into the center of Hackensack. As it will there connect with cars through Ridgefield to Leonia, this line will then afford an opportunity for a round trip that will be among the pleasantest in New Jersey.

3. Northern Railroad of New Jersey.

This railroad, which is leased to the New York, Lake Erie & Western Company, and has its terminus at the Erie station in Jersey City, is a convenient means of reaching the pretty district along the base of the Palisades, described in the bicycle route from New York to Nyack. As soon as its train emerges from the tunnel under Bergen Ridge, it turns to the right and runs along the edge of the meadows, with the tracks of the New York, Susquehanna & Western on the left, and Snake Hill and Secaucus in the distance. At Homestead the Paterson plank road is crossed and the line of the electric cars to Passaic. At New Durham the West Shore Railroad comes in and keeps a parallel course for two miles, then crosses over, and strikes off to the left in company with the Susquehanna line, and disappears. Then follow Fairview and its old mill, and Ridgefield with its antique church. The Hackensack is now left behind, and the course lies up the valley of the English or Overpeck Creek, passing Palisades Park, a very modern settlement of New Yorkers, and the older towns of Leonia, Nordhoff, and Englewood (p. 104). Many trains run thus far. A fewer number run on north through a beautiful region, where every station invites the rambler to long walks. The stations in succession are Tenafly, Cresskill, Demarest, Closter, Tappan, and Sparkill. This brings the line into the high hills at the northern end of the Palisades, among which it finds an exceedingly picturesque path to Nyack-on-the-Hudson. The station is on the main street half a mile above the summer hotels on the shore of the Tappan Sea, and the ferry to Tarrytown.

4. The West Shore Railroad.

The West Shore Railroad passes through one of the most beautiful stretches of country near New York. Its station is in Weehawken, reached by ferry from the foot of Jay Street, or, principally, from the foot of West Forty-second Street; and the trains almost immediately enter and pass through the tunnel beneath Bergen Ridge, emerging at New Durham, where are large yards. The road then turns sharply north beside the tracks of the Northern Railroad of New Jersey and of the Susquehanna & Western, and exciting races between trains often take place for a couple of miles along this level course; then it turns to the left above the track of the former road, and passes out across the meadows on each side of Bellman's Creek, a tidal tributary of the Hackensack, which presently appears on the left, while the broad expanse of Overpeck Creek spreads blue and breezy at the right. The beautiful hills of Bergen Ridge and the Palisades, on the summit of which is Fort Lee, rise in green terraces, dotted with villages in that direction. In the angle between the two views a long avenue of old trees crossing the marsh will be noticed; there ran anciently the Albany post-road, and the ruined stone house of the ferryman still stands near the track. Then the Overpeck is crossed upon a drawbridge, and *Little Ferry* is reached (6 m. from Weehawken). This village occupies the lower end of the Ridgefield Peninsula, projecting southward between the Overpeck and Hackensack valleys, and is a very old settlement, taking its name from the fact that in colonial times a ferry was maintained here on the upper road from Weehawken to Hackensack. It was short and unimportant as compared with the Newark and Paulus Hook ferry below Snake Hill, and hence distinguished as the "little ferry." It was the scene of lively skirmishes during the Revolution, and its picturesque surroundings have attracted several well-known artists as residents within recent years.

Just above Little Ferry is a suburban village, Ridgefield Park, where the Susquehanna road leads off to the left, while the West Shore keeps straight north past the little station West Englewood, along Teaneck Creek to *Bergen Fields* (12 m.). This is a lovely spot on cross-roads leading east to Tenafly ($1\frac{3}{4}$ m.) and west (turning to the right at the first corner beyond the church, and then to the left at the next corner) to Riveredge, on the Hackensack ($1\frac{3}{4}$ m.; p. 134). At each place you will find a railroad, by which you may return to New York. The church with the lofty spire on the hill at the left is the house of an old Dutch Reformed society, which took a very prominent part in the religious history of this part of the State, when the policy of the neighborhood churches had a much more important influence upon social and political affairs than at present. It has a large but not particularly interesting graveyard beneath its shadow. *Schraalenburgh*, the next station ($12\frac{3}{4}$ m.), is a still older and quainter relic of Dutch society, where the Teaneck road, north and south, crosses the straight road, east and west, between Cresskill and New Milford, each about $1\frac{3}{4}$ miles distant. At Schraalenburgh is a very old stone meeting-house—the best relic of colonial church architecture in this region—and its antique graveyard. The local roads are rather soft and uneven for bicycling, and there is little shade.

The landscapes seen from the car windows as the train moves

northward are quietly beautiful. The whole land has long been under cultivation, and aged orchards, brushy hillside pastures, and shady lanes bordered by stone walls, diversify the fields and meadows. On the right are always the hills, growing ever higher and more rugged; and presently swampy woods denote an approach to the channel of the Hackensack, which here bends far enough to the east to touch the railroad's north-and-south course. A glimpse is caught of the river at the left, and then the train reaches Harrington Park (16 m.), where old farms have lately been cut up into building lots, and several fine, modern houses have been built, whose owners are impatiently awaiting nature's effort to renew, according to the landscape gardener's ideas, the beauty which the ax and hoe have too ruthlessly destroyed.

This is an excellent point of departure for rambling afoot or on a 'cycle. Closter (p. 105) is only a mile east, and a three-mile walk up the ever-growing ridges east of Closter will carry you to *Indian Head*, the highest point of the Palisades, overlooking the Hudson half-way between Yonkers and Hastings. A rather rough road leads south from that point along the brow of the Palisades as far as you please to follow it.

A short distance north of Harrington Park, along the railroad track, is **Old Hook**, an ancient designation of the elbow in the Hackensack, where it receives the Tienekill and other streams from the east, and the larger Pascack Brook from the west. These flow together in the midst of a swampy grove of trees, among which gigantic buttonwoods and elms are conspicuous; and for miles above and below, the river is shaded by great trees, and bordered by bushy meadows very enticing to the rambler and naturalist. Something of a path follows the winding stream all the way from Rivervale, 3½ miles above, to Oradell, three miles below Old Hook; and it conducts one through tangled woods and lush meadows, out of sight, and almost out of hearing, of civilization.' Several fine old-fashioned houses and many picturesque features of rural life as practiced by the Dutch may be found in this neighborhood, where pleasant roads lead west to Westwood and other stations on the New Jersey & New York Railroad. A good long walk would be to follow the river downward from this place. Cross the iron bridge and go west for three-quarters of a mile, then turn to the left (southward), walk on and cross the river again, and straight on, 2½ miles, to Overton. Here the east-and-west road, spoken of on page 105, crosses east through Schraalenburgh to Cresskill. Turn to the right upon it (⅜ m.) until you come to the river road, and then to the left, leaving New Milford behind you and heading southward to Riveredge station (⅝ m.). The next stage is to New Bridge (1¼ m.), where you cross the river, pass the interesting old Steuben house, and go on to Hackensack, through the highly cultivated suburbs of Cherry Hill and Fairmount, to the

square (2 m.). The total distance is about eight miles, and it is
fair to good riding for bicycles all the way. The route may be varied
by crossing the river at Oradell, New Milford, Riveredge, or by *not*
crossing at New Bridge, but continuing on down the left bank to
Anderson Street bridge, where, if you wish, you may turn to the left
and run straight over a fine road to Englewood.

The next station is Norwood (17½ m.), followed by *Tappan* (19 m.)
where the revolutionary army headquarters, occupied by Wayne
at the time of the execution here, in 1780, of the spy, André, and
often temporarily used by Washington and other officers during their
frequent visits to this central point in their northern campaigning, is
plainly visible from the train, in a field at the right, under some great
trees a short distance before reaching the station. The hill upon
which André was hung was that west of the track and a few rods
south of the road leading over the hill from the station. A large,
square stone marks the place. This road is an ancient one, leading
over to Rivervale (3½ m.).

Tappan is the first station in New York State (Rockland County).
The next is *Blauvelt* (22 m.), where the Piermont branch of the
Erie Railway crosses, following between here and Suffern nearly
the course of the revolutionary military road, over which the allied
armies marched and remarched, and communications were maintained
between the northern and southern departments. *West Nyack*
(24 m.) and Valley Cottage (26½ m.) are in a delightful region for summer residence or excursions, and then comes *Congers* (28½ m.), the
station for *Rockland Lake*. The village, which is a summer resort
for a certain class of people, covers a hill at the right; and this hill
conceals the lakes from which is derived a large part of the ice
supplying New York City. Smaller ponds, made by damming the
outlet for the sake of enlarging the ice-producing surface, appear on
this side of the hill. A road descends a ravine to Rockland Landing
on the Hudson, where the ice-boats load, and where a daily steamboat stops on its way to New York every morning, except Sunday.
This is directly opposite Sing Sing. The road striking west from
Congers reaches the Hackensack in about a mile, and winds its way
on, some two miles farther, to New City. It opens an interesting
country for cycling or walking, and is elsewhere described (p. 135).

Two or three miles beyond Congers brings the train to the base
of the Verdrietig range of mountains, which terminate in the Hook
Mountain, so conspicuous from the river, the basal promontory of
which is called Verdrietig Hook. These are rough, wooded, rocky

hills, the peaks some 800 feet high, which will furnish scrambling enough to satisfy any amateur in mountaineering, and reward him with glorious views from their summits. They are penetrated beneath Long Clove, where the ancient Dutch road ran over to "Haverstroo," by a long tunnel, in which the train is speedily engulfed.

West of this clove is the highest peak of the range (820 ft.), *High Tor*, whose precipitous summit makes its ascent difficult, except by following a path which leads up the eastern slope from the road through the clove. This climb is well worth the exertion; but a word of warning should be uttered to those inclined to wander about the ledges of these rude hills, on the subject of poisonous snakes, since copperheads, although not plentiful, are sufficiently numerous to make caution prudent. This is true of the Ramapo Mountains, the Watchung ranges, and, indeed, all the hills of New Jersey. Rattlesnakes, however, are very rare, although said to exist in the more northerly and wilder parts of the Palisades.

The West Shore train emerges at full speed from the tunnel upon a lofty ledge overlooking Haverstraw Bay, and the brilliant picture made by this broad, sail-dotted, steamer-plowed reach of the Hudson and its farther populous shore, bursts upon the view of the traveler with an effect as soul-inspiring as it is startling. This sudden leap out into the sunlight and to the presence of that brilliant landscape is one of the finest incidents in American travel, and worth coming all this way to see. Take pains, therefore, to sit on the right-hand side of the car.

Haverstraw (32 m.) has little to attract the visitor. The best of it is the view from the cars, which overlook the town and its profitable but ugly brickyards. Here was the scene of the conferences between the British emissary André and the traitor Arnold, in 1780, the full account of which, and of the other revolutionary incidents of this region, may be read in "Ingersoll's Guide to the Hudson River" (Rand, McNally & Co.). Beyond Haverstraw the road skirts the river, passing beneath the high, wooded, rocky banks past Stony Point (35 m.), where the site of the old fort that Wayne stormed and captured may easily be visited; past the stone-shipping wharves of Tompkins Cove (37 m.), along the base of Dunderberg, where there is a ferry from Jones Point (39 m.) over to Peekskill; past the fine wooded picnic grounds of Iona Island (41 m.), and underneath the revolutionary fortifications and battleground of Fort Montgomery (43 m.), to Cranston's and **West Point** (47½ m.), Cornwall (52 m.), and Newburg (56½ m.).

5. New Jersey & New York Railroad.

The New Jersey & New York Railroad serves the people in the valley of the Hackensack. Its terminus, in Jersey City, is that of the Erie Railway (its present lessee), and its trains use the track of that railway across the meadows, taking a northwest course from the Bergen Ridge tunnel, across Secaucus Island, the Hackensack River, and Berry's Creek, as far as the shore, when it swerves to the north through Carlstadt ($9\frac{3}{4}$ m. from Jersey City). The next station is Corona, in the midst of countless market gardens, and then Hackensack (14 m.). The principal station is on Central Avenue Street, at some distance from the center of the town. A mile farther there is another (Anderson Street), in a newly settled part of the city, near the bridge leading to the Englewood road. The road goes straight on through the woods, leaving Fairmount somewhat on the left, to *Cherry Hill* (1 m.). This is a modern village that has grown up near what has been known since colonial times as **New Bridge**.

This bridge, first built long anterior to the Revolution, stands a short distance east of the station, where the original road (only parts of which are now used) led down to Liberty Pole (Englewood) and Bergen. It was over this bridge that the defeated army of patriots was led to Hackensack in November, 1776, when the fall of the forts on Manhattan Island rendered the sudden abandonment of Fort Lee necessary. Here, later, a battery and small garrison were placed on the high ground at the western end of the bridge, and several severe skirmishes took place here and in the immediate neighborhood, where the British and Americans alternately held possession, and nearly all the farmers were Tories. One of the best and oldest examples of primitive farm-house architecture is found in the Zabriskie house, so called, at this end of the bridge, where the site of a mill, famous in the country a century ago, is also apparent. This house and farm figured largely in those troublous times, and was again and again made a military headquarters. After the war, it having fallen by confiscation or otherwise into the hands of the State, it was given to Baron Steuben as a popular recognition of his services; but he seems to have held and occupied the property only a short time.

A very pretty run of a mile and a half takes the train to *Riveredge*, which is a most picturesque spot, the stream expanding there into a quiet, deeply shadowed pool above a little harbor, which is the head of sloop navigation on the river. The old roads that lead east and west from here are all interesting; and the place is an excellent terminus for a day's outing. At New Milford, three-quarters of a mile above, is another bridge, and here are the fine waterworks which supply several cities below with water taken from the upper river. Botanists will find this an admirable place to collect plants, especially those growing in wet woods. Roads lead westward over to Paramus and the Saddle River Valley, and east to Schraalenburgh, etc. (p. 130). Oradell, just above here, is a more modern village, full of summer residents, who find the river, here dammed into a large pool, a means of great amusement. North of here the Hackensack makes a great bend to the eastward (see Old Hook, p. 131), which the road cuts off by a straight northerly course through the pretty villages of Kinderkamac and Westwood (21½ m.). Between Westwood and Hillsdale, a new and uninteresting place, Pascack Brook is crossed and then accompanied northward through the hill-town of Park Ridge (25 m.), where many New Yorkers reside; and so out of the State and into Rockland County. Here it swerves to the left through Spring Valley and then on around the Verdrietig Mountains to Haverstraw (42½ m.). A branch line, however, keeps straight on to the county seat of Rockland, New City (33 m.).

A delightful walk, of about three and a half miles, may be taken from New City across to Congers station (Rockland Lake), the most interesting point in which is the valley of the Hackensack River, where you may be tempted to diverge and follow its course downward until tired. The road crosses this river at the point where the old highway north and south also spans it—a mile below the Machiqua Kill. A queer little settlement of half-ruined stone houses amid worn-out fields surrounds a bridge in a hollow, approached by crooked roads, where the river feeds a mill pond long ago abandoned to the weeds and the fishes. This is Tom Pye's Corners. The Pyes were important people here in times past, and may be so yet; but just what distinguished "Tom," that he should have "Corners," I do not know. The mill is well into its second century, and its pristine redness has grown very gray, while the old wooden wheel long ago stopped hatcheling the current and tossing down its bright shreds to be re-knit in the foaming pool below. The pond, where the boys are wont to fish and the girls to gather cresses, has been almost filled up with the silt of half a century, until masses of lily pads and aquatic weeds flourish in a broad band along its shore and stand like islands in its middle. The dam is now a mere blockade of stones, dry for the most part, and covered with a thicket of brush and jewel weed, and against the wheel, rooted in the very ridge of the dam, stands a tree at least fifty years old.

The water trickles here and there over this decayed barrier and then rattles down a stony avenue arched with great elms. Where the road turns sharply eastward with the stream you can look back, straight up this water corridor where the air is dark and cool, and see the afternoon sun flashing upon the troubled current above, every ripple reflecting pure, white light. There is color enough — the foreground is full of it — yet the picture is such an one as a master could give us fully in black and white alone.

At night, sometimes, that star-proof arch is vividly illuminated by torches carried by men and boys fishing for eels, who stand in the ripples and spear the lissome creatures as they wriggle toward the light and put up their heads to inquire into it. This is the first intimation the river gets of its destiny in the far-away sea.

Nothing could be more picturesque in its way than the disorder of plant-life below this turn in the river, and we may follow it half a mile in the shadow of trees that form a continuous thicket between its current and the roadway. The riparian lands here are low meadows, originally, no doubt, a swampy woodland. In early times they were cleared and drained, but long ago passed into neglect, and were replanted by ever-thrifty nature with willow, hazel, and alder, and with multitudes of tall weeds now in full flower.

Here, as we walk on, are acres upon acres of coreopsis, primrose, sunflowers, and other yellow blossoms — yellow is the color of autumn; and masses of a dull purplish boneset, called Joe-Pye-weed. Through these flats, the very image of abandonment and nature run to rags, the river finds a tortuous channel. Here and there, for a little way below the dam, are ledges where the smooth current breaks into a cascade, but for the most part a canoe would ride easily, and in some places the river spreads wide and deep between the roots of great old trees, and there are clean turfy banks where the farmer boys go swimming at evening, and in the mornings the farmer girls come and make little picnics with acorn-cups, 'o drink imaginary tea from, taking wild grapes, thorn apples, and nuts for the solid parts of the feast. Tall rank grasses and sedges wade in the water on each side, hiding the real shore, and often crowding but never quite choking the rapid current.

This is a region of old fields gone to seed, and mossy, tumble-down fences and stone walls, that have been half leveled by the prying hand of time and overgrown by green interlopers. Some of these walls are quite concealed, for rods together, by weeds and ivy, or form long ridges of grapevines, which ran wild a generation ago, and the fruit of which is now gathered by the children of neighboring villages to make "jell."

One wonders why so much land is allowed to lie untilled, near the greatest market of the country, and left to the breeding of noxious weeds and vermin. The real explanation seems to lie in the malign influence of the city upon rural pursuits. Men are not content to delve and plod on lonely farms when they can make equal wages in the gay town, so near by; or, if they do not revolt as far as this, they would rather keep summer boarders, pasture a few fine cows, or practice some other side specialty, than to pursue plain farming. The real farmer not only prefers to live, but succeeds better farther away from the city. His land is less cut up by roads and railways; his helpers are more contented to stay with him, and to live after the rural fashion; and tramps, gunners, and vagabonds are less a nuisance, etc. These remarks increase in pertinence as we descend nearer and nearer to the town, until finally we enter that almost abandoned belt which surrounds all great cities, the owners of which are too busy staking out "parks" into town lots to plant and harvest their fields.

No part of this desolate belt is more thoroughly abandoned to nature than the courses of the streams; and the artist, the naturalist, or the ungainful lover of wild nature seeks their ravines and follows their windings, with the feeling that he is not far away from that primeval and poetic wildness which fascinates the most stolid of hearts.

Not much variety develops as we trace the river through its unkempt and wooded bottom lands for the next four miles or so. Three miles down, in the vicinity of Valley Cottage, there enters the tributary which drains Rockland Lake through the two ponds that the ice company have created by damming this outlet. This tributary the maps call the East Branch of the Hackensack, but, since the ice ponds were made, it adds very little water to the river's quota. Its first name was Kill Van Beast, and it was owned by the Remsens, who had a mill upon it as early, at least, as 1750, at the point where the ancient willow-grown dam now holds back the water of the lowest pond, just above the road from Congers Station to Rockland Lake.

Just below the mouth of this kill, where a country road and the upper of the West Shore Railway's two bridges cross the river, is the mouth of that Mattarnick Kill, which drains the fields about Borden's and was the southern boundary of "Welsh's Island." Walking on, we come to many deep, still pools in dense woods. This brings us to Old Hook (p. 131), and to a good place to stop.

6. The Susquehanna Railroad.

The route of the old Midland Railway of New Jersey, now called New York, Susquehanna & Western Railroad, leads through a very attractive region west of the Hackensack Valley. Its station in Jersey City is that of the Pennsylvania Railroad, reached by Desbrosses and Cortlandt Street ferries from New York, and it runs frequent suburban trains. Its course is along the eastern brink of the always beautiful meadows (p. 129), and across the Overpeck at the left of, and parallel with, the West Shore Railroad. A mile or so beyond Little Ferry, at Bogota, an old Dutch village, this road turns to the left and crosses into *Hackensack*, where its station is on Main Street, the principal and most central one in the town. Thence it curves to the left and takes a straight westerly course through the pretty suburbs of *Maywood* and *Rochelle Park*. The latter is at the crossing of Saddle River, and forms a good point of departure for a wheeling trip up the valley to quaint old Paramus (about 6½ m.; p. 108). Continuing, the road crosses Passaic River at Dundee Lake and curves round to the north through the eastern part of the city of *Paterson*, where there are three stations, the principal of which is near the station of the Erie Railroad in the center of the city. Another station is at Broadway, and a third, in the northern edge of town, called *Riverside*. Leaving the city by a second bridging of the Passaic, the road takes a northerly course along the vale of Goffle Brook, with the ridges of the Preakness at the left and such villages as North Paterson, Midland Park, and Wortendyke, which show that they are largely the homes of men who go to Paterson or New York to business daily. At Wyckoff (29 m.) a more rural appearance begins, and the region grows rougher. Here the line swings west, crosses over the bridge dividing the Hohokus from the Ramapo, and dips down to Crystal Lake station. This locality is full of ponds and rapid streams, by whose banks can be found old mills such as artists go into ecstasies over ; and it is only two miles, by the road leading south, to Franklin Lake, a circular pond more than half a mile wide. The Ramapo River is reached at *Oakland* (33 m.; p. 112) and soon afterward is crossed, when the line turns south along the base of the Ramapo Mountains, and with Pompton Lake close by on the left, though not much of it is visible. Here comes into view the wide, level, thickly populated Pompton Plain, and in the foreground is the pretty village of *Pompton* itself — one of the pleasantest in Northern New Jersey. A glimpse of the hard, level, and shaded

roads here justifies the high reputation of this broad valley among wheelmen and drivers. The train dashes across the Wanaque, intersects the New York & Greenwood Lake Railway, and there meets the dark, rushing Pequannock River, whose valley it thenceforth follows northwestward for fifteen miles to its source in Sussex County. The ascent of this river is a charming experience, despite the ruthless manner in which the hills have been stripped of their timber and the stream dammed at every curve; for nature has clothed the rocky steeps with second growth and turned the old dams into mossy cascades. An excellent macadamized road runs along the valley, so that cycling over this route would be a pleasure. The hills are rugged, but not very high, and broken by valleys and ravines with tumbling brooks where the skillful can surely get trout. Every two or three miles is a substantial village with factories run by waterpower. From *Charlottesburg* (44 m.) a stage runs to Macopin, or Echo Lake, two miles distant. This lake is twice as large as Pompton Lake, lies along the eastern base of Knouse Mountain at an elevation of nearly 900 feet, and is much frequented in summer. Southward from Charlottesburg run the mining railroad and wagon-roads to Green, and Denmark, and other large ponds along the base of Copperas Mountain, described on page 115. A narrow gap lets the railroad through to *Newfoundland* and *Oak Ridge* (48 m.), which lie in a depression where the Rockaway River heads in Mooseback Pond, and the Bear Fort Mountains fill the northern horizon. These names are suggestive of the unkempt beauty of hill, and forest, and mountain stream, which attract the rambler in this region, and of which there is no lack. Westward of this lie still loftier and more rugged ranges—massive granitic and gneissoid ridges clothed with forests and breaking into cliffs, cut by ravines and cañons where the streams are all cascades, so that little farming can be done. Here is the place for camper and fisherman; and a study of the map will show the opportunities that are open. This rude, picturesque region extends for many miles west along this railroad, whether you go north with the branch to Middletown, or southwest with the line to Pennsylvania; and there is no railroad out of New York which in forty miles will carry one to so remote, wilderness-like, and picturesque a region as will this one.

7. The Erie Railway.

The New York, Lake Erie & Western Railway, familiar to everybody as the "Erie" for nearly fifty years, runs a numerous and convenient service of local trains which penetrate an interesting region of Northern New Jersey. Its station in Jersey City is reached by ferries from Chambers and West Twenty-third Street, New York, and the trains pass beneath Bergen Ridge through a long tunnel. Emerging from this they turn northward and take a straight course across the meadows of Penhorne Creek, through the fields of Secaucus Island, with Snake Hill conspicuous at the left, then over the Hackensack into Boiling Springs township, whose marshes are drained by Berry's Creek, until dry land is reached in *Rutherford*. From there it is almost continuous town through Passaic — which appears to excellent advantage — to Paterson, a city having little in it to attract the out-door pleasure-seeker. From the station to **Passaic Falls** (p. 109) is about a mile and a quarter, and the white electric cars, in rear of the station, go directly to them. Beyond Paterson the line strikes north through *Hawthorne*, (where the Passaic River and the New York, Susquehanna & Western Railroad are crossed), *Ridgewood* (where a cut-off from Rutherford comes in), and *Hohokus* in the Hohokus Valley. Here the country begins to be wild and interesting, and pleasant wagon-roads may be followed east and west. *Allendale*, *Ramseys*, and *Mahwah* are successive stations among the hills, whose rills drain out through Hohokus Creek to Saddle River. All are centers for summer residents, who are scattered as boarders among the farmers' houses far and near. These villages are connected by a road good for bicycling, which extends through to *Suffern* (p. 112), where the Ramapo River is encountered in a lovely valley between lofty hills.

Here a branch road, which was the original line of the railway, runs straight east to *Piermont*, crossing various north-and-south lines, so that one may easily return to New York by this branch and the New Jersey & New York, West Shore, or Northern Railroad of New Jersey, making a very fine round trip.

At Suffern the Erie swings into the Ramapo Valley, through a narrow defile. For fifteen miles the valley extends, mountain-bound, and at times it is of barely sufficient width to allow the passage, side by side, of the river, the historic post-road and the Erie, while again it will widen out into a dell or ravine which marks the course of a mountain rill or torrent. Here and there, too, the mountains recede, and the valley spreads itself into a fertile plain, and in these occasional plateaus nestle, in the order named, the little hamlets of Hillburn, Ramapo, Sloatsburg, Tuxedo, and Southfields.

Tuxedo, named from a lake long famous for its fish, has become a household word by reason of the private club-park established there by the Tuxedo Park Association, composed of wealthy men in the highest social circles of New York. They acquired many years ago 6,000 acres, including the lake, for the purpose of creating a great game-preserve and sporting ground, and so much has been done toward accomplishing this object that this resort is now probably the most extensive and complete of its kind in America. The grounds are elaborately laid out in a system of boulevards and mountain drives. Tasteful cottages and villas abound, and on the shore of the lake is the extensive club-house of the association, which is provided with every modern convenience for the accommodation and entertainment of members and their guests. These privileges are carefully guarded, and an introduction or invitation is necessary in order to enter the grounds.

Turner's is an important station at the end of the Ramapo Mountains and one of the foremost shipping points for the milk and butter of the famous Orange County dairy farms.

The Newburg Branch strikes eastward from here through a region of delightful hills and glens, and finds a devious way around the western base of the Highlands of the Hudson and down to Cornwall and Newburg. This exhibits much wild scenery, and a novel view of Storm King, Cro' Nest, and other of the Highland peaks; and the last five miles of its course is over ground rendered historic as the last camp ground of the patriot army of the Revolution. This circuitous trip to Newburg (about 63 m.), and a return by boat on the Hudson, would form a thoroughly enjoyable one day's excursion, and one exhibiting well the character of the country west of the great river. The suburban service of electric cars at Newburg is very complete, penetrating far into the rural environment of that interesting and beautifully situated city.

The main line now pursues a course through the fine rural towns and farming districts of *Goshen* and *Middletown*, where the Shawangunk Mountains are in full view, to *Port Jervis* on the Delaware. The road then enters the Allegheny Mountains, by ascending the rushing Delaware, and finds its way across to the Great Lakes by one of the most picturesque routes open to the western traveler. Only one point more concerns us, and that is mentioned because this railroad runs cheap excursion trains thither every few days during the summer. This is **Shohola Glen**, twenty miles west of Port Jervis or 107 from New York. Here, near a village, the Shohola comes down to the Delaware through a rocky gorge, which has been fitted up by the erection of shelters, restaurants, dancing platforms, etc., for picnicking as understood by the crowds of holiday excursionists who travel out from town for such a day in the country as these arrangements provide for them. We are told that the falls of the Shohola are a great attraction, and also Panther Brook, once a fine trout stream, with fine cataracts, which enters the Delaware near by. In the neighborhood are many good fishing streams and lakes, and a deal of rough and more or less wooded country in Sullivan County.

8. New York & Greenwood Lake Railway.

This railroad uses the stations of the Erie Railway (see above), but diverges from the Erie tracks just west of the tunnel, and strikes straight across the Hackensack Meadows to Arlington, beyond which it crosses the Passaic and bears northwestward through the thickly settled districts of North Newark, Bloomfield, and *Montclair*, passing the latter city at a considerable distance from the business center. It then takes a northerly course through Upper Montclair and Montclair Heights, along the base of First Mountain, which it crosses through Great Notch, where the country really begins. The region beyond is high and beautiful, with an extensive outlook. Caldwell, Cedar Grove, *Little Falls*, and Singac bring the passenger to the banks of the Passaic, which is crossed just before reaching Pequannock. Then follow *Pompton Plains*, the crossing of the Pequannock River, at Pompton Junction (with the Susquehanna Railroad, p. 138), and the run northward along the pretty valley of the Wanaque River to the foot of Greenwood Lake. Here, at Cooper station, are the *Glens*, where the outflow of the lake is through a series of rapid cataracts in the midst of the woods.

Extensive improvements have been made to provide an agreeable place for excursions here, and many Sunday-school picnics and similar parties avail themselves of the facilities. " Shady walks have been constructed on the mountain side and along the margin of the stream, and a refreshment house of ample proportions has been provided, attached to which is a new and beautiful pavilion for dancing and other recreations. The view commands the entire lake, while on the front of the property, crossing the railroad track by a bridge, has been erected a spacious bath, with ample accommodations and dressing rooms for all who may desire to bathe within the house or in the lake. Boats, ball grounds, tennis courts, swings, and the usual appliances for enjoyment have been provided. The domain extends to many thousands of acres."

The village of *Greenwood Lake* is situated at the head of the lake, which stands a thousand feet above tide-water, and whose waters are deep, clear, and cold. Here the angler will find game fish of every variety—bass, pike, and pickerel being the most prominent.

Summer hotels and private boarding-houses are numerous; while those who desire to take their own equipage, and try a season of "roughing it," will find along the shores, or upon the wooded islands in the lake, choice spots for camping out. Here, at the lake itself, is every facility for rowing, sailing, fishing, and bathing; and in the adjacent mountains, easily reached by quiet, shaded pathways, are romantic ravines and dells, their rocky walls garnished with beautiful mosses, ferns, and wild flowers.

The Orange Branch of this railroad turns east at Woodside Park, and runs through Silver Lake and Watsessing to *Llewellyn Park*, where it turns south to Main Street, and connects with electric railways to Eagle Rock and South and East Orange.

9. Electric Lines to Passaic and Paterson.

The cars of this line leave the Hoboken ferry and proceed to the top of the hill by the Elevated road, then turn north until they reach the Bergen turnpike in West Hoboken. They then follow this down the hill to Homestead, and cross the Hackensack Meadows by the old Paterson plank road (p. 102). The course is then through Carlstadt, and into *Rutherford*, where the car turns down to a terminus at the Erie Railway station. Thus far, two fares (10 cents) are charged. For *Passaic* you change at the turn-off to another car, which goes along the plank road, and over Passaic Bridge into Passaic (fare 5 cents). Here, after some zigzagging, the car reaches the railway station, and then (not crossing the tracks) continues out Central Avenue to Paterson through Clifton. This region is very thinly settled, and is of little interest. Approaching Paterson it turns sharply to the left along Crooks Avenue (Lakeview road), then to the right, following the railway into the center of the city of *Paterson* (fare 10 cents).

☞ *A pleasant diversion* is to alight at the turn-off from Central Avenue (the southwest corner of Cedar Lawn Cemetery), and walk down the Lakeview road past the cemetery to Dundee Lake, and then up the interesting river road to the cemetery entrance, where trolley cars can be taken into the city along Vreeland Avenue and Broadway. This "lake" is a favorite resort in summer; steam launches run upon it, row boats may be hired; you may fish (but will catch nothing, probably, but a muddy carp); and light refreshments are on sale at the boathouse.

The Plank Road Line from Passaic to Paterson starts its cars at Garfield, east of Passaic, passes the station, and thence takes the straight course of the plank road past the handsome estates of Clifton and the disused Clifton race track into the business center of *Paterson*, where the cars follow Main Street, then turn to the left, and go out to Little Falls and Singac. The fares are: Passaic to Paterson, 10 cents; Paterson to Singac, 5 cents.

Various transfers are given free on both these lines in Hoboken (to all ferries), in Passaic, and in Paterson.

10. Electric Lines in Paterson and to Little Falls.

The city of Paterson has lines of trolley cars in all directions, reaching the outskirts of the city at Dundee Lake, Riverside, Haledon, Passaic Falls, Lincoln Bridge, and Totowa. The most important of these, however, is the line up the river to **Little Falls** and Singac. This comes up Main Street, turns west near Market Street, and makes its way by a circuitous course over the high ground of West Paterson to Lincoln Bridge, which carries the highway across the Passaic about a mile above the falls. Thence it follows the turnpike along the west bank of this beautiful river, past the city's West Side Park, and the private picnic grounds of Ryle Park, to the quaint, century-old, carpet-making town of *Little Falls*, which takes its name from the lofty cataracts down which the river is forced by the rocky obstacles it there encounters. The whole of this ride is along a shady old road, with wide and interesting views of the river, the valley, and the distant mountains; and it exhibits some of the quaintest old stone houses remaining in New Jersey. Little Falls has a neat hotel (The Eagle), and is growing into a place of suburban summer residence. The road terminates at *Singac*, about a mile beyond, where railroads and wagon-roads to Pompton and Boonton cross the river. This whole ride, costing 5 cents, is one of the coolest and most enjoyable in the country.

11. Boonton Branch, D., L. & W. Railroad.

This branch of the Delaware, Lackawanna & Western Railroad leaves the main line (p. 145) just west of the Bergen tunnel, and strikes northward across the Hackensack Meadows, with the Erie Railway on the right of it and the Greenwood Lake Railroad on the left. It passes through Kingsland to *Lyndhurst*, crosses the beautiful Passaic, and skirts the southern parts of *Passaic* and *Paterson*, upon

THE PASSAIC RIVER, ABOVE PATERSON, N. J.

pretty region, along the foot of the ridge, and beside the East Branch of Rahway River, to *Maplewood*, where it begins to bear west through the park-like streets of Wyoming, until it comes to *Millburn* (p. 122). Its course is then west through a charming country to *Short Hills*, one of the prettiest suburbs of New York. Here a community of wealthy families have built a collection of elegant homes, which appear to be set irregularly in a great grove, unbroken by fences or gardens. A single large supply store and post office are the only indication of business, apart from the numerous greenhouses and fields of flowers that betray the industry of the place, which is horticulture, more particularly in the direction of exotics.

Several large nurseries exist here and near here, of which the most prominent is the great establishment of Pitcher & Manda. Their fields of flowers, and their extensive and wonderful greenhouses, in which many acres of rare flowers are cultivated, are a sight worth going far to see. One large house is devoted entirely to tree ferns and similar tropical growths; two or three others to the rarest and most curious orchids, recruited by agents in all parts of the world, and many others to blossoming plants less remarkable, perhaps, but no less beautiful. Short Hills is identified with much of the most stirring history of the colonial and revolutionary periods, and has been the home since of several men and women famous in literature and art.

Two miles farther comes *Summit*, a sightly little city, crowning the summit of hills that overlook a large area of the Rahway Valley, even down to the coast of New York harbor. Its streets, which run with the irregularity belonging to an old-fashioned village, are well paved and closely shaded; and costly and beautiful homes extend far out from the center in all directions. The general elevation is about 400 feet, and the highest part is distinguished as *Hill Crest*, where along Woodlawn Avenue stand many of the finest houses in town. Most streets and windows command fine views, but if one will climb to some loftier outlook, such as the attic of the Hotel Beechwood, he will find himself able to overlook a surprisingly wide and varied landscape. In the north, Boonton lies like a map upon the flanks of the hills that roll up far behind her; and all the villages can be picked out in the Whippany Valley down to Morristown and Madison, whose spires stand well above the trees and sharp against the farther hills. Eastward, Second Mountain cuts off the view north of Millburn, but southeastward the land sinks away in a great smooth hollow so green that it can have appeared little different when the Indians, one of whose highway trails came up through

this gap in the hills, looked out upon its aboriginal forests. Countless spires, tall chimneys, and pillars of smoke, stand above the treetops, however, and show where a score of well-known towns have their sites. Far away gleams the great metropolis, her cathedral and bridge-towers conspicuous, and the shining surface of her bay reflecting the light close to the horizon.

This healthful and sightly situation, the excellent social tone which prevails, and the highly civilized comforts provided, are bringing forward more and more the claims of these highland villages to attention as summer residences for city folks, especially Millburn, Summit, Madison, and Morristown. Each year additional boarding-houses are opened, and the hotel accommodations are increased. It is such patronage which has created the large and handsome *Hotel Beechwood*, in Summit, which is really a luxurious city hotel in a country park, uniting the qualities of both in an admirable degree. It is capacious, elegantly furnished, proud of its table and service, and has attached to it large wooded grounds and several furnished cottages. One prominent feature is a music room adapted to theatrical and other entertainments, dances, etc., and this opens upon an extensive piazza inclosed in glass and heated by steam, which forms a winter sun-parlor. A number of other hotels, smaller but prospering, are catering to a similar custom in this and the neighboring towns.

At Summit the railroad makes a northward kink in its line along the slender upper stream of the Passaic, then turns west and follows the old Morris turnpike through *Chatham*, *Madison*, and the station for St. Elizabeth's R. C. Convent and School, into **Morristown**. Here small local railroads run down the Whippany and Rockaway valleys into quiet country districts, attractive to ramblers, artists, and fishermen. From Morristown westward the Morris & Essex line turns northward through Morris Plains to a junction with the Boonton Branch at Denville, a few miles west of Boonton (p. 114). This gives an excellent opportunity of making a round tour by rail, which would give an admirable idea, with the least possible expense of money and exertion, of all Morris and Essex counties.

13. Electric Cars to Newark and Beyond.

From Jersey City to Newark and its surrounding towns two lines of electric trolley cars may be used; fare, 10 cents:

1. *By the Newark Plank Road.*
2. *By the Newark Turnpike.*

The former route leads from the Jersey City ferry-landing at the Pennsylvania Railroad station, foot of Montgomery Street, up Montgomery and Grand streets, and over the Heights to the old Plank road, which crosses the meadows beside the Morris & Essex Canal, not far from the confluence of the Hackensack and Passaic rivers, and enters Newark through the crowded southern part of that city, then passes up Market Street and out to Irvington. This is a most unpleasant route from one end to the other.

The latter route is from the Pennsylvania Railroad ferry, as before, up Montgomery Street and Newark Avenue, past the old Hudson County Court House, on " the hill," or up Pavonia Avenue from the Erie Railway station. These routes join at the "five corners," where in ancient days stood the village of *Bergen*, the original Dutch settlement, whence the name Bergen Ridge is derived, and around which clings many historical associations of local importance. Lines of cars north and south along Summit Avenue lead from here southward to Bayonne, and northward to Hoboken and beyond. From Bergen the Newark line descends the hill to the Hackensack bridge, close beside the Pennsylvania and the Lackawanna railroads, and then follows the ancient turnpike, which was the first improved wagon-road across the meadows, and dates back to long before the Revolution, straight across to that part of Newark east of the Passaic, called Harrison—a flat and muddy assemblage of small wooden houses, factories, and railroad yards. Having passed through this, and crossed the Passaic River, the cars enter *Newark* proper, and go straight to Broad Street, just above Military Park, where they turn down to Market Street. This line is as disagreeable as the other.

The intersection of Market and Broad streets is the center of Newark for commercial and transportation purposes, and here cars may be taken for all suburban termini, namely:

Jersey City, via the Turnpike.
Arlington, via Kearney Avenue.
Passaic, via Belleville, Avondale, and Franklin.
Woodside and Forest Hills.
Bloomfield, Glen Ridge, and Chestnut Hill. (See No. 15, p. 149.)
Orange, via Roseville and Brick Church to Eagle Rock (p. 150).
South Orange, via South Orange Avenue, to the Mountain Railway.
Irvington, via Springfield Avenue.
Clinton Avenue, via Broad Street.
Elizabeth, via Waverly.
Jersey City, via the Plank road.

Free Transfers are given between nearly all these lines, but the

passenger is required to ask for the transfer he wishes *at the time of paying his fare*, or it will not be given him.

Certain of these routes fall within this chapter, and others belong to the next chapter.

14. Electric Line to Arlington.

The cars of this line go north from Market and Broad streets, *Newark*, cross the Passaic into *Harrison*, and turn north through the open residence district east of that river along Kearney Avenue to the village of *Arlington*, a pretty town on the Greenwood Lake Railway, identified with colonial copper-mining.

This line is the starting point of a projected line north along the Ridge road, through Kingsland, Lyndhurst, Rutherford, and Carlstadt to Hackensack, which is likely to be built before the end of 1897.

15. Electric Line, Newark to Passaic.

This line sends its cars from Newark north on Broad Street, and along Belleville Avenue through Woodside, North Newark (where the Greenwood Lake Railway and Second River are crossed), to and through *Belleville* (p. 121). Here rural appearances begin, and the line occupies high ground overlooking the valley and across to the Arlington Ridge. The Jersey City waterworks and, a mile above, the Newark waterworks are conspicuous buildings. Washington Avenue leads straight on through *Essex* to *Avondale* and *Nutley*, where the cars turn to the left as far as the romantic Yantecaw or Third River, when they turn to the right (north) on Franklin Avenue, through *Franklin*, where the " Paterson & Newark Branch " of the Erie Railway is crossed. All four of these are agreeable old villages fast assuming the appearance of modern towns, and this part of the route is one of the pleasantest experiences of electric railroading in Northern New Jersey—a trip one may well take for the pleasure of it. From Franklin to South Passaic the line passes along Franklin Avenue, over a high, sparsely-occupied tract, giving a very pleasing view across the valley eastward to Rutherford, and proceeds to its terminus at the Erie Railway station in **Passaic**, where it is but a few steps to the electric cars for Rutherford and Hoboken, or for Paterson and beyond. Fare, 15 cents.

16. Electric Cars to Bloomfield and Montclair.

From Broad and Market streets, Newark, these cars pass north along Broad Street to the forking of Belleville and Bloomfield avenues, and strike out the latter, an ancient thoroughfare to the northern interior via Bloomfield and Montclair. Much half-rural and pretty country is passed over, with First River, the Morris Canal, Silver Lake, and Watsessing Village (the original name of the Bloomfield settlement) as incidents, until old *Bloomfield* is reached. The trolley line passes on along the principal street to the northwestern suburb called *Glen Ridge*, where it terminates at the D., L. & W. Railroad tracks. Fare, 10 cents.

Stages run from this street-car terminus along Bloomfield Avenue through Montclair and up to the top of the mountain, where a line of electric cars runs upon the highway out through Verona to the western border of Caldwell.

17. Electric Cars to the Oranges.

From the Pennsylvania Railroad station, on Market Street, in Newark, electric cars pass out through the northeastern part of the city and on through " all the Oranges " along the old country highway, which is now the main artery of traffic.

This road was laid out in 1709 as the Crane road—the first to the foot of the mountain from Newark. It " began at the head of Market Street, near the present Court House, in Newark, and passed the residence of Jasper Crane, on High Street, and ran thence through the present Warren Street to Roseville . . . It occupies the original Indian trail, and turns to the right or to the left just as the natives had deviated from a straight line." South Orange Avenue is of about the same age and crookedness.

This street cuts diagonally across the checkerboard of modern streets and reaches the outskirts of Newark at *Roseville*, where it bears west and becomes Main Street—a name it retains to the foot of the mountain. It is not particularly interesting until Grove Street is reached, its corner marked by the fine Congregational Church of brownstone, with a lecture-room annex. The railroad station (Morris & Essex Railroad) is one block at the right. It is by the churches that one mainly marks progress along this old thoroughfare, which is more and more becoming a business rather than a residence street. The new building in yellow brick and with a great square tower, on the corner of Hawthorne Avenue, is the First Baptist Church, built in 1891. A few steps farther brings us to a brownstone Gothic house of worship, increased by a large extension in the rear, which stands at the corner of Munn Avenue, one of the finest streets; this is the First Presbyterian Church of East Orange, whose pastor is the Rev. J. M. Ludlow, more widely known as the author of " The Captain of the Janissaries " and other stirring novels.

MUNN AVENUE, EAST ORANGE.

East Orange centers at the railway station, where there are a number of fine buildings, especially that of the Water Company, which also contains banks, the post office, etc. Arlington Avenue intersects Main Street here. Crossing the railroad, which henceforth will be upon our left, and going by the cluster of stores, we notice, a block away at the right, the tall new East Orange High School, with its ornamental clock tower and glass dials, four square to the dense city around it. At the corner of the next block is the dark stone Calvary (Methodist) Church, built in 1885. This is on the corner of Walnut Street; and the further half of the same block is occupied by the unfinished but beautiful white sandstone structure of Christ Church (Episcopal). The spaciousness of this building becomes more apparent when the extension on Mulford Street comes into view. A little farther on, at the corner of Clinton Street, a new Roman Catholic Church is building. A block beyond, on the left, is the brownstone Reformed Church, at the corner of Halstead Street.

Two prominent clubs have quarters on Halstead, nearly opposite this church. The first, in an elegant and comely building, having a façade in the colonial style, is the house of the Riding Club of Orange, which now has about 150 members and is flourishing. The club-house is in this Halstead Street front, and is commodious and pretty within. Its principal feature is that it is arranged for ladies as well as men; and its parlors, on the second floor, look out through a glass partition upon the riding hall. This arena or "riding ring" is 140 feet long by 92 wide, roofed by arches of a single span, filled with electric lights, and surrounded by galleries sufficient for several hundred spectators, having a music stand and communicating with the street by a driveway, and with the stables in the rear. Next door is the spacious cottage-like Athletic Club, whose grounds are near the railway station, where public as well as practice games and exercises of various kinds are often held. These two clubs often unite in athletic exhibitions and social entertainments, and form an active center for the fashionable life of these highly social communities, in which are the homes of so many wealthy men of business in New York. The amateur circus held here in April, 1896, will be remembered.

The next corner beyond Halstead brings us to **Brick Church**, one of the most important of the "Orange" centers. The railway station is one block to the left. This important nucleus in the teeming population of this region derives its name from the village church, remarkable then because of brick, erected long before the Revolution. The present edifice, also of brick, and on the same site, was erected in 1831 and rebuilt in 1878; its proper designation is, Second Presbyterian Church of Orange. Just beyond, the old Swinefield road, now called Washington Street, slants off toward the northwest through the ancient Tory Corners, and forms a straight road to Eagle Rock (p. 153). This highway, which leads on over to the Pompton Plains, was laid out as long ago as 1705. The yellow campanile and graceful architecture of Trinity Congregational Church, founded in 1870, but built in 1892, attracts attention on the left at the next street (Harrison Street —another name going back a century or more in local history), near the railway. Having passed the business center of Brick Church and descended the slope toward Orange proper (but it is continuous city from each of these centers to the other), we find the street suddenly widened and three rows of magnificent elms forming a park of the highway. Through this hollow originally ran Perro Brook. At the left is another Presbyterian church-building, of cut brownstone, half overgrown with vines. Then on the right comes the pretty Grace Church (Episcopal), and next to it the square, schoollike building of the Young Men's Christian Association, whose hall is a popular place for lectures and enterta.nments. On the left again, opposite this, stands the North Orange Baptist Church, of great size and highly ornate appearance. Just beyond it is the Windsor Hotel, and straight opposite McChesney's Park Hotel, both good houses, largely patronized in summer. This brings us to the business part of **Orange**, which includes some noticeably large and fine buildings, especially that occupied by the Orange National and the Half Dime Savings Banks. Music Hall and Davis' Restaurant are opposite. The railway station is one block at the left, down street, and the corner of this, the principal cross street (Day Street) is occupied by the old First Presbyterian Church.

☞ Along this cross street runs the *north-and-south electric line* of the Suburban Company, whose cars run from Chestnut Hill through Bloomfield and Orange to Highland Avenue and the cable road up the mountain. This cross-line might form part of a delightful round tour by trolley cars from Newark through the Oranges.

The cars continue straight on along Main Street, passing the Free Public Library on the corner of Essex Avenue, and the lofty St. Mark's Church a little farther on; then descend into the hollow where the biggest trees grow, and out past the terminus of the Orange branch of the New York & Greenwood Lake Railroad, to the foot of the hill, where it turns north through the newer part of the town, and sweeps along the eastern edge of *Llewellyn Park*, of whose beauties, however, little is seen.

GORDON -SOFT- POMMEL SADDLE

Construction: Steel Base; Seat, felt padded, and especially soft pommel; leather-covered top and bottom.

DOES NOT Chafe.
" " Lose its Shape.
" " Blow Up.
" " Get Hard.
" " Get Soft.
ALWAYS THE SAME.

Price, $3.25 each.

FOR COMFORT,
DURABILITY,
STYLE AND FINISH
THE GORDON
IS UNEQUALED.

ALL DEALERS; or sent prepaid to any address on receipt of price. Money refunded if unsatisfactory and returned prepaid within 10 days.

MADE BY

THE BECKLEY-RALSTON CO.
26 WEST BROADWAY, NEW YORK.

Smith's Roller Spring

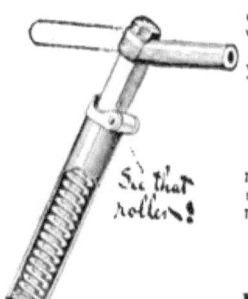

The Roller is of same importance to a Spring Seat Post as Balls are to a Hub or Ball-Bearing.

SEAT POST....

NO SQUEAK.   NO FRICTION.
NO VIBRATION.

ASSURES COMFORTABLE RIDING.

Sent PREPAID to any address on receipt of price. Returnable within 10 days if not satisfactory and money refunded.

GIVE SIZE WHEN ORDERING.

Price, $2.50 each.

JOS. N. SMITH & CO.
26 WEST BROADWAY,
NEW YORK.

Llewellyn Park is a private reservation (but any orderly person may wander through it) of about 800 acres, laid out in a grove with winding park-like roads, adapted to the primitive irregularities of the surface, whose knolls have been smoothed and occupied by the highly-cultivated grounds and costly houses of the various owners, while the hollows and glens have been left, as far as possible, in their natural condition. This was begun as early as 1852, so that now the whole forms one of the most princely and beautiful suburban localities in the world. It lies on the slope of First Mountain, just beneath the escarpment of basaltic rocks which form striking cliffs on each side of Eagle Rock, and it includes the site of the first house in all this part of the country. This first settler was a man named Smith, according to tradition. Soon after him Anthony Oliff "located" sixty acres there in 1678, and built a house just north of the stone bridge, where the present park roads, called Tulip Avenue and Oak Bend, intersect; and Tulip Avenue is laid out on the path to his house from the highway — Tony's Path, it was called by all the colonists for many years. His tombstone is the oldest one in the very interesting old burying-ground, which ought to be visited by every visitor to Orange who loves to recall the past.

The road and car tracks then bend toward the mountain, up the valley of the little Wagwan River, which rises at the foot of Eagle Rock and is the ultimate source, on this side the mountain, of Rahway River; and the line comes to an end at the cross-roads in *West Orange*. Just before reaching that point the Ridgehurst Road strikes off to the left. At this terminus of the track are two or three places where beer and luncheon may be obtained, and the Bramhall Park Hotel, a summer resort, which gives a regular dinner from 5.00 to 8.00 p. m., for 50 cents.

The cars to Eagle Rock pass this cross-roads-settlement just around the corner, and ascend the Wagwan Valley to the Rock, about ten minutes' ride. This line takes a more northerly route through West Orange than the Main Street line, connects with the Suburban Company's cross-line mentioned above, and returns to Main Street at the Orange railway station.

Eagle Rock is the name given to the gap in the mountain where several roads converge and pass over to the west. There are restaurants there, and the summit of the cliffs, here some 620 feet above the level of the sea, affords an exceedingly interesting view over all the Montclair Orange, and Newark region, the Rahway Valley, New York Harbor, and Staten Island, while New York City and the hills of Brooklyn are plainly visible on the horizon. The very highest point on the range is not here, however, but just north of the gap at the head of Bloomfield Avenue, in Montclair, three miles north, where you may climb to a bare pinnacle 665 feet in altitude.

From the West Orange car terminus the road at the left (Mount Pleasant Avenue) leads over the mountain to Mount Pleasant and St. Cloud, old-time settlements in the valley beyond, whence it is a lovely ride, or wheeling route, or walk of about four miles northeast to Verona and the notch in the mountain at the head of Bloomfield Avenue, above Montclair.

The Valley road, to the right from the car terminus, is continuous with Harrison Avenue, Montclair, and leads straight northward into that city. It is high, commanding pleasing outlooks, passes through wooded places, and enters Montclair along one of its finest streets. Keep upon it for about a mile to Union Street. Here, if you wish to climb the mountain, keep straight on; if not, turn down to the right one square to Fullerton Avenue, and then to the left a long square to *Bloomfield Avenue*. This gives a glimpse of Montclair's best houses and churches, and some of them are very fine. At the foot of this street, facing Bloomfield Avenue, Montclair's main thoroughfare, is the large, handsome house of the Montclair Club, one of the most complete and flourishing of suburban social associations. The Free Library has quarters close by.

Upward, toward the left, the old highway leads through a fine residential quarter to the pass in the mountain, and so west through Verona, Caldwell, Franklin, etc., in the Upper Passaic Valley; it is a beautiful drive northward through that notch to Cedar Grove and Little Falls (6 m. from Montclair Center), whence you may recross the mountain, through Great Notch, and return through Montclair Heights, Upper Montclair, and Watchung, having fine roads and a charming variety of rural and urban surroundings all the way.

Turning southeastward, or down from the Club House, Bloomfield Avenue is followed through the business part of Montclair, a quarter of a mile to the Lackawanna Railroad station, for Newark and Hoboken. There are no street cars in all this part of Montclair; but a half mile farther down the avenue, just beyond the railroad crossing, is the *terminus of the North Jersey Railroad's electric line*, which will carry you a mile farther to Glen Ridge and the Bloomfield line. The fare is 5 cents; but for 6 cents you may buy a ticket which entitles you to a transfer (by walking about 100 yards) to the trolley cars from Bloomfield to Newark (p. 149).

V.

CENTRAL AND SEASIDE NEW JERSEY.

The district included in this chapter is all the suburban region from Newark and the line of the Morris & Essex Railroad southward to the Raritan, and along the coast of Raritan and New York bays and the shore of the Atlantic within easy reach of New York. This region is mainly a plain, touching the hills only in its northwestern part, which rests against the Watchung Mountains; and that part of it abounds in good level roads, admirable for driving or bicycling; while the sandy region nearer the coast has been made accessible by at least one improved road, which affords excellent wheeling to all the maritime villages and seaside resorts. The principal bicycling routes are as follows:

BICYCLING ROUTES.

1. New York to Somerville.

From New York to Newark the wheeling is so bad, by whatever route one follows, that there is little pleasure in it; and the wheelman is advised to go by rail, unless it suits him to take the round-about route through Hackensack and Rutherford, from Fort Lee.

From the corner of Broad and Market streets, in Newark, which is the center of that city (and where the law requires all wheelmen to dismount), you go up Market Street one block to Halsey, turn south on Halsey (asphalt, save for a short distance) direct to Clinton Avenue. Turn to the right on Clinton Avenue one block to La Grange, then left to Pennsylvania Avenue, and right on that avenue to Wright, and right one block to Frelinghuysen Avenue, all asphalt; then turn to the south over a fine, level, macadamized path

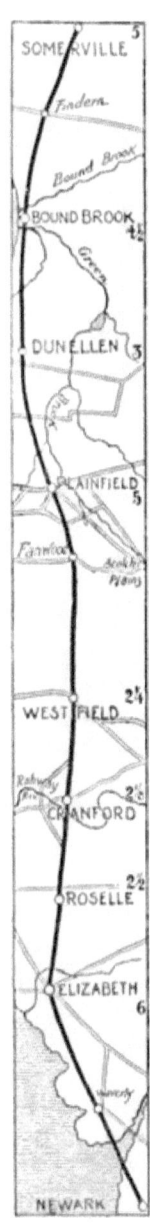

straight to Elizabeth. This is everybody's highway and crowded with traffic between the two cities, whose borders are scarcely separated by the diminishing marshes along Bound Creek and other trifling inlets to Newark Bay. Here go the electric cars and innumerable carts and beer wagons — special enemies of bicycles — and there is nothing to tempt us to slacken pace until this dusty highway has been left behind and the shady outskirts of Elizabeth are entered. The railway under which we dodge is the Lehigh Valley — the branch reaching across Newark Bay to Bayonne, and having its terminus on New York Harbor at Black Tom Island, below Communipaw. The parallel railroad at the left is the Pennsylvania Company's main line. Midway between the two cities are the State Fair Grounds at Waverly. *Elizabeth* is entered by Newark Avenue, which passes straight to the old town-center between rows of fine estates. After passing the railway stations bear to the left through Pennsylvania Avenue to Broad Street (6 m.). The Sheridan House, at the corner of Broad Street and Rahway Avenue, is the choice of the L. A. W., at $2.50 to $3. From Broad Street turn to the right into North Avenue, a broad, level, macadamized street of handsome houses, which leads directly to *Roselle* (2½ m. = 8½ m.), and through this pretty suburb to *Cranford* (2¼ m. = 10¾ m.). These are stations on the Central Railroad of New Jersey, and Cranford (hotel near the station) is astride the winding Rahway River. The tall spire belongs to a Presbyterian church, as is usual in this part of New Jersey. North Avenue keeps straight on, connecting villages so closely that it is difficult to tell where one stops and the other begins, until we reach *Westfield* (2¼ m. = 13 m.), where we leave it, turn to Broad Street, cross the tracks (Park Hotel, near the station), and take South Avenue — the first road to the right. This road is of fine macadam, and runs straight and parallel to the railroad through *Fanwood* and *Netherwood*. At the latter is a large summer hotel;

and here fine roads diverge to Scotch Plains (p. 161) and interesting upland localities to the west and north; and also southward to Perth Amboy. The grades along all this part of the route are very easy, and the scenery is that of a prosperous, long-cultivated countryside, with occasional pictures that we pause to study with pleasure, the Watchung or "Orange" Mountains forming an ever-present and pleasing background at the right. We enter Plainfield by Fifth Street and turn to the right into Park Avenue (5 m. = 18 m.). McVey's Hotel and restaurant, on North Avenue near the railroad station, is the L. A. W. headquarters ($1.50). The Revere House ($3), out Park Avenue, is also popular.

Plainfield is one of the larger and more beautiful of the suburban cities of New Jersey. Having had a steady growth of over two hundred years, it has accumulated wealth and conveniences of every sort, and its trees have had time to mature, making almost every street a shady park.

The streets are hard, smooth, and in good repair, furnishing excellent driving and wheeling all over the town, and out upon macadamized roads in all directions for many miles. Plainfield is mainly a city of homes, and a large proportion of its citizens go to New York daily. It has, however, many shops and stores, a public library and art gallery, an opera house, and other institutions for the pleasure and profit of the people. In the direction of outdoor sports much is done, here, in an organized way. The Union County Club has a fine clubhouse here, with an exceedingly attractive casino. The Park Club is a social organization of ladies and gentlemen, owning an elegant clubhouse, with tennis courts, etc., which pays much attention to outdoor sports, and holds the championship trophy of the American Whist League. The driving association has a fully equipped half-mile driving-track, where members match their fast horses each pleasant Saturday afternoon. There is also a riding academy sustained by the Riding Club (of ladies and gentlemen), which practices horsemanship and cavalry evolutions. The game of tennis is cultivated heartily by the Hillside Tennis Club, which has a clubhouse and spacious courts. Bicycling interests are led by the Crescent Wheelmen, who have a commodious house on Second Street; but there are three other smaller clubs, one of which is composed of young women. Another active club is that of the Y. M. C. A. Athletic Association, which also attends to track athletics, and has a gymnasium, bowling alley, etc., in its new building on the main street of the city—Springfield Avenue. Plainfield is one of the principal points on the New York to Philadelphia century-run, no matter what other variations of route are indulged; and on Sundays, in good weather, several hundred strangers may visit or pass through the town or their wheels. Electric cars run south as far as Dunellen.

☞ *For a pleasant excursion from Plainfield*—which is not only open to wheelmen, but to others—take the electric car marked "Somerville Street," and ride to its terminus at the foot of the hills west of the town, and then follow the straight road up Stony Brook through Washingtonville, passing the little Wetumpka Falls, and many other pretty bits of scenery by the way. Climbing on up the hill, you presently reach the *Washington Rock*. "The view from the rock," we are told, "is the widest and most agreeable to be had anywhere in the neighborhood. It may, or may not, be true that Washington used to go up there to study the movements of the British troops. As the British were out of sight from the rock it is very likely that he didn't. But if, as is more likely, he went up there to rest, and think, and enjoy the prospect, it speaks well for his taste. There is a green plain twenty miles wide, stretching away to the Kill, that cuts off Staten Island from the main land; and the Navesink Highlands, Statue of Liberty, and Brooklyn Bridge are in sight on a clear day." On the other side of the mountain lies *Washington Valley*, a region of broad farms and quiet, old hamlets, "where the fathers are still voting for Andrew Jackson"; and pleasant roads entice you to walk in many directions. Washingtonville is a village cross-roads, at the foot of the pass, and it is only four miles northeast to Scotch Plains, whence you may return to Plainfield by stage or go down to the railway station (1½ m.) at Fanwood; or make an interesting tramp across the hills to Morristown or Millburn.

Leaving Plainfield we turn to the left on Front Street and proceed direct to Dunellen. The road is level and has a good macadam surface, following the valley of Green Brook, and giving attractive views of the mountains at the right across a rolling country dotted with farms, while handsome villas line the way. We enter *Dunellen* on Main Street and draw up at the Park Hotel ($2), opposite the railroad station (3 m.=21m.). Quitting Dunellen we take the left fork, after crossing the little bridge. The road now becomes poor, it being sandy loam, barely ridable in good weather, but the lovely scenery compensates us for this discomfort; and presently we turn to the left by a road-house, then bear to the right and cross the bridge over Bound Brook. The road now improves, having a telford surface, and we enter the city of *Bound Brook* via Union Avenue, then turn to the left into Mountain Avenue which leads directly to Main Street (4½ m. =25½ m.). The Berkeley Hotel ($2) is opposite the station.

Bound Brook is more important as a railway junction than otherwise, but is a pretty village going back to early history, without any special present characteristics, except the periodical floods in the Raritan, which annually submerge a large part of the town. There is a good road down the river to New Brunswick (p. 160).

Leaving Bound Brook we keep on out Main Street — a clay pike and good riding — through a long, rolling ascent, at the summit of which we command a wide and beautiful landscape. The road improves as we pass through Findern. On the right, outlined against the rich green background of hills, stands Findern Hotel, a handsome structure of yellow brick, popular as a summer resort. Toward the left (southward) we enjoy pleasing glimpses of the Raritan, as it winds among the hills, and presently enter the quaint and quiet county town of Somerset — **Somerville** (5 m. = 30½ m.) — and halt at the Somerset House — the L. A. W. headquarters ($2).

2. Newark to Plainfield, through Orange.

Another route is outlined by an experienced rider as follows: Go out Market Street, Newark, to Halsey Street, turn to the right and run to Central Avenue, then to the left along that street to South Grove (3 m.). Turn to the right on South Grove to Park Avenue, *East Orange* (2 m. = 5 m.), and on to *Llewellyn Park* (1½ m. = 6½ m.), where you turn to the left and proceed through Orange to the Valley Hotel, in *South Orange* (1½ m. = 8 m.). Here you take the road to the right as far as the church, about a mile ahead, on the left of the road, where you turn to the left, cross the railroad, and, at Griffiths drug store (a short distance after crossing the tracks), turn to the right. This road leads to *Maplewood*, where a turn to the right is made, until *Millburn* is reached (3½ m. = 11½ m.). From Maplewood to Millburn is part of the celebrated Irvington-Millburn road. From Millburn keep to the left, to *Springfield*, then to the right, and at first turn, to the left again into an almost straight stretch of about eight miles, to *Scotch Plains* (9½ m. = 21 m.). From this village there is an almost straight run of five miles to Plainfield (5 m. = 26 m.). A part of this run passes through country described in Chapter IV, and other parts are further mentioned in Routes 1 and 3 of this chapter. It makes an excellent part of a round trip when combined with Route 1.

3. New Brunswick to Newark, via Springfield.

For the sake of making it more useful as a part of a round trip in connection with other bicycle routes, we give this run toward, instead of from, New York, as usual.

Leaving **New Brunswick** at the Mansion House, we wheel up Albany Street into George Street, passing on the right the fine buildings of Rutgers College, and turn to the right onto College Avenue, skirting the campus, then keep directly down the hill to the river road. From the hilltop we have an extended view of the Raritan

River and valley hemmed in by wooded heights beyond, then turn to the left onto the river road skirting the canal, with the river below, half a mile to Raritan Landing, when we turn to the right by the mill, cross the canal, and then the long bridge over the river, from which we may enjoy a splendid view of this beautiful and historic stream in both directions. After crossing the bridge we turn to the left, by a fine old homestead nestling in a bower of trees on the steep hillside to the right, and follow the river bank. The roadbed is of red loam which makes a fine riding-surface in good weather, but is apt to be very sticky and heavy after a rain, or somewhat dusty in very dry seasons.

Upward on the right rise huge rocky bluffs, the red sandstone cropping out in a myriad of fantastic shapes, here and there a tiny stream trickles down over its time-worn bed, while scraggy trees and low bushes cling tenaciously to the scanty turf and thrust their roots into the rocky crevices to strengthen their precarious tenure. On the left lies the river, calm and peaceful under the summer sun, bordered with green trees and water-brush, and shadowed by the low, irregular wooded hill rising on its farther shore.

We cross an old stone bridge under which a stream rushes down from a rock-bound glen on the right to the river below. The road winds back inland, and then bears again to the left to the riverbank. Several old farmhouses, bearing evidence of many a season's weather marks, stand along the roadway, and broad fields of grain wave gently in the summer breeze. Beyond the peaceful breadth of the river we see the canal, closely following the outline of the bank, and watch restfully the lazy plodding tow-mules dragging the coal-barges that steal with ghostly silence across the picture. Inland again swings the roadway, now through a redolent pine grove, now between ancestral fields, soon to return again to the river's brink and skirt a high bluff overhung by stunted cedars. We now swerve to the right as the road forks under the railroad tracks, then to the left again a third of a mile, and again to the right under the tracks, and turn to the left into Main Street, *Bound Brook*, to the Berkeley Hotel, $2, on the square opposite the railroad station (7¼ m. from New Brunswick).

☞ For the road to Newark from here, via Plainfield, see Route 1.

Continuing from Bound Brook northward, we turn up the first street beyond the hotel—Mountain Avenue. This gives us a stiff climb to Union Avenue, when we turn to the right onto a good macadam roadway, which very soon gives away to a sandy red loam pike. We cross the bridge over Bound Brook, and go straight on to the cross-road, then turn to the right by the *road-house* over the worst bit of road on the trip, hardly ridable even in good weather. The scenery, however, is very charming. Broad meadow lands stretch northward to the mountains, while on our right the landscape is a pretty commingling of meadow, wood, and hill. We keep to the right at the next fork, and bear directly into Main Street, *Dunellen*, following the trolley tracks directly to the Park Hotel ($2) on the depot square (4½ m. = 11¾ m.). Leaving Dunellen we keep directly out Main Street over a surface of smooth macadam, with charming views of the mountains on the left, directly into Front Street, *Plainfield* (3 m. = 14¾ m.; p. 157). Continuing straight out Front Street (the city name of Springfield Avenue) we pass along one of the oldest and most perfect roads in New Jersey, between the beautifully kept country places of city men to the center of the ancient and attractive village of *Scotch Plains* at Emery's Hotel (2½ m. = 17¼ m.).

Scotch Plains is in the midst of a very pleasant and enjoyable country. It lies at the foot of the mountain in the opening of a gorge that contains the sources of Green Brook, between hills rising 350 feet above the plain; and it abounds in mementos of a long and interesting past.

Proceeding on our way, we turn to the left at the hotel, and then to the right beyond the red brick church. The road is broad and level, and lies up a depression along the base of the mountains and hills, ever increasing on the right. Presently we come to and pass by the beautiful estate of Warren Ackerman, and wheel through a cool avenue of broad-leaved maples ; now through broad fields, dotted with masses of flowering weeds and low bushes, the distant hills a mass of green and furzy coverts, clusters of evergreens prettily diversifying the deciduous shrubbery. The road winds in and out among low hills, until, as it swings to the right through a cut in the hillside, we emerge at a junction, where a branch road from Westfield comes in from the south. Here a wee box-like structure, painted bright yellow, attracts everybody's notice; it is the United States Post Office of *Baltusrol*, and the famous golf links are near by. We bear onward toward the left, through low hills, and gradually descend into meadow lands studded with the neat farms of *Locust Grove*. The Westfield road leads south, and a road strikes off west across Washington Valley to Feltville, and over to the

Passaic at New Providence. On we go along the highway through hilly rural scenes, run smoothly over a little stretch of macadam, halt a moment at "The House that Jack Built," and wheel into *Springfield* (6¾m.=24m.), where we alight at the Springfield Hotel ($1.50). Here comes in Route 2.

Leaving Springfield we turn to the right by the hotel onto Main Street, and a quarter of a mile farther take the left fork (Springfield Avenue) on through the towns of Hilton and Irvington. The surface is smooth macadam, the country rolling, and the surroundings interesting. Irvington is really a suburb of Newark, and is the terminus of an electric road. Leaving Irvington take the right fork, Clinton Avenue, of good macadam direct to Halsey Street, left to Market Street, Newark. A short stretch of block pavement is encountered on Clinton Avenue as you enter the city, but is succeeded by asphalt.

This route is not only very interesting for what one sees, but for its memorable associations, since it passes through a region identified with some of the most stirring and creditable history of the revolutionary struggle.

It was along this old road through Scotch Plains and Springfield that Washington's army advanced, after the victories at Trenton and Princeton had enabled him to resume the offensive against the British; and he kept it open as his line of communication between the Northern and the Southern colonies during all the war, in spite of the efforts of the enemy. None of these attempts were more vigorous than during the winter of 1780, when Washington's troops were in winter-quarters at Morristown, and Springfield was an outpost guarding the camps against attack. Staten Island was then covered with British camps under the command of the Hessian general, Knyphausen, who chafed at the annoyance given him by patriot raiders, and who was taught to believe that so much discontent was rife in the American army that the people of New Jersey were desirous of returning to their allegiance to the British crown. To make an opportunity for them to do so, Knyphausen determined to invade that State, and on June 6, 1780, crossed over to Elizabethtown with an army of 5,000 men. From this place he marched toward Springfield, by way of Connecticut Farms, where he halted. "Before reaching that place, however," to quote *Clute's Annals of Staten Island*, "he discovered that the reports of disaffection among the people were entirely without foundation; . . . the hostile demonstrations of the people were more decided than ever; out of every ditch, from every hedgerow, from behind every tree in orchard or forest, in the line of his march, he was met by the leaden messengers of death. . . . The German general's disappointment was not only great, but he was exasperated to such a degree that he caused the village, with its church, to be burned, before he attempted

A STREET IN SHREWSBURY, N. J.

The Road to Joy

Has been found by millions of cyclists who use

HALF-SIZE

3 in One

It prolongs the life of wheels, guns, typewriters, etc., and makes them work smoothly.

An Ideal Lubricant

Because it never will gum.

A Positive Rust Preventive

For all nickel and steel parts.

A Thorough Cleaner

Which cuts away dirt and gives a brilliant lustre.

ASK YOUR DEALER FOR IT.

SAMPLE BOTTLE FREE.

SEND TWO-CENT STAMP FOR POSTAGE.

G. W. COLE & CO.

.......111 BROADWAY, NEW YORK.

to retrace his steps. The minister's wife, who had remained at home, supposing that her sex would be her protection, was deliberately shot through a window; permission, however, was graciously given to remove the body before burning the house. This cold-blooded murder of Mrs. Cauldwell produced a thrill of horror throughout the country, and no act of British brutality more excited the indignation and hatred of the people than this."

4. To Long Branch, Asbury Park, etc.

A bicycle tour to the seashore resorts of the New Jersey coast may be made in five ways, namely:

1. By wheeling the whole distance, via New Brunswick.
2. By rail to New Brunswick or Matawan and wheeling.
3. By steamer to Keyport and wheeling.
4. By steamer to Red Bank and wheeling.
5. By steamer to Atlantic Highlands and wheeling.

The consideration of the course of the first route will enable us to include all the others as they join it.

From New York to New Brunswick a route may be chosen from those already outlined within the last few pages.

From New Brunswick to the coast the good wheeling road strikes southeast to Old Bridge, or Herbertsville, where it crosses Matchaponix Creek, near its junction with Deep Run to form South River (6 m.).

☞ There is a sort of road between this place and South Amboy, but it is almost unridable, and no bridge spans the Raritan at the Amboys, except the railroad bridges, consequently no practicable route for cycling exits between Perth Amboy and the seacoast.

From Old Bridge the road, which is macadamized but rather hilly, takes a curving course to the eastward up Deep Run, through a pleasant country and past the hamlet called Browntown, to *Matawan* — a flourishing village that has grown up at the head of navigation on Matawan Creek, and around the crossing of the railway from Amboy to Long Branch with that from Keyport to Freehold.

☞ *To Freehold* (about 8 m.) a road runs nearly due south, accompanied by the railroad. It passes through Mount Pleasant, Wickatunk, and Marlboro. At Wickatunk is the burying-ground of the old Scots Church, built by the Scotchmen who were wrecked at South Amboy in the ship *Caledonia* about 1687. Beacon Hill, 385 feet high, is two miles northeast. Marlboro is so called, not after the English noble family, but because here was first used the famous marl whose presence in great amount in this part of the State gave Monmouth County the leading place in productiveness. *Freehold* has been the county seat of Monmouth since 1715, and is a beautiful little town, steadily growing and becoming more and more attractive. It is chiefly as an historical locality, however, that Freehold interests the stranger, for the *Battle of Monmouth*, one of the most important of the War for Independence, was fought here on June 28, 1778. The British commander, Clinton, having abandoned Philadelphia, was attempting to march his army to the ships inside of Sandy Hook and thus transport it to New York. Washington successfully endeavored to intercept him, and the armies met three miles west of here, where Clinton was marching along the road to Middletown. The Americans attacked fiercely, and a series of skirmishes followed, until finally a considerable body of troops were gradually brought face to face, when Lee ordered a retreat, which Washington managed to stop in time to save his lines, at the same time berating Lee, who was afterward convicted of treason by a court martial. Finding that they must fight, the British commanders sent in their best men, but failed to break the American line, and were glad when night enabled them to take their shattered army away to safety amid the Navesink Highlands. The importance of this battle — in which, among other thrilling incidents, occurred the episode of Molly Pitcher, and the death of Colonel Monckton — was the invigorating moral effect it had upon a weak and discouraged country, and the confidence it gave the patriots in their ability to stand up before the well-fed and disciplined regiments of Great Britain. The battle-ground is easily visited; and a monument has been erected upon it. *The old Tennent Church*, which was Washington's base of operations, and in whose cemetery are buried many who fell in the battle, is still there; and the whole neighborhood abounds in historical mementos. A very pleasant, but rather difficult, road may be followed from Freehold to Red Bank.

This stage of the journey from New Brunswick terminates three miles north of Matawan on the shore of the bay at Keyport.

Keyport to Red Bank.— Coming from New York by steamboat to Keyport — interesting only as a fishing place — the cycler would have time to run down to Freehold over the turnpike through Matawan that night, if he wished; or could make his way as far as Red Bank before halting for the night. The road from Keyport to Red Bank is a graveled turnpike, hard, smooth, and fairly level, and eleven miles in length. It is the continuation of Main Street, and, at the outskirts of Keyport, bends to the left (eastward). Half a mile farther it is joined by Atlantic Street and two cross-roads; and a little beyond forks prominently. Take the left (turnpike) branch.

☞ *The right-hand branch* leads south by a fairly ridable road through Hazlet to Crawford's Corners (about 2½ m.), and thence eastwardly by a wild and hilly road south of Oak Hill to Red Bank (8½ m. = 11 m.).

The turnpike continues nearly due east to New Monmouth, half

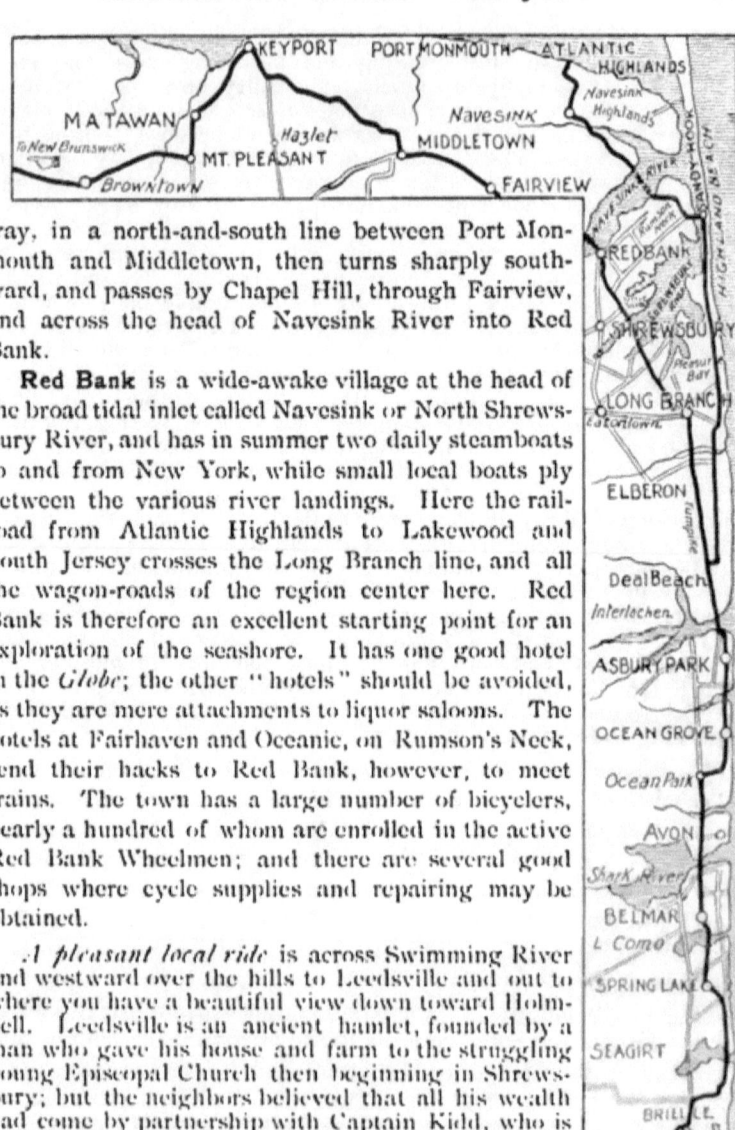

way, in a north-and-south line between Port Monmouth and Middletown, then turns sharply southward, and passes by Chapel Hill, through Fairview, and across the head of Navesink River into Red Bank.

Red Bank is a wide-awake village at the head of the broad tidal inlet called Navesink or North Shrewsbury River, and has in summer two daily steamboats to and from New York, while small local boats ply between the various river landings. Here the railroad from Atlantic Highlands to Lakewood and South Jersey crosses the Long Branch line, and all the wagon-roads of the region center here. Red Bank is therefore an excellent starting point for an exploration of the seashore. It has one good hotel in the *Globe*; the other "hotels" should be avoided, as they are mere attachments to liquor saloons. The hotels at Fairhaven and Oceanic, on Rumson's Neck, send their hacks to Red Bank, however, to meet trains. The town has a large number of bicyclers, nearly a hundred of whom are enrolled in the active Red Bank Wheelmen; and there are several good shops where cycle supplies and repairing may be obtained.

A pleasant local ride is across Swimming River and westward over the hills to Leedsville and out to where you have a beautiful view down toward Holmdell. Leedsville is an ancient hamlet, founded by a man who gave his house and farm to the struggling young Episcopal Church then beginning in Shrewsbury; but the neighbors believed that all his wealth had come by partnership with Captain Kidd, who is credited with retreats and treasure burials along these coasts, as in so many other places. Another interesting memory of Leedsville is that, for many years, it was the abode of a large community of philosophical enthusiasts, who practiced the form of socialism taught by Fourier. This was a "phalanx" similar to that more famous, if less successful, one, at Brook Farm, and tried in Pike County, N. Y., and elsewhere. It had great material as well as social success and happiness for a time; but after a few years the shrewdest men saw that they were carrying many incapables, and declined to continue to bear indefinitely an unequal burden; the phalanx therefore went to pieces. The buildings remain, and the people of the neighborhood tell interesting stories of the ideas and methods of these kindly communists.

Rumson Neck, the peninsula between the Navesink and Shrewsbury rivers, affords the best riding near Red Bank, however, for it contains some of the best roads in New Jersey. One of these skirts the south shore of the Navesink, through the summer port of Fairhaven to Oceanic, where the Navesink is bridged. Here comes in the road from Atlantic Highlands, which zigzags through the hills from that port. It is thence a short ride to the eastern extremity of the neck, where the river is bridged into Seabright. This bridge is at the extremity of the *Rumson road*—a broad, smooth avenue running along the south shore of the neck, between fine country seats, to Little Silver, one of the most picturesque of the shore villages, near the head of Shrewsbury River. An excellently paved road runs straight from Red Bank to Little Silver and the Rumson road; and from Little Silver across Parker's Creek to Pleasure Bay, Long Branch village, and the Long Branch shore, so that several good roads combine to form pleasant round-trip runs between Red Bank and the shore towns. Rumson Neck also has excellent cross-roads, which offer charming views, and it is probably the most attractive and highly cultivated district in this whole region, and the favorite driving ground of summer residents in Long Branch and Elberon. It has been the scene, in the past, of a vast deal of stirring history, which everyone should familiarize himself with, since rambling around these old roads brings one to many a place and object that "might a tale unfold."

The Main Road to the South from Red Bank leads out Broad Street, and straight on through Old Shrewsbury to Eatontown. This is a turnpike and usually in fine condition. At *Shrewsbury* it is crossed by the Rumson road, continued to Tinton Falls, a very pretty place, full of colonial traditions, 2½ miles west.

Shrewsbury is the most fascinating village in all Central New Jersey. Gigantic trees shade its antiquated houses and venerable churches, and arch over its four historic highways. "This little town

HIGH CLASS,

SUPERB FINISH,

EASY RUNNING,

EASY STEERING,

ROYAL BLUE.

The Napoleon •
A Man's Wheel.

• The Josephine
A Woman's Wheel.

They are built to please the fastidious.

• • •

Write for Catalog.

• • •

JENKINS CYCLE CO.,
18-20 Custom House Place, CHICAGO.

• • •

NEW YORK AGENCY: BROOKLYN AGENCY:
C. A. NELSON,   DOWN & FLEET,
8 GRAND CIRCLE.   1191 BEDFORD AVENUE.

was settled in 1664 by a number of immigrants from Shrewsbury in England, several of whom had tried Connecticut and Long Island. The Quakers were the first to organize there, and eight years after the settlement George Fox visited them. . . . George Keith, a famous convert from Quakerism to the Church of England, came there in 1702, and drew a number of the Friends into the Episcopalian meetings, of which there are records dating back to 1689. . . . The present picturesque shingled edifice was built in 1769. Bullets riddled the walls of its belfry when the patriots shot at the crown on the spire. . . . Queen Anne gave the communion silver that is used there. Opposite the old church building is an ancient dwelling, which also has a place in history. It was the scene of the massacre of some continental soldiers by Tory refugees." The Quaker Meetinghouse was built in 1816, replacing one dating from 1695. Library Hall, near by, is the building where formerly the Orthodox Friends worshiped. The Presbyterian Church opposite the Friends' Meetinghouse is comparatively modern (1821, enlarged in 1845), but its predecessor dates back to a century before it. This is only a suggestion of the historical lore to be gathered in this locality.

Eatontown is a place nearly as old, but its traditions are of seafaring men rather than of farmers and preachers. Stories of Captain Kidd are rife, and more trustworthy legends of privateering during the Revolution. The most interesting object here is the extremely picturesque old gristmill on the creek, which was built in 1780, but stands upon the site, and is fed by the pond, of mills first set going there more than a century before.

From Eatontown the road leads straight eastward, passing both the old and the new Monmouth Park race courses, and going through Oceanport (long ago a prosperous seaport), and Long Branch village to Broadway in Long Branch. At Long Branch village, however, you may turn to the right and run straight down the old turnpike, a fair road for cycling, to *Elberon*, a wealthier and more exclusive settlement than even the West End of Long Branch, and which will ever be memorable because it was the summer home of President Grant and of President Garfield, the latter when dying from an assassin's wounds. Here Ocean Avenue may be said to end, and wheelmen who have come down the shore turn inland and go on along the turnpike. The next settlement — also a wealthy colony of private houses — is *Deal Beach*, a name that goes back to the seventeenth century. The long narrow pond here is Deal Lake, and the settlement along its northern shore is now called Loch Arbour. It was opposite here that the dreadful wreck of the *New Era* occurred in 1854, when over 500 emigrants lost their lives. Deal Lake divides inland into two prongs, between which lies *Interlaken*. Here the lake is crossed by a wagon bridge, and its southern end admits the traveler to **Asbury Park**, where he may turn to the left and go around by the beach, or turn to the right and pursue his way straight through the town and on southward without detour or interruption.

The course outlined above has been inland and direct from Red Bank; but if the rider prefers to move along the beach he will find in **Ocean Avenue** a magnificent road, which in summer is thronged with carriages and wheelmen, extending from the heel of Sandy Hook to Elberon, and represented by beach roads through all the shore towns southward, though frequently interrupted by inlets.

The northernmost place to which Ocean Avenue extends is *Highland Beach*, where a bridge crosses the mouth of the Shrewsbury to Navesink Highlands. Some maps indicate a first-class road between this point and Atlantic Highlands; but none that is ridable for bicycles now exists. Navesink Beach is the name of the shore about Life-Saving Station 3. Then comes Normandie, followed by Rumson Beach. These are park-like communities of private owners, who discourage excursionists and idle visitors of all kinds. *Seabright* has a similar exclusiveness, but is older and more numerous in population. Here is a drawbridge across the Shrewsbury, connecting the Rumson and Atlantic Highlands roads with the beach. South of Seabright, Low Moor and Galilee are the names of the railway stations for a continuous line of cottages, extending on to where the strip of shore land broadens out toward Pleasure Bay. Here is the elegant settlement of *Monmouth Beach*, consisting of handsome summer homes scattered about lawns created with extraordinary pains and care, and having only the pretty Episcopal Church of St. Peter of Galilee, an elegant clubhouse, and a picturesque railway station, as public buildings.

Long Branch begins a mile further down, and in place of the studied privacy of the shore villages above, there is now an equally studied publicity. The show begins at the foot of Broadway, where the roads from the interior and the electric railway approach the beach. A block below is the iron steamboat pier, and here are clusters of summer stores, bathing places, candy shops, liquor saloons, and what not, reaching around the corner on the street that leads to the railway station. The white cottage of the Ocean Club, standing amid half an acre of flower-beds, will next attract admiration; and then follow two big but ugly hotels and half a mile of cottages, in which the gig-saw and paint-brush have worked unrestrained. They face the road and look across it to the sea through an endless glare, for there is not a tree or shrub to break the rays of the sun or relieve the eye. Iauch's, the United States, and some other large hotels break the line of private houses down to the southern part of Long Branch proper, which is known as *West End*, not because it is either the end of or west of anything in particular, but because that sounds well—the only principle in view along this coast, where Long Branch and Deal Beach are the only historic designations, and Navesink Beach and Shark River the only really appropriate ones, in the whole list. Here the scene is dominated by the huge West End Hotel, whose cornices are supported upon square posts, reaching clear from the ground, in the fashion of fifty years ago. It has a bridge crossing Ocean Avenue to a large pavilion overhanging the beach, where, in the season, music, flirtation, and the sipping of beverages go on *ad libitum*. Just here the shore road bends inward a few rods, and on the south side of it, is a large annex to the hotel, beyond which stands the white, gilt-topped, flower-decked cottage of the Pennsylvania Club. North of the West End is the Howland House, and in its rear the Casino, an amusement institution. Turning south from the West End, you glide imperceptibly into the streets of Elberon, where every house is worth a fortune, and then turning to the right, reach the turnpike that leads directly to Asbury Park.

Asbury Park affords good riding upon nearly all of its streets, and possesses a great army of cyclers in summer, whose headquarters, probably, is the clubhouse of the Asbury Park Wheelmen.

Ocean Grove also offers plenty of good riding roads, and you may follow the beach down for a long distance, or, if you prefer, go straight along Main Street, due south from Asbury Park, for some miles. This will carry you along the inner edge of a succession of shore villages and resorts—Ocean Grove, Bradley Beach, Neptune City, Ocean Park, and Avon, coming rapidly one after the other to the bank of *Shark River*. This is a salt-water lagoon, narrow at its inlet, but expanding inwardly, and forming a place of deservedly high repute for boating and fishing. This river is bridged, and upon its southern bank, near the inlet, is the large summer town *Belmar*. Thence the good road continues southward along the turnpike through Como, Spring Lake, *Sea Girt*, Manasquan, and Brielle, on Manasquan River, and *Point Pleasant*, to *Bay Head*, below which are the lagoons of Barnegat Bay.

RAILROAD AND STEAMBOAT ROUTES.

1. Pennsylvania Railroad.

This magnificent line of railroad runs from Jersey City across the State to Trenton, and also penetrates the suburban territory by its Long Branch line from Monmouth Junction, and its coöperation with the Central of New Jersey in certain seashore traffic. Its splendid station, at the foot of Montgomery Street, Jersey City, is reached by handsome double-decked ferry boats from Desbrosses and Cortlandt streets, New York, and from Fulton Street, Brooklyn; and it runs beautiful trains at short intervals as far, at least, as New Brunswick. These pass through a gap in Bergen Ridge at Marion, and straight across the Hackensack Meadows beside the ancient turnpike. This was the first line of rails laid across the meadows, and was completed in 1837. It passes through *Newark*, accommodation trains stopping in succession at Centre Street, Market Street (the central station), and Chestnut Street. Then it takes a straight course southward past Waverly to *Elizabeth*, where the line crosses the town and the tracks of the Central Railroad of New Jersey upon a lofty viaduct. The next station, Linden, is half way to *Rahway*, which is an attractive village in the valley of the Rahway River, and in the midst of a lovely bicycling region, for the district is level and abounds in excellent roads. One of these is a direct route south along the coast to Perth Amboy; another is the macadamized Westfield road, which leads west and north up the valley through Westfield and Montclair to Millburn and the Oranges. On the further edge of the town the Perth Amboy branch leads off to the left. Houtenville and Iselin (whence there is a good road to Woodbridge and Sewaren, on the shore of Staten Island Sound) are small stations, followed by Menlo Park. Next comes the rural station of *Metuchen*, from which there is a straight macadamized road across to Perth Amboy east, and Plainfield west, and a very attractive country for rambling. Five miles more brings one to the Raritan, which is crossed upon a high bridge, giving a picturesque view of this river, the Delaware & Raritan Canal, and the pleasant old town of *New Brunswick*. Rutgers College is in plain view on the right; and, beyond, the train proceeds through a farming region to *Monmouth Junction*, where a branch line for Long Branch and the coast strikes off. Then follows *Princeton Junction*, whence a short branch leads up to the famous college town, whose towers are visible on the hilltop three miles north; and ten miles beyond that is Trenton (60 m.), where the line crosses the Delaware into Pennsylvania. **Trenton** is an extremely interesting city for a day's visit; and the Trenton House, which is centrally located and well furnished and managed, enables one to be comfortable while there. An excellent excursion would be to go to Trenton by train and return by cycle through Princeton to New Brunswick, and then home by Routes 1 or 3, by the excellent road, originally the "King's Highway," which follows the line of the Pennsylvania Railroad to Jersey City.

2. Central Railroad of New Jersey.

The Central Railroad of New Jersey owns the principal lines into this suburban district. Its ferry station in New York is at the foot of Liberty Street, one block below Cortlandt, and its station in Jersey City is amid the marshes of Communipaw.

The main line runs down the shore of New York Bay to Bergen Point, with stations every mile or two, and then crosses Newark Bay upon a very long, pile bridge to Elizabethport and *Elizabeth*, where its station is just beneath that of the Pennsylvania Railroad in the center of the city. It then takes a straight southwesterly course through the beautiful country described in Bicycle Route 1 (p. 155), with stations at El Mora, Lorraine, *Roselle*, Aldene, *Cranford*, Garwood, *Westfield*, Graceland, *Fanwood*, Netherwood (hotel), *Plainfield*, Grant Avenue, Clinton Avenue, Dunellen, and *Bound Brook*. Here the line divides, the main stem striking west through Somerville to Easton and the Delaware Valley; while the line to Philadelphia diverges southward.

The Atlantic **Coast Line** of the Central Railroad of New Jersey diverges from the main line at *Elizabethport*, and runs down the flat shore of Staten Island Sound to *Perth Amboy*, passing through the new summer-residence village of *Sewaren*, where the Sewaren Improvement Company have brought to the notice of persons seeking a suburban home a beautiful area of shore, easily accessible and offering all sorts of aquatic pleasures for one's leisure moments. A large and comfortable hotel stands on the shore of Staten Island Sound; and many fine houses are clustered between it and the railway. From Perth Amboy the Raritan is crossed by a drawbridge to South Amboy, where the road turns to the east and runs along the marshy shore of Raritan Bay, with an occasional glimpse of blue water, and now and then a sight of some fisherman's hut and gear to break the monotony of salt marsh and sand dune. *Matawan* is the first station of any importance. Here passengers change cars for Keyport (which may also be reached by horse car), Atlantic Highlands, and Freehold (p. 163). Hazlet and Middletown are small stations before reaching *Red Bank*. From here onward the railroad follows substantially the bicycle route already described, with stations at Little Silver, Branchport, *Long Branch, West End, Elberon, Deal Beach*, Interlaken, North Asbury Park, *Asbury Park and Ocean Grove*, Bradley Beach, Avon, *Belmar*, Como, Spring Lake, *Sea Girt*, Manasquan, Brielle, *Point Pleasant*, and the terminus at Bay Head.

It should be noted that Asbury Park is also the station for Ocean Grove; and that on Sunday no trains stop either way at Bradley Beach, Asbury Park, or North Asbury Park, though they may be taken at Avon or Interlaken, a quarter of a mile outside the Sabbatical limits.

The Sandy Hook Route consists of a service of steamers, which run at the highest speed seen on New York Bay, from the foot of Rector Street to *Atlantic Highlands* — a landing on the mainland just inside of Sandy Hook, and the northern terminus of the old New Jersey Southern Railroad. It has a large summer population housed in hotels and cottages. Railways connect this station with Matawan and Freehold to the west, and eastward with Navesink Highlands, Sandy Hook Beach, and the shore villages and hotels north of Long Branch. Southward the trains follow the old Southern tracks through Chapel Hill and across the Navesink Hills to Red Bank, and then on through Shrewsbury and Eatontown, where they turn somewhat westerly into the pine woods and take a straight course through Pine Brook, Shark River, and Farmingdale (crossing of the Pennsylvania Railroad's line to Sea Girt) to *Lakewood* and Southern New Jersey.

The newest enterprise in this region is the opening of a tract for summer homes on the slope of the Navesink Highlands overlooking the entrance to Shrewsbury River, and about half a mile from the ocean at Highland Beach. It is named Water Witch Park, has a large hotel, a club, and residents of social prominence who propose to make one of the best seaside parks.

3. The Lehigh Valley Railroad.

This railroad takes very little part in the suburban business of the metropolis, since its line pursues a rather out-of-the-way course, striking no suburban towns conveniently until Metuchen is reached. It has one specialty, however, in the form of cheap excursions to

Mauch Chunk, Pennsylvania. As this is a very interesting coal mining and iron smelting town, in the heart of the mountains, and as the whole journey thither is through an extremely picturesque country, these excursions are largely and wisely patronized by those who can ill afford to go pleasure traveling at ordinary rates. This company uses the stations of the Pennsylvania Railroad.

4. Electric Lines.

The electric lines in this district are not so connected and useful for suburban travel as in the district northward.

From Jersey City to Bergen Point an electric line follows Avenue C, on the center of the ridge, and terminates at the ferry to Port Richmond; but there is nothing to see but dusty streets and commonplace houses from one end of it to the other.

From Jersey City to Newark an electric line from the Pennsylvania station and ferry follows Grand Street and Communipaw Avenue over the Greenville Ridge to the Hackensack Meadows, and then runs along the old *Plank road* and through the manufacturing district of Newark along the Passaic River to Market and Broad streets. The fare from any point in Jersey City to any point in Newark by this line is 15 cents; but a passenger is entitled to the benefit of all transfers in each city. The trip is a very dreary one.

The Turnpike Line is another route of electric cars to Newark. This goes out Newark Avenue and past the court house to the old Bergen village "five corners," where civilization began on Bergen Ridge, whence it descends to the Hackensack River, in Marion. This ride is rather more interesting than that over the Plank road, but is by no means amusing.

To South Orange a line runs out South Orange Avenue from Newark past Fairmount Cemetery and the Schuetzen Park, and through a sparsely built district around the Roman Catholic College, Seton Hall; but the trip is uninteresting. This road is continuing on northward along the base of the mountain to West Orange, where it connects with inclined cable road up the mountain and the Orange local lines.

To Irvington a line runs straight out from Newark along Springfield Avenue; and another out Clinton Avenue approaches Irvington; but neither forms an interesting excursion, though the former sets you well on your way toward an interesting country, beyond, about Springfield, etc.

To Elizabeth a line from Newark follows a rather circuitous course as far as Waverly, whence it runs straight to the railway station in Elizabeth. Here a branch line goes out to Lyon's Farms at the end of North Broad Street, and another line into the residence district of North Elizabeth, between the Pennsylvania Railroad and the water. The cars continue out South Broad Street to the end of that street, which contains about all of interest Elizabeth has to show, for this town retains less than almost any other, except Newark, of the signs of its antiquity and honorable history. A branch line runs out West Jersey Avenue to El Mora, and forms the beginning of a through line, which sometime, no doubt, will connect the towns as far as Plainfield at least.

To Elizabethport goes a branch down Third Avenue from near the City Hall. This, with a smaller horse-car line, reaches the Central Railroad station, and serves the needs of that manufacturing quarter of the city, where life centers in the sewing-machine factories. It would not interest readers of this book, except for the fact that, before the close of 1897, a ferry having been put into operation across the strait to Staten Island, and the Staten Island electric railroads extended westward to Howland Hook, and thus connected with the trolley lines of New Jersey, there will be put into running order a continuous rapid-transit route between Newark and South and Midland beaches.

Local Lines are found in Plainfield, Rahway, New Brunswick, Perth Amboy, and between Keyport and Matawan.

On the Seashore electric lines now run from Broadway, in the northern edge of Long Branch, southward along the general course of the steam railroad to Asbury Park, where a local system of tracks surrounds and crosses the town. Fare, 15 cents. From Asbury Park southward an electric line follows Main Street straight south to Belmar. Fare, 5 cents. This is the beginning of a proposed system which shall extend from Tom's River to Red Bank, or some port north of there.

Steamboats to New Jersey Ports.

To New Brunswick.—The steamer *New Brunswick* makes a daily round trip from New Brunswick to New York and return. She leaves her wharf at the foot of Harrison Street at 3.00 p. m., and reaches New Brunswick soon after 6.00 p. m. The fare is 50 cents, and no charge is made for a bicycle accompanying a passenger. The course is down the harbor, through the Kill von Kull, and then down through the windings of Staten Island Sound, stopping at Chelsea, Rossville, Boynton Beach, and other places. The handsome houses and large summer hotel at Sewaren, below Rossville, will be admired. Then a stop is made at Tottenville, S. I., after which the steamer crosses to Perth Amboy, then over to South Amboy, and then takes its course up the Raritan River to New Brunswick. This is one of the pleasantest boating experiences open to the New Yorker.

To Keyport.—The steamers *Minnie*, *Cornell*, and *Holmdel* make a daily trip between New York (foot of Vesey Street) and Keyport, N. J., leaving New York at 4.00 p. m. Fare, 30 cents; no charge for bicycles with passengers. These boats ascend the river to Matawan.

To Atlantic Highlands.—Central Railroad of New Jersey's train boats from the foot of Rector Street.

To Red Bank, etc.—Steamers *Sea Bird* and *Albertina* from the foot of Franklin Street, daily to the Navesink River, stopping at Highlands, Highland Beach, Oceanic, Locust Point, Brown's Dock, and Fairhaven, and ending the voyage at Red Bank. Fare, 50 cents. No charges for bicycle accompanying through passengers. This is a very pretty trip, and an excellent method of going to the coast, for wheelmen.

To Long Branch, etc. (Inside.)—The steamers *Elberon* and *Pleasure Bay* make daily trips from the foot of Jane Street to ports on the Shrewsbury River, stopping at Fort Hamilton, Seabright, Long Branch, and Pleasure Bay. Fare, 50 cents.

The possibilities for enjoyment held out by an excursion on any one of these boats are gracefully set forth in the following narrative of experiences:

" At nine o'clock in the morning, every day in the week," writes a recent excursionist, " boats leave New York for the Navesink and Shrewsbury rivers. Not the big excursion boats with their rushing and crushing crowds, . . . but quiet, unpretentious little crafts that take you thirty-five or forty miles into a country that you've probably never heard of, and bring you back again in time for a late supper, with an appetite that would ruin a boarding-house, and only charge 50 cents for doing it. You can even get a dose of *mal-de-mer* thrown in, if you choose a blustering, windy day or try to smoke a cheap cigar on the quarter-deck. We know little or nothing of these salty rivers, sweet with the odor of sea-grasses, spreading out, with their beautiful bays and inlets, like the arms of an octopus, over the Jersey coast. . . . Let us make the trip some bright summer day and have something beside baseball to speak of in after years. Let us get up early some morning and take the nine o'clock boat for Red Bank. Red Bank don't amount to much; it's a pretty place, but is nice chiefly as a good starting point for pleasant rambles of many sorts. A ting-a-ling of the bell and a toot of the whistle and we are off down the river, past the Battery, and before we have made up our minds which is the shady side of the boat, we have passed Quarantine and are running out through the Narrows, with the frowning forts on either side of us, and what appears to be the ocean in front; having run through the finest harbor, in every sense, in the world. Sheering off to the right, we get a glimpse of South Beach, the Coney Island of Richmond County, and in a few moments are passing the Quarantine Islands and steaming across the lower bay at a lively gait. The city is fading from our view; the domes and minarets of lower Broadway are 'hull down'; the castles of Brighton Beach are hidden in the haze, and for aught we know the captain may be heading us for Europe. But we are soon in sight of land, and, in answer to our anxious inquiries, learn that it is Jersey. From dreams of Europe to the sight of Jersey is about ten minutes, dead reckoning, but we greet it as a long lost friend, and feel like sharing the contents of our lunch basket with the gentleman in the pilot house.

"Taking a seat at the front of the boat, we look out upon a scene, strange and beautiful. On our right, the Highlands, studded with pines, and on our left a narrow strip of land, terminating, about a mile behind us, in Sandy Hook, and separating us from, but not hiding, the ocean beyond. The scene, from our places on the upper deck, will never be forgotten. Pleasure boats of every description dotted here, there, and everywhere. Sailing, rowing, fishing, and crabbing canoes dodging in and out; bathers on the beach; saucy little launches puffing away for dear life, and a brightness over everything. We run through the drawbridge, steer to the right, under the shadow of the lighthouses — those guiding stars to the mariner, which stand high up on the edge of the cliffs — call for a moment at the Highlands, and on again, to the right, up the Navesink, making several more stops, and reaching Red Bank by about noon. If we have our wives or sweethearts with us, as we should have, we can seek a quiet spot, easily found within a mile, in the woods or on the shore, by taking the road toward Oceanic, or over the river, and eat our lunch and otherwise disport ourselves until the boat returns. But if we are still novices, of 'maiden meditation, fancy free,' let us put our lunch in our pockets and start for a walk. Let us go the way we came. Follow the river back again and see where it takes us. We have plenty of time. The boat doesn't leave again for four hours, and we can take it at any of the landings lower down.

"We go through Red Bank with its crowd of summer cottages — mansions for the rich and cabins for the poor — and out among the green fields. A walk of two miles brings us to Fairhaven, and we wander down by the river, exploring the shell-covered beach, sit on an up-turned boat and eat our lunch. Some one tells us it is four miles to Oceanic; what of it? The roads are good and shady, our spirits are high, and we've plenty of time. The walk to Oceanic is a treat. The sky and earth kiss each other, o'er sunlit waves or emerald fields, and the roads and paths are through enchanting combinations of farms and villas. We meet the organ-grinder with his monkey; the itinerant merchant with his warehouse on his back; we see the fish-hawk's nests high up in the trees — and we reach Oceanic as fresh as the proverbial lark. There are still the same good roads to tempt us on, and Seabright three miles ahead. We gradually leave the Navesink, and another hour finds us crossing the Shrewsbury River at Seabright, and once again on the narrow strip of sand, and the ocean at our feet. From here we can take the Pleasure Bay boat for home, but the walk along the shore is tempting, as the breakers come rolling gently in, and in twenty minutes we are down at Highland Beach, over the swing bridge and back again at the Highlands, where those of us who have any 'grit,' climb the hill to the lighthouse and obtain a view that alone is worth the whole trip. The boat steams up about five o'clock and we take our seats, prepared to thoroughly enjoy a two-hours' rest; pleased with ourselves and the chance that took us there. A whole day of fresh air of the freshest kind, and exercises of the very best sort."

The LATEST ACKNOWLEDGED STANDARD MANUAL

FOR

Presidents, Secretaries,

DIRECTORS, CHAIRMEN, PRESIDING OFFICERS,

And everyone in anyway connected with public life or corporate bodies

IS

Reed's Rules

BY

THE HON. THOMAS B. REED,

Speaker of the House of Representatives,

"I commend the book most highly."
   WILLIAM McKINLEY,
   President of the United States.

"Reasonable, right, and rigid."
   J. STERLING MORTON,
   Ex-Secretary of Agriculture.

CLOTH, 75 CENTS,
LEATHER, $1.25.

RAND, McNALLY & CO., Publishers,
CHICAGO.

INDEX.

	PAGE
ALBANY Post Road	9, 12, 17
Amagansett	82
Amityville	69
André Monument	14
Aqueduct, a walk along the	57
Ardsley	48
Ardsley Avenue	21
Asbury Park	168, 169, 172
Astoria	60, 72
Atlantic Highlands	172
Avondale	121
BABYLON	69, 81
Bartow	28
Baychester	28
Bayport	71
Bay Shore	70
Bath Beach	77
Bedford	52
Bedford Avenue, Brooklyn	63
Bedford Road	22
Belleville	109, 121
Bellport	81
Bergen	148
Bergen Fields	130
Bergen Ridge	102, 106, 130
Bergen Turnpike	102, 103
BICYCLE ROUTES—	
Across Staten Island	93, 94
Astoria to Roslyn	72
Babylon to Northport, L. I.	70
Bay Shore to Port Jefferson, L. I.	70
Boonton to Morristown	116
Brooklyn to Westchester	25
Bronx Valley	19
Croton Valley	23, 38
Freeport to Patchogue	68
From Hackensack, north and west	108
Harlem Valley	19
In Northern New Jersey	101
Jersey City to Westchester County	26
Keyport to Red Bank	165
Newark to Plainfield	159
New Brunswick to Newark (via Springfield)	159
New York to Croton Falls	19
New York to Fort Wadsworth	92
New York to Freeport, L. I.	64
New York to Portchester	24
New York to Somerville	155
New York to Tarrytown	9
New York to Tottenville	91
On Staten Island	91
Paterson to the Ramapo Valley	113

	P.
BICYCLE ROUTES — *Cont'd*	
Peekskill to Lake Mahopac	
Portchester, east and north	
Patchogue to Port Jefferson	
Port Jefferson to Patchogue	
Sawmill Valley	
Tarrytown to White Plains and Portchester	
To Coney Island	63,
To Englewood and Nyack	
To Greenwood Lake	
To Hackensack and Paramus	
To Jamaica and the Jericho Road	
To Lake Hopatcong	116,
To Long Branch and Asbury Park	
To Morristown, via Orange	119,
To Morristown, via Paterson and Boonton	
To North Shore of Long Island	
To Paterson	
To Rockaway	
To South Side of Long Island	
To Throggs Neck and Fort Schuyler	
Up the Ramapo Valley	
White Plains to North Salem	
White Plains to Rye Pond	
White Plains to Tarrytown	
White Plains to the Sound Shore	
Yonkers to Mt. Vernon and New Rochelle	
Bicycling, Laws relating to	62,
Blauvelt	
Bloomfield	117,
Boonton	
Boston Post Road	
Bound Brook	
Bowery Bay	
Brentwood	
Brewsters	
Briarcliff Church and Road	
Brick Church	122,
Broadway (see Albany Post Road).	
Bronxdale	
Bronx Park	
Bronxville	
Bronx River	19,
Bull's Ferry Road	102,
CALDWELL	
Canarsie	
Carlstadt	
Castleton Corners	
Century Runs (Long Island)	
Chappaqua	
Charlottesburg	

(179)

INDEX

	PAGE
Chatham	122
Cherry Lane	125
City Island	28
Clifton	95
Closter	105
Cold Spring	85
College Point	60, 74
Congers	132
Connecticut Border, Country along the	32
Cornell's Neck	54
Cornwall	39
Coytesville	127
Cranstons	39
Cresskill	105
Crom Pond Road	19
Croton River	17
Cycle Path Across Long Island	72
Cycle Pathway in Brooklyn	64

DARLINGTON Road ... 113
David's Island ... 60
Dover ... 119
Dundee Lake ... 143
Dunellen ... 158
Deal Beach and Lake ... 167
Dobbs Ferry ... 11, 44
Drives on Long Island ... 76, 83

EAGLE Rock ... 153
Eastchester ... 34
East end of Long Island ... 80, 88
Eastern Parkway ... 63, 65
Easthampton ... 82
East Orange ... 151
East River ... 58, 73
East View ... 48
Eatontown ... 167
Edgewater ... 39, 103
Elberon ... 167
ELECTRIC LINES—
  Along the Palisades ... 125
  In Long Island ... 87
  In New York City ... 55
  In Westchester County ... 55
  Jersey City to Bergen Point ... 173
  Jersey City to Newark ... 173
  Newark to Passaic ... 149
  On Staten Island ... 99
  Paterson to Little Falls ... 144
  To Irvington ... 173
  To Montclair ... 141
  To Newark and Beyond ... 147, 148
  To New Jersey ... 173
  To Passaic and Paterson ... 143
  To South Orange ... 173
  To the Oranges ... 150
  To Arlington ... 149
  To Elizabeth ... 174
  To Elizabethport ... 174
  To Fort Lee and Englewood ... 127
Elmsford ... 36, 48
Englewood ... 103, 127

FAIRVIEW ... 102
Featherbed Lane ... 26
Fingerboard Road, Staten Island ... 96

	PAGE
Fire Island	81
Five-mile Pike	19
Flushing	74
Fordham	26
Fort Hamilton	77
Fort Lee	39, 127
Fort Lee Road	103, 127
Fort Schuyler	27
Fort Wadsworth	96
Freehold	163
Freeport	68

GLEN Cove ... 84
Glen Island ... 30, 60
Great Neck ... 75
Great Notch ... 117
Great South Bay ... 69
Green Pond ... 115
Greenport ... 80
Greenwood Lake ... 142

HACKENSACK ... 107
Hackensack Valley ... 101, 104, 107, 120, 129
Halsey Mansion, East Chester ... 35
Harlem River ... 47
Harrington Park ... 131
Harts Corners ... 21
Hartsdale ... 21
Hastings ... 10, 44
Haverstraw ... 18, 39, 133
Hellgate ... 59, 72
Hempstead Plains ... 79, 81
High Tor ... 133
Homestead ... 120
Hudson Heights ... 127
Hudson River Steamboats ... 38
Huntington ... 85
Hunts Point ... 54
Hutchinson Creek ... 53

INDIAN Head ... 131
Irving's Washington, home (see "Sunnyside").
Irving's Grave ... 13
Irvington ... 39, 44
Islip ... 70

JAMAICA Bay ... 66
Jackson's Mill ... 74
Jericho Road, L. I. ... 66

KAAKEOUT ... 37
Katonah ... 52
Kensico ... 51
Kitchawan ... 49
Kill von Kull ... 89, 100

LAKE Hopatcong ... 119
Lake Mahopac ... 53
Lake Ronkonkoma ... 71, 79
Lake Waccabuc ... 52
Leedsville ... 165
Leonia ... 103
Lincoln Park ... 114
Little Falls ... 109, 144

INDEX.

	PAGE
Little Ferry	107, 130
Little Neck Bay	75
Llewellyn Park	153
Locust Grove	161
Long Branch	168
Long Island, general remarks	62
Lynbrook	67

	PAGE
MADISON	122
Mamaroneck	31
Maplewood	122
Massapequa	69
Matawan	163
Mauch Chunk	173
Metuchen	170
Merrick Road, L. I.	66
Midland Beach	100
Millburn	122, 146
Montclair	117
Monmouth, Battle of	164
Montville	114
Moriches	81
Morristown	123, 147
Mosholu Avenue	19
Mott Homestead, Tarrytown	13
Mountain Railway (incline)	125
Mountains of Northern New Jersey	115
Mountain View	110, 113
Mount Kisco	52
Mount Vernon	33, 50, 60

	PAGE
NEPARA Road	13
Nepperhan Avenue	48
Nepperhan River	35
Newburgh	39
New Dorp	92, 93
New Durham	129
Newfoundland	138
New Milford	134
New Jersey—Northern Suburban District	101
New Rochelle	30, 55
New Springville	93
Nordhoff	163
North Beach	74
Northfield	124
Northport	85
North Shore of Long Island	60, 83
North Shore, Staten Island	94
Norwood	105
Nyack	13, 106, 129

	PAGE
OAKDALE	71, 112
Oak Ridge	139
Ocean Avenue	168
Ocean Grove	169
Old Hook	105, 131
Old Place	94
Oradell	134
Orange	152
Orange, (First) Mountain	117, 122
Overpeck Creek	103
Oyster Bay	84

	PAGE
PALISADES of the Hudson	11, 126
Paramus, (Church)	108

	PAGE
Parks in Brooklyn	78
Paterson	138
Paterson Plank Road	120
Passaic Falls	140
Passaic River	109, 118
Patchogue	71, 81
Paulding Manor	45
Payne Monument	30
Peekskill	39, 46, 118
Pelham Bay	28, 55
Pelham Manor	30
Pelham Priory	29
Pelham Road	28
Philipse Manor	14, 41, 43
Piermont	140
Pipe Line	51
Pipe Line, Bronx Valley	19
Plainfield	157
Pleasantville	51
Pompton Plains, Lake, etc.	110, 112, 137, 139
Portchester	60
Port Jefferson	86
Port Morris	54
Port Washington	76
Prospect Park	63, 77
Prohibition Park	99

	PAGE
QUARANTINE and Lighthouse Stations, U. S.	95

	PAGE
RAHWAY	170
RAILROADS—	
Brooklyn Suburban Roads	86
Central R. R. of N. J.	171
C. R. R. of N. J., Sandy Hook Route	172
D., L. & W., Boonton Branch	144
D., L. & W., Morris & Essex Branch	145
Harlem	49
Hudson River	43
In Northern New Jersey	125
In Westchester County	40
Lehigh Valley	172
Long Island Railroad	79
On Staten Island	98
Newburg Branch (of Erie)	141
New Jersey & New York	134
New York & Greenwood Lake	142
New York & Putnam	46
New York, New Haven & Hartford	53
Northern Railroad of New Jersey	129
Pennsylvania	170
The Erie	139
The Susquehanna	138
West Shore	129
Ramapo River	112
Ramapo Valley, The	140
Rapid Transit, Staten Island	90
Red Bank	165
Richmond Turnpike, S. I.	91, 100
Ridgefield	103, 107
Ridgefield Park	130
Riveredge	134
Riverhead	80
Rockaway Beach	67, 87

	PAGE
Rockaway River	115, 118
Rockaway Road	65
Rockland Lake	132
Rockville Center	67
Rosebank	95
Roslyn	83
Rumson Neck and Road	166
Rutherford	121, 140
Rye Beach	31
Rye Pond	24

STEAMBOATS —

	PAGE
For Ports on North Shore of Long Island	60
On East River	58, 60
To Atlantic Highlands	175
To Hudson River Landings	38
To Keyport	175
To Long Branch	175-177
To Long Island ports	87
To New Brunswick	174
To New Jersey	174
To Red Bank	175
To Staten Island	90, 100
Saddle River Valley	108
Sag Harbor	82
Sayville	71
Scarsdale	21, 51
Schraalenburgh	105, 130
Scotch Plains	161, 162
Sea Cliff	84
Secaucus	120
Second Mountain	117
Setauket	86
Shadyside	39
Shark River	169
Shelter Island	80
Shinnecock Bay	82
Shohola Glen	141
Short Hills	146
Shrewsbury	166
Singac	110
Sing Sing	17, 39, 46
Sleepy Hollow	14
Smithtown	86
Southampton	82
South Beach	98
South Orange	145
South Oyster Bay	69
South Side Club	71
South Shore Staten Island	94, 98
Sparkill	106
Sparta	16
Sprain Brook	50
Springfield	162
Spuyten Duyvil	40
St. George	91
Stapleton	92

	PAGE
Staten Island, general remarks	89
Steinway	73
Suffern	113
Summit	146
"Sunnyside"	12, 44

	PAGE
TAPPAN	105, 129, 132
Tarrytown	12, 39, 45, 49
"Tea Neck"	103
Tenafly	105
Tennent Church	164
Three Pigeons Tavern	102
Throggs Neck	26
Tompkins Avenue	36
Tompkinsville	93, 94
Tom Pye's Corners	135
Tottenville	93, 99
Travers Island	29
Trenton	171
Trolley Lines (see Electric Railroads).	
Tuckahoe	50
Tuckahoe Road	21
Turner's	141
Tuxedo	141

	PAGE
UNDERCLIFF	128
Underhill Mill	20

	PAGE
VAN CORTLANDT Manor	9, 17, 46, 47
Van Cortlandt Park	47, 57
Valentine's Hill	33
Valley Road, The	154
Valley Stream	67
Verdrietig Range and Hook	132, 133
Verona	117
Verplank's Point	18, 46

WALKS —

	PAGE
Along the Croton Aqueduct	57
On Staten Island	97, 100
West Farms to Bedford Park	55
Washington Rock	158
Washington's Headquarters	124
Weaver Street	31
Weehawken	126, 129
Westbury	79
Westchester Avenue	38
Westchester County, as a field for outings	7
Westhampton	81
West Point	39
Whippany Valley	116, 118
White Plains	22, 51
Whitestone	75
Willet's Point	75
Woodlands	48

	PAGE
YAPHANK	80
Yonkers	10, 35, 39, 41

Will you be convinced?

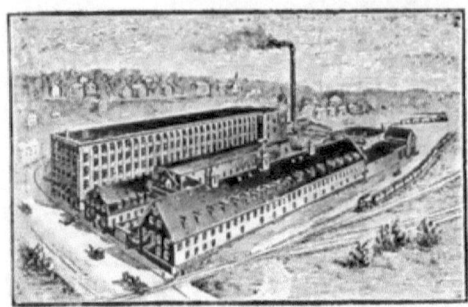

... If so, ask your Dealer in Bicycle Sundries, or send to us for an illustrated Saddle circular describing what we can furnish in Bicycle Saddles for your HEALTH and COMFORT, and, consequently, your ENJOYMENT.

We have a full line of Divided and Solid Top, Padded and Plain Saddles, mounted upon a highly finished and serviceable frame, with a strong and easily adjustable clamp.

We especially commend our Oak Saddle Leather to every manufacturer of saddles, and solicit estimates upon all requirements.

GRATON & KNIGHT MFG. CO.

Capital Stock, $700,000.

Oak Leather Tanners, Belt and Saddle Makers

Main Office, WORCESTER, MASS.

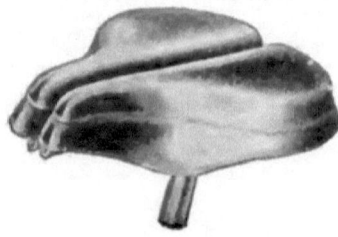

Branches:
ATLANTA, GA., 36 and 38 West Alabama St.
BOSTON, MASS., 94 Pearl St. and 126 High St.
CHICAGO, ILL., 14 South Canal St.
NEW YORK, N. Y., 112 Liberty St.
PHILADELPHIA, PA., 132 North Third St.
PORTLAND, ORE., 54 First St.

A Mount For the Fastidious

The Perfection of Bicycle Excellence

THE QUAKER WHEEL

If You'll Take The Trouble To Examine You'll Buy It.

It is not built for price competition, but, in material excellence, in mechanical excellence, and in finish excellence, competition is courted and welcomed.

♣ ♣ ♣ ♣

If you ride for pleasure or for business, it will, in every particular, please you.

♣ ♣ ♣ ♣

Only the one grade, that the highest.

♣ ♣ ♣ ♣

PENN MFG. CO.,
ERIE, PA.

STARR WHEEL CO., Agents,
132 East 23d Street,
NEW YORK CITY, N. Y., U. S. A.

The King Cushion Saddle.

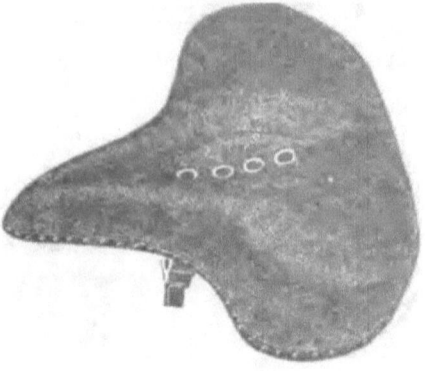

PRICE, $4.00.

AN UPHOLSTERED SADDLE
HAS ALL OF THE VIRTUES OF A PNEUMATIC
WITH NONE OF ITS FAULTS.

THE ONLY PERFECT SADDLE MADE.
CONFORMS TO THE RIDER.
SUPERBLY FINISHED.

USED BY SEVEN OF THE FINISHING RIDERS
IN THE LAST 6-DAYS' RACE AT MADISON SQUARE.

Owing to the manner in which the saddle is padded, it being constructed from coil springs and curled hair, there arises none of the soreness at the points of the hip bones. Again, the padding will not pack down hard as it does with other saddles in which the padding is made from felt or other substances without springs. The construction is such that it gives all the advantages of an air cushion with none of its faults. It is easy as a chair to sit upon, yielding at every point, causing no discomfort or friction, and yet avoids the faults of the pneumatic styles in which there is found the faults of heating, leakage of air, a rolling motion, and finally and most objectionable the forcing of the air in the pommel when sat upon, causing great injury. The pommel on a bicycle saddle is a necessity to give a sense of security to the rider, and to prevent lateral movement; but in the **King Cushion Saddle** it is so constructed that it does not come in contact with the person, except accidentally, and it is so soft and yielding that then it could cause no injury. The base of the saddle is made of Vulcanized Fiber and is positively unbreakable.

. . . FOR SALE BY ALL DEALERS . . .

KING MANUFACTURING CO.,

35 WARREN STREET, NEW YORK.

You See Them Everywhere

COLUMBIA
Bicycles

Standard of the World. $100 to all alike.

POPE MANUFACTURING CO.
HARTFORD, CONN.

HARTFORD
Single-Tube Tires

Are the Standard Tires

The Hartford Rubber Works Co.
HARTFORD, CONN.

www.ingramcontent.com/pod-product-compliance
Lightning Source LLC
Chambersburg PA
CBHW031752230426
43669CB00007B/592